04

A HISTORY OF LANGUAGE

GLOBALITIES

Series editor: Jeremy Black

GLOBALITIES is a series which reinterprets world history in a
concise yet thoughtful way, looking at major issues over large
time-spans and political spaces; such issues can be political,
ecological, scientific, technological or intellectual. Rather than
adopting a narrow chronological or geographical approach,
books in the series are conceptual in focus yet present an array of
historical data to justify their arguments. They often involve a
multi-disciplinary approach, juxtaposing different subject-areas
such as economics and religion or literature and politics.

In the same series

Why Wars Happen
Jeremy Black

A History of Language

STEVEN ROGER FISCHER

REAKTION BOOKS

Published by Reaktion Books Ltd
79 Farringdon Road, London EC1M 3JU, UK
www.reaktionbooks.co.uk

First published 1999
Copyright © Steven Roger Fischer, 1999

Printed and bound in Great Britain by
St Edmundsbury Press, Bury St Edmunds, Suffolk

British Library Cataloguing in Publication Data:

Fischer, Steven R.
   A history of language. – (Globalities)
   1. Linguistic change 2. Sociolinguistics 3. Linguistic change
   – Social aspects
   I. Title
   417.7

ISBN 1 86189 051 6

Contents

PREFACE   7

1   Animal Communication and 'Language'   11
2   Talking Apes   35
3   First Families   60
4   Written Language   86
5   Lineages   112
6   Towards a Science of Language   139
7   Society and Language   172
8   Future Indicative   204

REFERENCES   221
SELECT BIBLIOGRAPHY   232
INDEX   236

Preface

This book is an introduction to a history of language. Addressing the topic in its broadest sense, its intention is to prepare someone, who is perhaps only generally familiar with foreign languages and language study, for professional linguistic tuition. In this sense, the present volume is a useful preliminary reading before commencing a university or college introductory linguistics course. No previous training in linguistics is needed to read this book. It requires no foreknowledge of special linguistic terminology or of particular linguistic methods.

As a history of language in general, this overview differs greatly from traditional linguistic histories – that is, from formal descriptions of linguistic change in known or reconstructed human languages. It goes beyond human restrictions to include animal languages. It is a short, concise account of the historical significance of 'language' in global terms.

The first chapter begins with Nature and the past; the final chapter ends with Technology and the future. This introductory history also commences with macro issues and proceeds to micro issues: from the languages of all animates to those specifically of primates; from those of *Homo sapiens* in general to macro families of human languages; and from specific families of languages to our new global society's usage of language and the possible future of English as humankind begins colonizing the Solar System. It is a story of the commonplace and the unique, featuring the natural world's most fascinating faculty: language.

The many facets of what humankind means by this amorphous word 'language', with its two dozen different definitions, and even more connotations in specific contexts, will become evident as this introduction to a history of language progresses. The current formal definition of 'language' is experiencing a semantic change too, with 'language' no longer the exclusive franchise of *Homo sapiens*. It is now appreciated that any living being, in any epoch, that has used some means of conveying information to other animates has used 'language' of some sort. Language is apparently a universal faculty.

It would be absurd to claim that, 'Someone, somewhere, uttered the first word. *And someone else understood*'. At present such prose might be especially appealing. But its message is historically invalid, as we now realize. Language did not 'begin'. Language, in all its myriad forms, evolved over hundreds of millions of years. Only at the end of this protracted evolution did 'language', essentially an anthropomorphic concept, appear in the form that modern humans can identify with and better understand.

A history of language must include non-human language, then, as has been revealed particularly in groundbreaking avian, cetacean and primate experiments conducted since the 1960s. Primordial forms of language still exist throughout the world, and only now are being recognized as such, principally as a result of modern technology that makes use of sensitive monitoring equipment in order to register the hitherto unperceived communications of the natural world.

Early on, hominids turned into talking beings, too. It is this story of emerging human language, and of the subsequent evolution of human languages, that comprises the principal theme of this book. There remain no definite answers to the major questions concerning human language: What is 'language'? How does 'language' relate to other intellectual abilities? How does human language differ from non-hominid communication? One of the purposes of a history of language is to find ways to answer these and similar questions.

This book does not address the theoretical specifics of linguistic evolution. The topic is mentioned, but only within a larger history of language in general, as a global overview. For in-depth coverage of specific theoretical controversies – the origin of 'words', the emergence of syntax and so forth – relevant texts are cited in the References and Bibliography. The evolution of the human brain's ability to process specific vocal references is a similarly fascinating field which, unfortunately, is beyond the scope of this introduction to a history of language.

Jeremy Black suggested I should write this book, and I am extremely grateful to him for the idea and his inimitable support. Thanks are owing also to Michael Leaman of Reaktion Books, who kindly discussed the specifics of the project with me and offered many constructive comments and suggestions.

A special debt is owed, too, to many special people who have played an important role, each in his or her distinctive way, in my linguistic and philological career. Their profound knowledge of languages, the science of linguistics and/or philology over the past thirty years have influenced, shaped and honed my linguistic and philological knowledge and beliefs. Out of the many who deserve mention, I should like to express my indebtedness particularly to Eli Sobel (†), Noam Chomsky, Raimo Antilla, Theo Vennemann, Terrence Wilbur, Stephen Schwartz, Arthur Groos, Thomas Barthel (†), H. G. A. Hughes, Margaret Orbell, Bruce Biggs, Andrew Pawley, Malcolm Ross, Ross Clark, Ray Harlow, Terry Crowley, Albert Schütz, John Charlot and Jack Ward.

And a very special thanks to Jean Aitchison, too, for showing all of us how one should write about language.

Above all, my wife Taki was both pillar and candle.

Steven Roger Fischer
Waiheke Island, New Zealand
January 1999

ONE

Animal Communication and 'Language'

Earth's earliest organisms evolved primitive mechanisms of exchange capable of informing of species, gender and intent. This conveyance occurred through what was then nature's most sophisticated medium: chemocommunication. Continuous need over millions of years to contact another of the same evolving species in order to procreate necessitated ever more complex methods of communication. Out of this evolutionary process 'language' in its broadest sense was born.

Each type of language used in nature differs. The deeper one probes, the more one discovers each species's communicative ability distinguished by ever more elaborate definitions of the concept 'language'.

In its simplest definition, language signifies 'medium of information exchange'. This definition allows the concept of language to encompass facial expressions, gestures, postures, whistles, hand signs, writing, mathematical language, programming (or computer) language and so forth. The definition also accommodates the ants' chemical 'language' and the honey-bees' dance 'language' (we now understand that both insects simultaneously use additional modes of communicative expression, too).

The definition further recognizes the many bioacoustic exchanges of information (the sound emissions of life forms) that occur in frequencies beyond human hearing. For example, an average 15-year-old human can hear only about ten octaves at the loudness and closeness of normal conversation – that is, between 30 and 18,000 hertz (cycles per second). Birds, frogs, toads and dogs all vocalize within this range. However, most other creatures appear to communicate both below and above the range humans consider 'normal'. Infrasound comprises emissions below 30 hertz, such as many sounds made by finback whales, blue whales, elephants, crocodilians, ocean waves, volcanoes, earthquakes and severe weather. Ultrasound occurs above 18,000 hertz, frequencies commonly used by insects (Earth's most prevalent inhabitant), bats, dolphins and shrews. There is far more to language than vocal communication alone, however. In its most universal meaning, language is the nexus of the animate world, its limits drawn only by humankind's crayon.

More recent animal communication studies have attempted to be species-descriptive, linking animal communication to fundamental biological or socially specific processes.[1] Though a 'history of language' at the beginning of the twenty-first century is still implicitly a 'history of human language', it carries the suggestion that it might evolve to encompass many hitherto unsuspected forms of language. The vocal communication of many amphibians, especially frogs, has in the past few years been intensively researched – though one still looks in vain for any reference to a 'frog language'. Bioacoustics has turned its attention to fish as well, since, particularly during spawning, many fish emit a representative 'complex sound', the first part of which consists of a train of partially overlapping pulses, and the second part of which is composed of rapidly repeated pulses that overlap, producing a constant waveform similar to a 'tone'.

Vocal communication in its most primitive form, for example, is strikingly demonstrated by the 'humming' midshipman fish of the western coastline of the USA, whose nocturnal 'hums' were unknown to science until they recently disturbed a houseboat community in California and created international headlines. The male midshipman fish 'hums' to attract females to his nest for spawning. The noise – a loud, resonant drone very much like that produced by an Australian didgeridoo – originates from a pair of muscles attached to the swim bladder that contract and vibrate against the stomach wall, and will continue moving for up to an hour. Once a female arrives, the 'humming' promptly ceases.

Several orders of insects also possess sound-producing organs evidently used for communication. Many of these use ultrasound, whose very existence was unknown to science until the latter half of the twentieth century. During courtship, both male and female moths, for example, communicate through pheromones (secretions exuded through specialized glands); the entire sequence of moth courtship behaviour involves ultrasound production as well. This very recent discovery has necessitated a reconsideration of moth courtship behaviour, with greater emphasis now laid on the interaction between the several modes of communicative expression.

However, when one hears of animal communication or 'language' one commonly thinks of the languages of ants, honey-bees, birds, horses, elephants, cetaceans and great apes.

ANTS (FORMICIDÆ)

Ant species number between 12,000 and 14,000, each of their colonies comprising a million or more individuals. Occupying nearly every inhabitable spot on Earth, ants outnumber humans by trillions. None is alone. All communicate in some way. Each ant can transmit at least 50 different messages using body language and pheromones. Ants' mandibular glands secrete alarm odours; the hind gut terminates in a rectal gland that exudes scent for trail-marking; exudings from the sternal gland are used to call nearby workers, and so forth. These highly specific chemical messages, combined with body language, seemingly offer an economical package containing the necessary information an individual ant must exchange with its fellow ants for the colony's survival. Here language has been reduced to its bare minimum, essentially to a 'language of pheromones'. Some have called it Earth's primordial idiom.

However, it is possible that ants' linguistic ability is more complex than science currently admits. Ants' division of labour cannot be wholly explained by the present communication model. How does the group decide which leaf to fetch? How is mass organization and coordination achieved? This must involve a more elaborate exchange of information than has hitherto been identified. In addition, very recent bioacoustic research has revealed that ants also use stridulation; their sound and ultrasound production is still little understood and the precise contexts of its usage are still unknown. In any event, entomologists now suspect that for hundreds of millions of years ants have perhaps been communicating through a highly complex combination of pheromones, body language and sound emission.[2]

HONEY-BEES (*Apis mellifera*)

In the first half of the twentieth century the Austrian zoologist, Karl von Frisch, revealed that honey-bees use 'dance' to communicate, thereby stunning the world by demonstrating that even 'insignificant insects' were capable of exchanging complex information about things remote in space and time. By means of a 'waggle dance', the honey-bee forager informs followers of the type (through proffered samples), quality (quantity of 180 degree turns of 'dance') and location (tracing a figure-eight design for distance and direction) of food she has found beyond the nest. In the past, the waggle dance of the honey-bee has often been cited as a classic example from the animal kingdom of the use of 'true language'.

Recent research has additionally revealed that the foragers of dwarf bees dance only in the open, on top of their nests; followers merely watch. Those foragers from species who dance inside the dark nest, however, vibrate their wings to produce air currents, a 'voice' that the followers, after attending several figure-eight circuits, monitor from close proximity with their antennæ – indicating that bees can 'hear'. Followers thereupon request food samples by pressing their bodies down and emitting a sudden vibration of the thorax, sensed in the dancer's legs. These combined modes of expression – body language, food exchange and 'voice' – constitute among these honey-bees their 'language'. 'Robot bee' experiments have now shown that both waggle dance and acoustic message are essential to establish proper communication among most honey-bees. If one of these modes is omitted, most followers fail to find the food.

Keen birdwatchers have long thrilled to the March wren's vast repertoire of songs. And since antiquity it has been appreciated that some birds in the wild learn their songs in different contexts, a fact that suggests birds attach different meanings to their vocalizations. Recent field research has apparently confirmed this.[3]

Birds display great individual differences in vocal abilities and inclinations, even among the most loquacious species. Some birds say nothing; others, it seems, never stop chattering. Larger parrots are perhaps the animal kingdom's most phenomenal 'linguists', especially African Greys and Amazons (yellow napes, double yellowheads, red loreds and blue fronts). Scarlet and blue-and-red macaws can vocalize well, too; but they are commonly hoarse and loud. Cockatoos, fine 'talkers', possess mellifluous voices; however, like the macaws, they are difficult to teach.[4]

Already in the 1940s it was demonstrated that African Grey parrots were perfectly capable of learning non-vocal tasks, such as matching quantities of objects, that are commonly believed to require complex intelligence. Later researchers observed that parrots, in particular, seemed to be using natural vocalizations among one another in a variety of 'meaningful' ways, vocalizations certainly learned from other members of the flock.

The last quarter of the twentieth century saw a major breakthrough in our understanding of what has, for centuries, only metaphorically been called bird 'language'.[5] In June 1977, Irene Pepperberg began teaching a 13-month-old African Grey parrot named Alex to communicate with her in English, using new techniques and borrowing from research on human social learning. The results of the experiment are impressive. To all appearances, Alex, now fully trained, is not 'parroting' human speech at all but understands its meaning and can express a similar semantic content in reply, in a variety of conceptual modes, with remarkable statistical accuracy.

For example, a researcher holds up a purple metal key and a larger green plastic key. 'Alex, how many?' Fifteen seconds' pause. 'Two', replies Alex. 'Which is bigger?' 'Green key.' A wooden ice-cream stick is then lifted. 'What matter?' Long pause. Finally: 'Wood.'

Within twelve years, Alex's trainers had taught him a variety of linguistic tasks. Alex could name 40 different objects (banana, cork, chair, water and so forth). He possessed a functional use of 'no', 'Come here', 'I want X', and 'Wanna go Y'. He was able to name seven colours, describe varied shapes and count objects up to six. In the end, Pepperberg found that Alex was combining all the vocal labels to identify, request, refuse, categorize and quantify more than 100 different objects, including some that differed from his regular training exemplars. When tested on these abilities Alex's accuracy averaged 80 per cent.[6]

There were limits. Though Alex was apparently able to communicate with humans at a seemingly advanced level, he could not 'talk' to his trainers in the same way that they could talk to each other. Unlike great apes, Alex could also not relate what he had done the day before or what he would like to do on the morrow. Alex has indeed demonstrated to humankind that perhaps birds can also use language creatively and therefore can also reason at a level of complexity that is comparable to that of great apes (orangutans, gorillas, chimpanzees and bonobos) and cetaceans (whales and dolphins).

Recent neuroanalytical tests have revealed that birds possess left-brain control of song, similar to humans' left-brain control of speech. A connection has been drawn from this fact. However, the scientific jury is still out.

If, in the end, science concludes that birds do indeed have and use some sort of elaborate 'language', would this then imply that their remote ancestors, the dinosaurs, also used some sort of language, perhaps in similar fashion? The implication seems apparent.

Acoustic communication is also used extensively by all mammals, those higher vertebrates that nourish their young with milk secreted by mammary glands. Serving mammalian survival by enabling social coherence and adaptation, language appears to be a primary trait of this entire class of vertebrates. The complicated sounds mammals produce make their study as difficult as that of non-mammals, for the similar reason that mammals' social contexts are extremely complex and variable. It is hard to associate specific sounds and/or sound patterns with particular activities and/or with same-species exchanges. To add to the difficulty, like birds in the wild there appear to be many regional variants ('dialects') in mammalian 'speech', as well as individual learning abilities and expressions ('ideolects').

Most research on mammalian communication has hitherto concentrated on their bioacoustics, the measurement and analysis of the sound emissions of life forms. The finest bioacoustic studies on mammals have been achieved in highly context-specific environments, such as mating or sonar surveying (echo-locating). In fact, only the latter has been able to satisfy nearly all the demands commonly placed on scientific experimentation, since its environment is limited by well-known physical laws and since these sound emissions are more uniform and easier to monitor than social activities, permitting simple comparisons of data. However, sonar surveying is not communication. It does prove that several mammals, such as bats, whales and dolphins, possess elaborate biomechanisms that might well be capable of providing sophisticated exchanges of information within a species. Bat studies, in particular, have concentrated on the constant-frequency sonar and modulated-frequency sonar with which these small mammals echo-locate for orientation and hunting prey; here, ultrasonic emissions comprise the most important component. The bats' social calls, however, are emitted at lower frequencies and are still not understood. Mammalian bioacoustic studies have also addressed the vocalizations of mice. As yet, few have written of a 'bat language' or 'mouse language'. It is a deficiency that has its cause in human unfamiliarity or in the preferred restriction of the term 'language' to humans, since complicated bioacoustic communication appears to occur with both bats and mice. Until very recently, humankind has simply failed to notice.

On the other hand, horse, elephant, whale and dolphin 'languages' have received an enormous amount of popular attention in recent years. Esoteric writers have even linked these communication systems to supernatural, even extraterrestrial, forms of 'super-communication'. Though this is absurd, there is no doubt that these mammals do communicate in some way. Their communication is merely different from ours. There is no scientific evidence to suggest that non-human mammalian communication is in any way 'superior' – that is, contextually more elaborate – to human language. Indeed, the cumulative weight of evidence during the last half of the twentieth century urges the conclusion that hominids (humankind and close ancestors) alone have evolved the most sophisticated forms of natural and unnatural communication in the natural history of the planet.

HORSES (*Equus caballus*, FAMILY EQUIDÆ)

That horses use some form of sophisticated body language (gesture, orientation, eye contact and avoidance), linked with specific vocalizations, to communicate with one another, even over great distances, has long been known. In recent years, human trainers have developed new techniques based on the observation of this horse 'language' to manipulate equine behaviour for human purposes, such as saddling and riding. The results have been quite remarkable, reducing the 'breaking' time of horses from many days to tens of minutes. There can be little doubt that some hitherto unknown form of human–horse communication has been achieved here. Similar accomplishments with deer (family Cervidæ) have followed almost identical techniques, though the process here has been much slower and more subtle. Vocalizations have not normally played a role in these interactions; as a rule, among themselves horses almost always combine body language and vocalization. None the less, a form of 'language' is evident here in that an exchange of specific information is taking place between humans and horses and between humans and deer. However, a scientific investigation into horse and deer 'languages', including context-sensitive vocalizations, is only now commencing.

ELEPHANTS (ELEPHANTIDÆ)

In the last two decades of the twentieth century investigators have also turned modern scientific methods and techniques towards the question of elephant communication. It has long been suspected that elephants constantly communicate to reinforce the social bonds that underpin a herd's survival. How far this communication is a 'language', however, in the sense of conveying significant information within a species, is generally still unknown.

Elephants use a variety of vocalizations: rumbles, roars, growls, snorts, trumpets and barks.[7] Each of these vocalizations appears to represent a different mode of communicative expression, within which various sounds represent significant sub-units. Rumbles are doubtless the most meaningful of all elephant vocalizations, emitted between 14 and 35 hertz; above 30 hertz elephant rumbles are audible to humans as a deep organ bass, sensed as a subcutaneous 'tingling'. Such low frequencies are little hampered by their passage through grasslands and forests. Research in Zimbabwe, Namibia and Kenya suggests that elephants (probably uniquely among land mammals) use these infrasound rumbles below the usual audible limit in order to communicate in some fashion with other elephants far away. Remote sensors, with timers, have proved infrasound communication between elephant females and males to have occurred over a distance of four kilometres. It appears that, among many other uses, these rumbles allow male and female elephants to meet for reproduction (adult males and females live apart, with unpredictable migrations and no fixed breeding season). A female elephant, during her oestrus, emits a unique sequence of infrasound 'calls' that, since they always preserve the same form, one might label a 'mating song': they begin with slow, deep rumbles that gradually grow in strength while rising in pitch; these then sink into silence. A 'concert' may continue for half an hour.

Female elephant vocalizations are rich and varied, implying many different kinds of messages. Their calls seem at times to indicate how far the herd should wander, when to nurse, who is present in the group and so forth. Also, females react to far-off events. Adult males vocalize far less; one researcher has jocularly concluded that this is because the males are too busy listening to the garrulous females. Scent is always used together with hearing; pheromones evidently play a significant role in elephant sexual reproduction. Musth males in search of a mate, who might be in oestrus for only two days every four years, react acutely to such musth-alerting 'chemo-communication'.

Elephant communication as a form of 'language' would of course include those rumbles that allow varied kinds of messages, not merely reproductive signals. Some of the strongest infrasound recordings of elephants have documented rumbles evidently signalling panic; it has been suggested these 'panic calls' are emitted to summon help from one's distant herd. Though separated by kilometres of woodland, individual herds are able to continually adjust their foraging direction in almost perfect synchrony, apparently using infrasound rumbles to maintain contact with one another. Such networking might also allow the maintenance of an elaborate hierarchical society even among sparse elephant populations, some investigators have suggested.

WHALES (CETACEA)

For a wide variety of reasons, often of secret military nature (sonar studies), most international research into mammalian acoustics involves cetaceans: the aquatic, mostly marine mammals including whales, dolphins, porpoises and related forms. With birds and hominids, cetaceans appear to be the only other creatures on Earth with readily audible, spontaneous, complex, vocal exchanges. Current research into cetacean acoustics concentrates on social calls and echo-locating signals, analysing recordings of underwater sounds detected by towed arrays of hydrophones with digital signal-processing workstations. However, this method fails to reveal cetacean social contexts; for this, one needs video and real-time group monitoring whose results can then be analysed in a laboratory for comparative data. For whales in particular, such data gathering is extremely difficult.

Whale vocalizations can rise to 256,000 hertz – twelve times as shrill as the human ear can detect. For this reason, it was not until the development of electronic sensing devices in the second half of the twentieth century that humans became aware of the whales' true range of vocal communication. There are many types of whale 'languages', depending on genus.[8]

Research on orca whales since the 1970s has revealed that their vocalizations comprise clicks, whistles, and short piercing screams which are termed 'pulsed calls'. The clicks are simple echo-locating sounds. Whistles are heard among resting or socializing orcas and seem to involve sexual activity and play. Pulsed calls, likened to the 'screeching of a rusty hinge', probably serve to keep track of pod members when out of sight, since they can be heard by other orcas as far as eight kilometres away. Each pod shares a number of pulsed calls with other pods in the region. However, a discrete pod frequently demonstrates unique versions of these shared pulsed calls; in addition, each possesses one or two distinctive pulsed calls not shared by other pods. It is these differences that appear to isolate a local 'dialect'. Individual orca pods can be readily identified by their unique dialect. Unlike humpback whales, orcas maintain individual dialects without intentional change over very long periods, possibly a lifetime.

Finback whales are now known to emit intense infrasonic calls; whether this serves finback communication is still unknown. It is also unknown whether the groans, grunts, buglings, and elephant-like trumpetings of the bowhead whale, one of the most vocal cetaceans, comprise some sort of communication.

Among the most powerful sustained sounds from any living source on Earth is the call produced by the blue whale. As measured by the US Navy off the coast of South America its 188-decibel 'song' – comparable to the noise level of a cruiser travelling at normal speed – would be detectible for hundreds of kilometres. Usually in infrasound, blue whale songs comprise perfectly timed notes repeated at intervals of 128 seconds. Throughout most of the year a blue will sing for eight continuous days, repeating only five of these timed notes in different combinations. If there is a pause, then the next note will come in at exactly 256 seconds. Some experts believe the blue whales 'sing' to pinpoint their exact position in the ocean, timing the reflections of their emissions from continental shelves, undersea islands and seamounts. These songs would not, then, be fulfilling a communicatory function. However, the fact that the songs are audible for such enormous distances seems to contradict this hypothesis.

We now realize that humpback whales – next to primates perhaps the only other composers in nature – similarly broadcast 'songs' across hundreds of kilometres of ocean. Humpbacks apparently make use of a special 'language' that must truly be one of nature's most fascinating. They display a wide variety of vocalizations: whines, creaks, grunts, roars, and bellows which can sometimes be associated with specific types of behaviour, suggesting a social significance. But it is the songs of the humpback that most closely approximate our concept of true 'language'. For more than twenty years the songs of the Bermudan humpbacks were investigated. They were discovered to comprise 'long love songs' – that is, regular sequences of repeated sounds emitted for mating. The songs varied widely in pitch and lasted between six and 30 minutes; when recorded and artificially speeded up some fourteen times, the songs remarkably resembled bird song. There are humpback solos, duets, trios, even choruses of dozens of singers. Each humpback is singing the same 'song', though not in unison. And the song changes diachronically, that is, over time, which appears to be a constant, intentional process very similar to forms of human language change: new elements are composed, kept, then elaborated on. This is quite different from bird 'dialects', which are simply regional. Like humans, humpbacks are intentionally modifying their own ritual vocalizations over time. One regional group of humpbacks will sing the same 'song' one year, then replace this with another the next year. It is significant that the songs of two consecutive years are more similar than two separated by several intervening years. The song seems to be 'evolving' and each humpback participates in this evolution of song.

When the Hawaiian humpbacks were compared over four years with the Bermudan humpbacks, it was found that in any one year the two groups were singing a different song. Yet both were observing a diachronic change and demonstrating the same song structure (not content). For example, each song comprises about six themes, with several identical or slowly changing phrases. Each phrase holds from two up to as many as five sounds. One song will maintain the themes in a given order, but humpbacks will sometimes omit one or more themes. Those themes that remain are always sung in a predictable sequence based on earlier performances. Though Bermudan and Hawaiian humpbacks are not in contact, their songs share fundamental humpback 'linguistic rules'.

The laws of humpback composition appear, then, to be universal, whether Atlantic or Pacific. This suggests that humpbacks (indeed, perhaps all cetaceans) inherit a set of vocalization laws within which each generation then improvises. It is not known whether these supposed vocalization laws are transmitted genetically or by learning. It has been suggested that, since humpbacks do not sing at summer feeding grounds and since their songs are so complex, perhaps they are merely forgetting the song between seasons and devising a new version based on partial recall. This hypothesis was tested off the island of Maui in Hawai'i and found to be wrong: the old song was first sung by returning humpbacks then gradually altered during the breeding season.

Humpbacks always sing new phrases at a quicker tempo than old phrases, and new phrases are sometimes fashioned by connecting the start and finish of consecutive phrases. Middle parts are simply omitted, like the abbreviations used in human speech ('can't' for 'cannot'). This process has also been likened to evolving language in human communities. Because the songs of the humpback whales are different, though the song form is shared in both the Atlantic and Pacific Oceans, experts agree that one can speak here in general terms of true regional 'dialects'. It also strongly indicates that in humpback song one is encountering a form of 'language' that closely approximates human expectations, though its precise nature still needs to be understood.

The celebrated codas – distinctive patterns of clicks – of the great, timid, sperm whale appear to be different for each individual; that is, they do not seem to constitute the same sort of shared 'language' that humpback whales display. Unfortunately, these codas have still not been deciphered. It is known, however, that they vary from ocean to ocean and therefore might represent (at least for human trackers) a 'dialect' marker. For example, the sperm whales of the Galápagos emit 23 distinctive codas during social interludes. There is a five-click coda that often begins conversations, like a 'hello'. There is also a seven-click coda that usually follows an eight-click coda, both of whose meanings are unknown. Bulls announce themselves with a clang called the 'Big Click', repeated every seven seconds; likened to 'a jail door being slammed', the sound is perhaps used to attract females or intimidate rivals. Sperm whale codas are often heard at midday when the whales are socializing close to the surface of the sea. It has been suggested that the codas enable individual sperm whales to identify themselves to others. Various other clicks (not codas) that sperm whales use may act as sonar to echo-locate and, as some claim, to stun prey with sound.

DOLPHINS (DELPHINIDÆ)

Dolphins, a term which generally includes porpoises, a subspecies, also frequently vocalize, as has been observed for thousands of years with the Mediterranean striped dolphin which simultaneously whistles to communicate and clicks to echo-locate. Producing these clicks by forcing tough nasal plugs against bony edges in their skull, dolphins then focus these by passing them through fatty tissue in the forehead. Dolphins possess no outer ear; sound is received through a thin 'window' in their lower jawbone.

In the 1960s the American neurophysiologist and psychoanalyst John C. Lilly, convinced that dolphins already possess an elaborate natural language, began teaching dolphins to 'speak English'.[9] The design of Lilly's Project Janus was to enable human and dolphin, each in their respective element, to exchange vocalizations adjusted to their 'comfortable hearing range' using a code of 64 sounds. Lilly expected rapid human–dolphin communication: 'I want to find out if they have sagas, teaching stories, histories'. His anthropocentric wish – perhaps naive in retrospect, though realistic and thrilling at the time – was not to be fulfilled. Similar attempts later, such as that by Marineland of Florida, which was patterned after contemporary experiments to teach primates an artificial language, also yielded unsatisfactory results. Human–dolphin communication, often entailing simple symbol matching, seldom conveyed more than a dozen coded words in English.

It is evident that dolphins' vocal repertoire includes emotional messages of some sort. Experts have isolated one rising-falling, almost bird-like, cry that must signify something like 'Help!' Other isolated signature signals of dolphins must mean 'I am Flipper' or the like. Yet current scientific opinion, in stark contrast to the optimistic enthusiasm of over one generation ago, holds that the dolphin 'language' in nature (as opposed to human–dolphin artificial communication) is perhaps closer in analogy to a human groan, giggle, or sigh than to what one generally expects from true 'language'.

As we have seen, cetacean acoustics has indicated discernible 'dialects', and even marked evolutions of structure, that one would expect of a knowledge-based exchange of information. For all this, human attempts to establish cetacean 'dialogues', as we understand this concept, have hitherto failed. We truly do not comprehend the natural mode of cetacean information transfer. Cetaceans are communicating with one another in some fashion; above all, dolphins and the humpback whale seem to share a richly vocal society. But we have yet to grasp cetacean 'language' in these elaborate vocalizations.

With primates one is on more familiar ground. As the primatologist John Mitani has written, 'You cannot look closely at a great ape and fail to sense something very special'. It is the ultimate vanity: we are sensing ourselves. Some seventeen million years ago, during the Miocene period, there existed at least three times as many ape genera as today. Their surviving descendants are the lesser apes, or gibbons; the great apes (orangutans, gorillas, chimpanzees and bonobos); and humans, last of the Hominidæ.

All great apes appear to display linguistic abilities that come close to what we understand as true 'language', principally because the concept itself is anthropocentric.

ORANGUTANS (*Pongo pygmæus*)

At the end of the 1970s sign language was taught to great apes for the first time on their home ground, to orangutans in Borneo. Their lessons were modelled after contemporary experiments with gorillas and chimpanzees in the USA. Two orangutans learned twenty signs of American Sign Language in less than a year, a rate similar to the other species' learning capacity. The experiment indicated that the 'language' ability of all great apes is probably about the same, regardless of species. Individual talent seems to show wider differentiation. Language experiments with orangutans have increased in recent years. They have yielded an ever more surprising display of linguistic comprehension and generation.

GORILLAS (*Gorilla gorilla*)

Temporary tolerance of humans by mountain gorilla society can be achieved through gesture (pretended leaf-eating), posture (half-facing, eyes turned away) and vocalizations (eating sounds, foraging grunts) – all simultaneously. Or so Dian Fossey demonstrated at the Karisoke Research Centre in Rwanda from the 1960s up to her murder in 1985. She had effected a basic study of gorilla vocalizations in nature, and even reproduced these sounds herself in an attempt to 'talk gorilla'. For the first time in history, trust was established between humans and gorillas in the wild – using their 'language', not ours.

At the same time, language experiments with the female chimpanzee Washoe had inspired Francine Patterson to attempt teaching an adapted form of American Sign Language or Ameslan, the 'hand language' of the deaf in North America, to a 13-month-old female lowland gorilla named Koko in July 1972. Within six years the world was acclaiming Koko as the 'first gorilla to achieve proficiency' in conversing with signs. The experiment became the world's longest ongoing study of ape language, and continues today.[10] Koko now displays an active vocabulary of more than 500 Ameslan signs; she also possesses a passive vocabulary of another 500 signs. Her total vocabulary now approximates that of human toddlers. Such linguistic capacity also proves a cerebral faculty for language to be present in great apes – that is, gorillas in the wild are already 'prepared' for language of some kind, which then enables their use of Ameslan in the laboratory. Koko's IQ, tested using the Stanford-Binet, ranged between 85 to 95; this is slightly below the average for a human child. However, several of her 'errors' on this anthropocentric test were incorrectly faulted: for example, to a gorilla a tree, not a house, is the logical shelter from rain. Koko's real IQ would probably be slightly higher.

Koko's accomplishments are both entertaining and sobering. When Koko saw a horse with a bit in its mouth, she signed, 'Horse sad'. Patterson asked Koko why. Koko signed in response: 'Teeth'. Imitating humans, Koko has even attempted to talk; she once tried to telephone (the horrified operator traced the call, thinking the caller was dying). In 1976 Koko was joined in her training by a three-and-a-half year-old male lowland gorilla named Michael. Patterson told Koko a new baby was arriving. When Koko saw 50-pound Michael she signed in reply, 'Wrong. Old'. Within two years the gorillas Koko and Michael were 'talking' to one another using Ameslan.

A special keyboard was devised to operate with a voice synthesizer. Koko and Michael push a key and the chosen word is spoken aloud through a speaker. Using Ameslan and the keyboard, Koko, in particular, displays the full panoply of a human child's emotions, humour, and intelligence.[11]

Patterson has gone even further. Recognizing a principal characteristic of human language to be displacement – the innate ability to refer to events removed in time and space from the actual act of communication – she tested whether Koko was in fact labelling simultaneous events or linguistically recreating using displacement. 'Does the animal use its symbols to refer to events earlier or later in time?' she dared to ask. It was soon discovered that Koko could readily converse about a past biting incident as well as describe a past emotional state.[12] Displacement was also patently displayed in Koko's telling lies, which she used primarily to avoid blame but also to express humour or cheekiness. For example, Koko began chewing a red crayon. Patterson asked, 'You're not eating that crayon, are you?' Koko signed in reply 'Lip' and started applying the crayon first to the upper lip, then to the lower, as if it were lipstick. This humorous anecdote conceals a deeper revelation: the use of language by a non-human to distort the listener's perception of reality. Until Patterson's experiments with Koko, such use was regarded as an exclusively human prerogative.

Contrary to naturalists' depreciatory estimations of gorilla intelligence in the mid-twentieth century, at the beginning of the twenty-first century primatologists now consider gorillas to be the intellectual peers of chimpanzees, mostly as a result of Patterson's research. But there are significant differences between gorillas and chimps. Compared to her signing chimp cousins, Koko signs more deliberately and carefully. She also signs more often and addresses a much wider range of activities.[13]

Even today, 27 years after the experiments began, Koko is still actively using her 46-key auditory keyboard. This bears the usual letters of the alphabet and numbers, but each key is also painted with a simple, arbitrary geometric pattern in one of ten different colours. Koko understands that these represent 'words' for objects, emotions, and actions; they also include pronouns, prepositions, and modifiers, allowing a primitive syntax. Patiently, Koko types with her index finger; one hand is kept free for signing. She types and 'speaks' simultaneously. Koko and her companion Michael regularly use hundreds of gestures of Ameslan. The ongoing project continues to revolutionize our understanding of animal communication and 'language'.

CHIMPANZEES (*Pan troglodytes*)

A milestone year in human–ape communication came in 1967, for it was then that the chimpanzee Washoe signed the sentence in American Sign Language: 'Gimme sweet'. The 1960s to the 1980s was the great era of experiments in human–chimp communication. Earlier experiments over many years with the chimps Viki and Sarah using plastic symbols or spoken words had generated only an extremely small vocabulary. In contrast, Washoe learned 34 signs of Ameslan in the first 22 months of training, and two years later, in 1970, had acquired a total of 132 signs, which she used in a similar manner to that of human children in the first stages of learning to speak.[14] It had been evident to Washoe's trainers, Allen and Beatrix Gardner, that chimpanzees' difficulty in acquiring language lay in their inability to control lips and tongue – that is, to produce articulate speech. Also, the great apes' pharynx prohibited human-like aspiration, allowing only the simplest vocalizations by means of the larynx: grunts, shrieks, whimpers, and so forth. The Gardners were the first to use sign language with primates. Their results were astonishing, and inspired Francine Patterson to use Ameslan with the gorilla Koko, as they also prompted Duane Rumbaugh to set the chimp Lana before a computer console at the Yerkes Regional Primate Research Center in Atlanta, Georgia: Lana eventually 'typed out' rational, non-random statements on an arbitrarily encoded keyboard.[15]

If in the early 1970s linguists, on the basis of chimpanzee research alone, unanimously concluded that Washoe and other great apes in fact did not possess language as we know it, by the end of the 1970s, principally as a result of Patterson's experiments with the gorillas Koko and Michael, linguists either wholly retracted or significantly modified this negative assessment: great apes, most linguists then conceded, do appear to possess some form of 'language ability'. Very recently, a feature of the brain considered essential to human language – the asymmetry of the planum temporale located just above the ear – was discovered in the chimpanzee brain as well; however, it remains uncertain how this may influence chimpanzee language ability, if at all. The exact role of this asymmetry in language reception and/or production must still be determined.

Human–ape experiments in two-way communication from the 1960s up to the 1980s, in which some apes learned sign language while others used invented symbolic languages, demonstrated that it made no real difference whether gestures or symbols were used. The great apes did learn to exchange information with their human trainers, some rather remarkably, which proved that their neural pathways for 'language' in some non-specific form were already present. However, the overriding question still remained: is human–ape communication proof that great apes are able to use language in a similar way to humans? Perhaps Washoe was signing vague associations for a reward. Koko might have been overinterpreted by human preconceptions. Other chimps might have been responding to subtle body, sound, and situational cues, not to actual language. Pessimism descended over the entire field and funding was greatly reduced. Then the bonobo Kanzi changed everything.

BONOBOS (*Pan paniscus*)

We share 99 per cent of our genetic makeup with chimpanzees, and even more human-like characteristics with miniature chimps, the bonobos. In the wild, individual bonobos have been observed to communicate constantly with one another using body language (gestures, facial expressions, postures, orientation) combined with simultaneous vocalizations. For example, there are at least twenty gestures and calls that indicate a willingness to copulate. Does this 'natural language' of the bonobos in the wild possess the neural pathways to allow bonobos to use language in a way with which humans are perhaps more familiar? Recent experiments by the American Sue Savage-Rumbaugh, hailed by the scientific establishment, have not only confirmed this, but have revealed a hitherto unsuspected dimension to great ape linguistic ability.[16]

The bonobo Kanzi was taught to communicate with humans using a 'lexigram', a keyboard of symbols representing set words or actions. Kanzi differs from a 'trained ape' in that his responses are motivated rather than conditioned: Kanzi is 'prompted' to use symbols spontaneously and creatively to communicate to humans and other primates. After many years in this artificial training environment, Kanzi has also learned to understand English voice commands, questions, and statements, to which he reponds using his lexigram. This can now also electronically activate a voice response for Kanzi. Seldom has a primate come so close to generating a lexicon and syntax that humans can readily identify and understand. Kanzi appears indeed to be on the threshold of using 'language' as humans comprehend this concept.[17]

In one instance, Savage-Rumbaugh had her keys stolen from her by one of the chimps at the research centre. She asked Kanzi to get them back for her. Kanzi went to the culprit, 'murmured' something in the latter's ear, and came back with the stolen keys. Kanzi also displays recognition of human voices over the telephone, and can signal appropriate responses to these telephonic messages. He appears to be sharing human-like vocal communication with his trainers, though his replies to vocal messages are necessarily either electronic or symbolic. At present Kanzi is using a lexigram of 256 geometric symbols. Chimpanzees are similarly learning to use Kanzi's lexigram. A curious upshot of this is that human children with learning disabilities are also now using and profiting from an adapted version of the bonobo's lexigram.

In a recent test in which 660 first-time requests were made to both Kanzi and young human children, such as 'put the apple in the hat', Kanzi scored higher than a human child of two years of age. Kanzi seems to be able to respond to and spontaneously generate language with the innate adequacy of a two-and-a-half year-old human child. Savage-Rumbaugh has proved to most experts' satisfaction that apes can both comprehend and spontaneously use language just as small human children do: through listening and relating to spoken words the objects, symbols, and actions that they represent.

If a two-year-old human's linguistic ability is termed 'language', then Kanzi the bonobo is 'speaking' to us.[18]

Is there truly non-human 'language'? Or are we merely 'bestowing' language on non-humans, perhaps reading language into what is really non-language? As the Austrian-born philosopher Ludwig Wittgenstein wrote: 'If a lion could talk, we would not understand him'. Great ape communication in the wild differs significantly from human–ape communication in the laboratory: the former comprises a rich combination of body language and vocalizations, whereas the latter is an artificial human environment prompting apes to respond using human symbols or words.[19] However, a wealth of controlled tests have demonstrated, perhaps beyond any critical doubt, that, though the medium is unnatural and trained, the result of these human–animal experiments is spontaneous and creative communication – that is, the vocal or signed exchange of significant information. Using pre-existent neural pathways, animals are indeed speaking to us, and with us, in a meaningful way.[20]

None the less, communication between humans and animals has furnished almost no information about what animals are communicating to one another in their natural environment. It is possible that primates are conveying complex messages; however, what the content of their exchanged information comprises is still unknown. Humans may be teaching African Grey parrots and bonobos to communicate humanly, but African Grey parrots and bonobos are not teaching humans to communicate non-humanly.

Human ignorance of, and arrogance towards, most animal species up to the middle of the twentieth century was replaced, in the second half of the century, by an exaggerated belief in animals' intrinsic equality, even postulating commensurate intellects. This irrational dialectic has now found a more rational balance that accepts that animals do indeed use 'some kind of language' in the wild; that they are capable of being trained to communicate, spontaneously and creatively, with humans and other non-humans using artificial and/or unnatural media; and that the limit of (human-defined) intelligence of such human–animal communication can sometimes approximate that of very young human children. One must accept, on the other hand, that the question of comparative intelligence of non-humans may simply not be worth posing.

The language that non-humans are taught and actively use is neither unimportant nor ephemeral to those animals. In the early 1970s the chimp Bruno learned Ameslan; in 1982 the project was terminated and Bruno was moved to a medical laboratory. In 1992 Bruno, unprompted, was still using Ameslan, and inspiring laboratory technicians to learn it in order to communicate with him. Other apes have voluntarily taught their kind, including offspring, human-learned modes of communication. To these animals, artificial language, once acquired, is recognized to be an essential element of social interaction. Perhaps the appreciation is innate.[21]

More importantly, the study of animal communication and 'language' allows us to speculate more intelligently on the evolution of human language. It is certainly no coincidence that those animals who appear most closely to possess 'language' as we conceive it – though vocalization is here achieved only by electronic means – are also genetically closest to us. Humankind's very concept of what language constitutes is, by necessity, anthropocentric. We are not looking for language in animals; we are looking for human language. When we devise various ways to elicit language from fellow creatures, we are generally limiting them to human artifices. Most human–animal 'language' researches, even the most objective, create an unnatural, human-centred medium that has little to do with natural languages. In this regard, it is admirable of researchers such as Patterson and Savage-Rumbaugh to consider also the semantic content of great apes' glances, gestures, postures, and orientations as 'communicative modes' that, also in the laboratory, are equal in consideration to utterance and keyboard ability.

What sets humans apart? We are no longer identifiable as the toolmaking species. We seem also no longer to hold the patent on language. Perhaps humans are the animals which have simply evolved a 'more elaborate communication' that has yielded unprecedented benefits for its innovators.

Concluding with its strictest definition, language might be understood as the medium through which one conveys complex thoughts using arbitrary symbols – grammatical utterances or their graphic expression – in a significant syntax. Though humankind has hitherto assumed this definition to be fulfilled only by *Homo sapiens*, the revelations from the most recent human–animal experiments have forced at least a reconsideration of this age-old assumption.

Perhaps it is best to regard fellow animals as similar manager-assessors who attempt, through a variety of combined communicative means, to get other creatures to obey in ways that are beneficial to the individual, the group, and the species. This interplay between management and assessment might then explain the evolution of animal communication in general: it is what communicative behaviour accomplishes, not what it says, that is truly important for survival and growth in nature. In this ever more elaborate evolutionary process of management and assessment, language in the form of vocal communication as not only the basis for all social interaction but also the vehicle for sophisticated thought – at least in comparative terms – has, it appears, naturally arisen in only one family.

The hominids.

TWO

Talking Apes

Our great ape antecedents evidently possessed precisely those neural pathways necessary for various modes of communicative expression to achieve an adequate conveyance of information. However, the great apes' lips and tongue lacked coordinated control; they were also incapable of controlled exhalation. Even if these great apes had been physically able to speak, their 'speech' would probably have been nothing similar to how we understand this word today. The modern human brain is two to three times greater in volume than that of any living great ape; it imparts an enhanced ability to use and further elaborate spoken language and to reason with it. A history of human language is also a history of the human brain and its cognitive abilities; the two go hand in hand. It is an ancient story.

Seven to five million years ago in Africa, probably as a result of differing diets, hominids split from other primitive ape species.[1] Two major genera of hominids have differentiated, the genus *Australopithecus* and the genus *Homo*.

Forced by Earth's changing climate to adapt in order to sur-vive, hominid Australopithecines – present in Africa's Great Rift Valley at least 4.1 million years ago – became more carnivorous than their great ape cousins and evolved bipedalism (walking on two legs) with an upright posture, allowing a greater range for food gathering and hunting with two free hands. According to some experts, because of a high-calorie diet, brain capacity increased relative to body weight. As the African forests continued to retreat, these robust Australopithecines adjusted physically and mentally to the new, arid, open savannas; they developed greater cooperation among small bands with longer hunting times and distances. No great ape has ever displayed the social coercion necessary for a successful savanna hunt (although chimps do band together to hunt monkeys in the forest); yet here on the African savanna the ancient Australopithecine thrived. However, an *Australopithecus africanus* of three million years ago, for example, would have demonstrated a linguistic ability in no way different from a modern gorilla's, chimpanzee's or bonobo's. As they had mastered bipedalism, Australopithecines were walking great apes, but most experts agree that they were not talking great apes.[2]

Human vocal language appears to have first emerged with the genus *Homo*, as the following will explain. Most experts presently assume that a species of genus *Australopithecus* – either South Africa's *africanus* or East Africa's *afarensis* – begat a lineage that eventually evolved into our genus *Homo* by about 2.5 million years ago. (However, it is equally possible that *Homo* represents an unrelated genus.) The oldest identified *Homo* specimen, at 2.4 million years old, belongs to the species *Homo habilis*. *Habilis* emerged when Africa's climate changed again: it became drier and cooler; the rain forests shrank; grassland covered larger expanses. With a brain capacity of 400 cc to 500 cc, Australopithecines were evidently unfit, in evolutionary terms, to adapt to this changed environment. With a significantly larger brain of 600 cc to 750 cc, *Homo habilis* possessed additional attributes that *Australopithecus* lacked and the new environment demanded – longer, more modern limbs – and so *habilis* thrived until about 1.6 million years ago. *Habilis* had no weapons; it scavenged the prey of faster, more powerful carnivores. However, *habilis* made simple stone tools, such as hammerstones. *Habilis* was also the first creature to control fire.

Habilis's bigger brain enabled larger bands to survive, achieving occasional food surpluses. This in turn allowed bigger and more complex groupings of *habilis* to develop which then demanded more elaborate societies favouring more propagation among those members with superior mental abilities. This synergistic process evolved ever larger brains in *habilis*. Only in the skull of *Homo habilis* does one first encounter the bulge of Broca's area, a region of the brain essential to the production of speech and sign language.[3] *Habilis* might have possessed the neural pathways for very rudimentary language.

However, human speech might not have been physically possible at such an early date. The physical attributes needed to produce vocal speech have generally been ignored in the search for the beginnings of human language. Only in the last two decades of the twentieth century has science begun investigating this question in earnest. It seems that 1.6 million years ago *Homo ergaster*, a hominid species succeeding *habilis*, still preserved the smaller hole in the thoracic vertebræ of the ribcage through which the spinal cord passes that is identical to the small hole also found in today's non-human primates. The nerves in this spinal region control the ribcage muscles that are used specifically in exhaling. With such a small hole the exhalations necessary for speech are uncontrollable: there is too little nerve tissue. The two earliest *Homo* species were thus capable of only short, slow, unmodulated speech patterns, not of articulate speech, which is the systematic arrangement of significant vocal sounds.

In addition, their larynx or voice box was still like that of human infants, who are anatomically incapable of articulating most human sounds until the larynx drops down in the throat at one year of age or later (the larynxes of great apes never drop). Early *Homo habilis* skulls show only a slight flexing at their base, indicating that the *habilis* larynx had not yet evolved into that of modern adult humans. Even if the neural pathways might have been present to allow speech, the physical organs for this were apparently lacking.

The physical attributes for human articulate speech appear to have evolved rather quickly, between 1.6 million and 400,000 years ago. From the latter date comes our earliest hominid fossil indicating a possible use of vocal speech. This possible use emerged with a wholly new species of hominid: *Homo erectus*.

HOMO ERECTUS

Modern science currently recognizes at least three crucial species of the genus *Homo*: *habilis*, *erectus* and *sapiens*, in this evolutionary order. It is possible that only two human species ever ranged beyond Africa: *erectus* and *sapiens*, and that they did so only because they had elaborated, through rudimentary speech, a higher degree of social organization which enabled group migration. One currently favoured model posits *Homo erectus* as the first hominid to leave Africa, following larger game and leaving a trail of finely manufactured hand axes.

In the 1890s, fossil discoveries of a human skullcap, molar and femur on the island of Java in Indonesia, dated 700,000 years, proved that an early hominid, first termed 'Java man', was inhabiting what was then the South-east Asian subcontinent of Sunda. Later discoveries enabled the identification of a separate species: *Homo erectus*. This hominid species might have evolved in Africa about two million years ago as it followed herds over the African grasslands during an interglacial expansion, slowly becoming almost entirely carnivorous. *Erectus*'s emergence signalled a major advance in hominid evolution. *Erectus* was leaner, taller, faster and smarter than all hominids before it. From neck down, *erectus* closely resembled modern humans. However, *erectus* boasted a powerful body and its head displayed protruding brow ridges with a forehead sloping backwards. Some experts believe that the extra energy supplied by its predominately carnivorous diet produced a larger brain: 800 cc to 1,000 cc (*Homo sapiens*: 1,100 cc to 1,400 cc).

The larger brain enabled *erectus* to invent in a way hitherto unprecedented in nature. *Erectus* manufactured the first hand axe (the world's oldest hand axe site, Konso-Gardula in Ethiopia, is dated between 1.7 and 1.37 million years). It butchered its kill with stone flakes and cobbles. It probably also worked with bone and wood. With versatile tools and ready supplies of meat, *erectus* apparently became the first globally adaptable hominid.

Erectus seemingly emigrated from Africa at an early date, almost at the same time *erectus* was first emerging as a species there. (Or a *Homo* ancestor had emigrated before this, who evolved into *erectus* elsewhere then emigrated to Java and back into Africa, as a competing theory proposes.) It seems that *erectus* was already settled in Java – that is, on the ancient Sunda subcontinent before the ocean rose – by about two million years ago.

The Java connection is critical. Until 1997 it was believed that *erectus* had never, presumably through lack of speech and intelligence, been able to cross Wallace's Line, the invisible boundary separating Sunda from the island of Lombok that divides the fauna of Asia from that of Australia. Indeed, up to then Wallace's Line represented the watershed delineating the differing capabilities and range of *Homo erectus* and *Homo sapiens*.[4] However, stone tools and dietary remains discovered in 1997 on Flores Island east of Lombok – across Wallace's Line – dating between 900,000 and 800,000 years ago appear to demonstrate that *erectus* was both intelligent and socially organized enough to construct bamboo-log rafts and to cross the seventeen-kilometre strait separating Sunda from its eastern neighbour, even at times of lowest sea level. (More than a decade earlier, a Dutch palæontologist had suggested that humans had caused the extinctions there of pygmy stegodons around 900,000 years ago.)

Complex planning requires complex thought processes. The social implementation of complex planning demands a high degree of social cooperation. This implies use of language allowing conditional syntax (meaningful phrase and sentence sequencing): 'If we do this, then this and this will happen'. It seems appropriate to infer from the Flores Island evidence that already nearly a million years ago *Homo erectus* was capable of expressing just such a form of conditional proposition in her and his speech. This is already far beyond humankind's 'first step' towards symbolic thought.

Experts have only recently entertained the notion that *erectus* might have been capable of vocal language. The admission derives from the recognition of *erectus*'s ability for social organization, as witnessed in his manifold achievements over the globe. However, *erectus*'s language is unlikely to have been speech as we know it. The hole in the lowest vertebra through which the spinal cord passes was still too small in *erectus* to control exhaling. Short, meaningful utterances were conceivably possible; perhaps a conditional syntax was indeed developing. But long, complicated utterances were anatomically impossible.[5]

Homo erectus seemingly populated all of the Old World (illus. 1). Ten thousand stone tools, including many hand axes, recently discovered at Ubeidiya in Israel near the Sea of Galilee

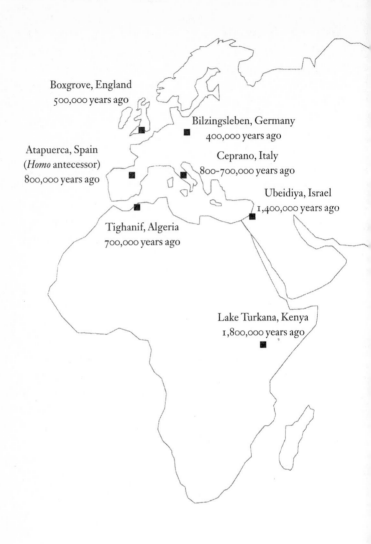

Boxgrove, England
500,000 years ago

Bilzingsleben, Germany
400,000 years ago

Atapuerca, Spain
(*Homo* antecessor)
800,000 years ago

Ceprano, Italy
800-700,000 years ago

Ubeidiya, Israel
1,400,000 years ago

Tighanif, Algeria
700,000 years ago

Lake Turkana, Kenya
1,800,000 years ago

1 Chronological range of *Homo erectus* (showing modern coastlines).

Lantian, China
1,000,000–700,000
years ago

rmada, India
oo (?) years ago

Flores Island
900–800,000 years ago

Sangiran, Indonesia
1.7–1 million years ago

have been dated at 1.4 million years old. Until the 1990s, it was believed humans had not entered Europe before half a million years ago. However, evidence for *erectus*'s presence there at a date much earlier than this is now appearing almost yearly in the archæological record. Of course, this relates immediately to the history of human language in Europe.

By early 1996, much of the skullcap of a (provisionally identified) *erectus* that had been found 80 kilometres south-east of Rome near Ceprano was pieced together and discovered to be up to 800,000 years old; it lacks the slight crest along the centre of the skull and its brain is significantly larger than that of classic *erectus*. In two recent seasons at the Gran Dolina site in the Sierra de Atapuerca in northern Spain, nearly 100 presumably *erectus* fossils and twice this number of stone tools have been discovered, dating at least 800,000 years old. Toolmaking does not require language, whereas the crossing of the Strait of Gibraltar as a 'folk migration' – like crossing Wallace's Line in Indonesia – does. The similarity of these latter fossils to *erectus* fragments found in Algeria in the 1950s suggests that *erectus* performed similar sea crossings from the North African coast over to Sicily and the Italian boot at roughly the same time. The lower jaw of an *erectus*, dating perhaps 1.6 million years ago (this is contested by several Western scientists), was found in 1991 in the Republic of Georgia. The cumulative weight of evidence currently suggests that *Homo erectus* may have entered Europe from various directions – south-west, south and east – more than a million years ago. However, not all palæontologists agree.[6]

These earliest Europeans appear surprisingly sophisticated when compared with earlier hominids. The Boxgrove site in south-eastern England demonstrates that, for a short period at least half a million years ago, early humans there were already hunting large dangerous animals, such as aurochs and horses, with wooden spears in elaborate orchestration. This was not the scavenging of early African *erectus* sites; this was cooperative hunting, on a scale far beyond that of chimps hunting monkeys in the forest. In order to plan, coordinate and ambush in such a way, speech is critical.

Most recently, Germany has revealed the sophistication of *erectus* society in central Europe nearly half a million years ago.

In 1995 near Schöningen, west of Magdeburg, five long throwing spears dating 400,000 years old were discovered amidst thousands of butchered horse bones and many campfire hearths. Another site, Bilzingsleben near Jena, appears to have been a permanent *erectus* settlement at least 412,000 years ago, with 'houses' of three to four metres in width and a large paved area that must have served for group ritual, including that of crushing and scattering human remains. The site has provided the largest collection of bone artefacts in the world and indicates the erstwhile presence of human workshops for fashioning bone, wood and stone. Several bones from Bilzingsleben appear to display intentional engraving, revealing cut lines in regular intervals. Though their discoverer sees in these cuts early graphic symbols, others hold any human intentionality to be improbable, as symbolic thinking is generally accepted to be a defining feature of the modern human mind.

About 350,000 years ago northern Europe was engulfed by glaciers. Humans became scarce, migrating south to warmer climes. Remains of at least 32 humans dating 300,000 years ago were discovered in 1993 in the Sierra de Atapuerca. One skull had held a brain as large as a modern human's. The facial features of these early humans would have resembled those of the first Neandertals (see below), but they stood as tall as we do. It is unknown whether this population comprised late *Homo heidelbergensis*, early *Homo sapiens* or an altogether new species of *Homo*. As a result of successive migrations, Europe at this time housed perhaps many different species of hominids. Fossil differences also suggest significant 'racial' diversity among *erectus* populations as well, indicating greater genetic freedom than has hitherto been appreciated.

Europe's harsh climate forced an almost exclusively carnivorous diet which, in turn, because of the enormous difficulties presented by a hunt in this climate, urged ever more complex planning, coordinating, organizing: early European hominid societies even detailed small hunting parties that were then separated from the main group for long periods. In order to survive in Europe during the Ice Ages, migrants from more southerly, warmer latitudes had to develop complex social networks, leave or perish. A recent theory proposes that human articulate speech possibly evolved first in the harsh northern ranges of Europe and only later was transmitted to other *Homo* species elsewhere. However, if language is genetically determined then its transmission to other species could only come about by interbreeding; this makes the recent theory sound unlikely. The inferred use of articulate language in Sunda to enable the crossing of the Wallace Line as early as 900,000 years ago, should this be true, similarly contradicts the suggestion.

Did *Homo erectus* 'cease' to exist? Recently, a collection of *erectus* fossils at the Ngandong site in Indonesia were redated to less than 50,000 years ago. Perhaps *erectus* coexisted there with arriving *sapiens*. In this regard, most recent fossil finds still appear to support at least a modified version of the 'Out of Africa' theory for the replacement of *Homo erectus* and appearance of *Homo sapiens* in this region.[7] That is, modern *sapiens* emerged in Africa between 150,000 and 100,000 years ago then expanded into the Middle East and Europe, where they replaced Neandertals by 30,000 years ago, and into Asia where they replaced the older *Homo erectus*. The Ngandong crania display higher vaults than those of earlier *erectus* crania from Java or China. Some experts believe that this could be explained either as convergent evolution – that is, the *erectus* crania simply evolved on their own like that of modern humans – or as a result of interbreeding with arriving *sapiens* less than 50,000 years ago (though the defining feature of a 'species' is its inability to breed with another).

With the species *erectus*, perhaps beginning as early as 900,000 years ago, a form of human articulate speech was seemingly evolving for the first time, possibly enabling complex planning and organization. It might be that humans were then already using names to identify individuals. To claim, however, as one neuroscientist has recently done, that a primitive marriage ritual seeded symbolism in the hominid mind and was the sole source of human language, ignores the complexity and antiquity of human speech development which, in reality, was a protracted process of anatomical and cerebral evolution compelled and nurtured by a multitude of external factors. That this process was already beginning specifically with *erectus* is perhaps further suggested by the shared physical and neural capabilities of speech with later *neanderthalensis* (Neandertals) and *sapiens* (modern humans) and the relative sophistication of their speech-based societies: a sophistication that argues for either a convergent evolution or a common origin.

What linguistic fundamentals was *Homo erectus* possibly evolving nearly a million years ago? It is to be regretted that the brain processes of earlier hominids are unlikely ever to be retrieved. One generally accepts that human vocal language does not derive directly from some pre-human trait. Human vocal language also does not resemble any known form of animal communication in the wild: the primitive 'Fire!' call of great apes and other animals, for example, does not constitute an embryo 'word'. And an indexical association – that is, a link between a physical object and a spoken or signed word like 'banana' or 'keyboard' – is not symbolic, but simply associative. So vocalizations or signs that reproduce these associations, such as those used in human–animal communication experiments, do not signal the human use of language; they merely express the human–animal use of language. Human vocal language is different. It is a dynamic, symbolic – not associative – and wholly anthropocentric process. This is because human vocal language evolved as a distinct and autonomous function together with human speech organs and the human brain. However, the implication that the human brain could only have evolved in conjunction with speech is unlikely.

At the core of the history of the emergence of human vocal language lie two fundamental questions: how did 'words' emerge and how did 'syntax' emerge?[8] These two questions might perhaps best be answered through an investigation of language universals. Universals might well have been present at the earliest stage of hominid language development. The basic class of 'lexicon' (understood here in its broadest sense to mean the collective of individual units of communication) might be shared by all creatures, made manifest through differing modes of expression: pheromones with ants, dance with honey-bees and vocalic language with hominids. One will note, however, that the vocal lexicon of a human toddler's language does not combine into longer structures; its lexicon also cannot be defined in terms of other words. The human toddler's language lacks syntax, just as that of all non-humans lacks syntax in their manifold modes of communication. (The counter-argument that bee dances must surely have a syntax would be begging the issue; choreography does not replace articulation.)

About a million years ago significant changes were apparently taking place in primitive hominid vocalizations, perhaps as one more result of evolving cerebral capacity because of diet, migrations and/or changing climate. Grammar was emerging from hitherto indistinct sounds. A basic vocal lexicon was probably now incorporating simple morphology: for example, a core word like 'hunt' could now become 'hunted' to express the past. (This is merely an illustrative analogy.) A more sophisticated phonology or system of sounds, perhaps because of better vocal control, allowed phonetic (spoken sound) distinctions to become phonemic (the smallest sound unit) distinctions: a word like 'dog' could now be distinguished from a word like 'fog'. It was at this time that the first specific language universals would perhaps have appeared. One may infer pre-*sapiens* universals in those types of universals one finds among today's *sapiens*.

There appear to be four basic types of language universals. Among the several *absolute universals* are, for example, the recognition that every language system contains at least three vowels and that black and white must be present in the colour complex. Among the many *tendential universals* is the perception that [p t k] are 'usually' the basic articulation points for stops (consonants that include a full obstruction of the breath passage) and that other stops are commonly not added to the language unless [p t k] are already present. *Implicational universals* are only true once certain conditions are met: for example, if red is a colour in the language then one can 'expect' that black and white are already present. *Non-implicational universals* hold no prior condition, but may also be absolute or tendential: this is observed in the seeming universal that all human languages contain at least three vowels.

American linguist Noam Chomsky has proposed that children possess some 'innate predisposition' to select certain formal principles of sentence construction in natural languages and not others. He is convinced that if, say, an artificial language were constructed, one that violated several of these principles, then this artificial language would simply not be learnable or would not be acquired with the 'ease and efficiency' that a normal child displays on learning a natural language. However, Chomsky's hypothesis is not subject to direct empirical verification. Also, there are several serious problems with the concept of 'innateness'.[9] Most significantly, the concept seems to require passive acceptance of some indefinable and inexplicable quality – 'innateness' – rather than identifying universal language features to be derived from dynamic thought processes that are related to the capacities of perception, cognition, social demand and information processing.

Let us move from syntax, from sentence construction, to a language's lexicon or constituent words, in order to broaden the discussion of universals for a moment (though one should note that Chomsky's position relates specifically to syntax). The black/white universal mentioned above is not truly a 'colour universal', but merely a product of the perceptual process of the human brain which might register brightness in terms of 'blackness' and 'whiteness', whereas hues are separately coded as 'yellow/blue', 'red/green' and so forth to build up the six focal colours of the rainbow that all language groups seem to respond to in various ways.

In the same vein, it is also formally inadequate to state merely that there is a minimum of three vowels in all modern human (that is, *Homo sapiens*) languages. One really must include the information that those languages that have only three vowels display exclusively [i] (pronounced EE), [a] (AH) and [u] (OO). (Recent studies have shown that even *Homo neanderthalensis* was anatomically incapable of producing specifically these three *Homo sapiens* vowels.) Then one must pose the question 'why?'. To this the answer will be that these three vowels provide maximal acoustic salience. Additional vowels will be positioned evenly between these three basic vowels according to the dynamic role of vowel separation.

A further example, and one associated with the cognitive processes of the human brain, would be the recognition in all languages that singular occurs more often than plural, and plural more often than dual. That is, the human brain registers one specific unity before a (collective) group, and a group before a type of group. From this one may generalize the dynamic universal that, in all languages, simple marking comes before less simple marking.[10] (Marking means qualifying through the identification of distinctive features.)

Are there then syntactic universals which may have been elaborated at such an early date with *Homo erectus*? There do indeed appear to exist a number of syntactic universals. For example, all languages seem constrained to put adjectives ('big') close to the nouns ('cave') they modify. A cerebral sense of 'belongingness' operates on human language to limit the distance between 'belonging' items. What belongs together mentally is then clumped together syntactically. Poetry's artificial, archaic and/or often strained syntaxes (for example that of Homer, Virgil or Bāshō) would simply comprise felicitous exceptions expressed in highly marked, or less frequent, modes of speech; this syntactic universal is found in most languages, too.

Homo erectus was perhaps already elaborating, over hundreds of thousands of years, similar forms of language processing that contain human language essentials. Of only limited, if connotative, significance are the obvious human language universals: all humans have to open their mouths to speak; all human languages have a verb (action or mode word) and a complement (subject or thing); all human languages have commands, statements, negatives and questions. Far more important for current research are the larger universal dynamics of languages: in all languages, for example, it appears that meaningful phrase and sentence sequencing stands in opposition to systematic word formation, that the compound ('beehive') stands in opposition to the phrase ('to the beehive'), and further similar oppositions.

An additional question addressing *Homo erectus*'s gradual elaboration of articulate speech would be the degree to which language's communicative function may influence language's own form. Innatists believe that language universals are characteristics inherent in an autonomous language module that our species has inherited. Functionalists would have cross-linguistic constraints – or universals – explained primarily by language processing and the pressures this imposes. An examination of the debate between Innatists and Functionalists argues perhaps for the compromise stance that both autonomous syntactic constraints and processing complexity serve fundamental and complementary roles in language production.[11] Language's communicative function does dynamically influence language's form ('beehive' versus 'to the beehive'), but within specific inherited constraints, it seems ('big cave' remaining close together, mentally and syntactically).

All experts agree, however, that in hominids language control and hand control are closely related cerebral functions. Gestures are so integral to human speech that they actually appear to facilitate the cerebral process that underlies language ability. Gestures are not only there to inform viewers and listeners but to enable the performer to think. At a very early date, the language of gesture would perhaps have contributed, in ways that are still unclear, to the growth of human vocal language.

HOMO NEANDERTHALENSIS (NEANDERTAL)

The distinctive features of the Neandertals began to appear in the Middle Pleistocene era between 300,000 and 230,000 years ago.[12] Neandertals are anatomically quite different from later *Homo sapiens*, though both probably diverged from the same ancestor. Their fossils were first found in the 1850s in a quarry near Düsseldorf, Germany; since then, Neandertal remains have surfaced from Gibraltar to Iraq. Apparently living in independent bands of about 30, Neandertals evidently never numbered more than a few tens of thousands at any one given time. The earliest Neandertals, the Pre-Neandertals, were tall and thin, preserving many characteristics of the earlier *erectus* in a region that experienced occasional periods of subtropical warmth.

About 180,000 years ago, another wall of ice descended on Europe. Many, but not all, Pre-Neandertals probably migrated south and south-east to the Middle East. When the ice slowly retreated, many groups then repopulated Europe. However, these were no longer the tall, thin Pre-Neandertals but stocky, barrel-chested Neandertals with short powerful limbs – a heat-retaining anatomical adaptation to the harsh, frigid climate of

Ice Age Europe. Gatherers of shellfish, plants and reptiles, and hunters of large game, the Neandertals killed through strategy and cooperation, not superior weapons. The rounding tooth wear of their fossils proves they frequently held hides with their front teeth when fashioning warm clothing, just as today's Inuit do. They buried their dead; they cared for their lame; they delighted in personal ornamentation. Their tools, often hide scrapers, were a craftsman's ideal. They were expert flint knappers, a highly sophisticated technology. Though Neandertals possessed a brain larger than that of modern humans, this excess capacity possibly managed their additional body mass. Neandertals seem always to have chosen brawn over brain.

Most experts agree that Neandertals used a rudimentary language close to our own; nothing else can explain their complex tool manufacture and high level of society. It has recently been proposed, from the discovery of an intact 60,000-year-old Neandertal hyoid bone (which supports the larynx at the back of the tongue) identical to a modern human's, that the Neandertal tongue was as dexterous as that of later *Homo sapiens*, indicating frequent and fluent speech. However, not all experts agree.[13] More recently, the width of the Neandertal hypoglossal canal (which carries the nerves that control the tongue through the base of the skull) was discovered to lie within the range of that of modern humans.

One might be persuaded to consider that by this time, more than 300,000 years ago, more complex human thought processes were possibly being enabled by more complex sentences.[14] The rapid enlargement of the human brain seemingly occurred hand in hand with the ever more sophisticated thought processes facilitated by more complicated human language. Early humans' 'toddler language' was being replaced – primitively with *Homo erectus* and then in more complex fashion with *Homo neanderthalensis* – by a medium that was rapidly evolving together with its functional apparatus: the enlarging brain enabled articulate speech, and articulate speech enabled the brain to enlarge even more. Already these two early hominids could seemingly transcend the immediate necessities of daily life – food, heat, sex – by mentally objectifying the achievements of one day, analysing and qualifying these so as to be prepared to achieve better on the morrow.

To attain this objectification, to create productive thought, a human brain requires more than referential words, that is, autonomous sounds relating to objects in real life, such as aurochs, fire, genitals. A human brain requires words that point to other words. The thought and language system must become *self-referencing*. To accomplish this, human language, perhaps already at an early date, could have elaborated an entire class of special words like 'to' and 'which', 'because' and 'why?' These new higher order words – not at all associated with the outside, objective world – might then have linked the lexicon of lower order, inherited words to form complex sentences. It is complex sentences that underlie the dynamic of multilevel thought. Modern human language is born through syntax, something that has become so utterly essential to humankind but is lacking in non-human 'languages' in the wild: rules which govern the way in which words and elements in phrases and sentences are connected to yield meaning.

Early hominids, perhaps as a result of a random mutation that generated a cerebral reorganization, made syntax the heart of their unique vocal language. This human syntax – which could evolve only when humans possessed both the neural pathways to process language at this level and the breathing apparatus to control aspiration, building on the foundation of a gestural language – evidently 'commenced' nearly a million years ago among *Homo erectus* (or possibly more than a million years ago since this process was apparently shared by early Asian and European *erectus*). It was probably approaching 'completion' only about 400,000 to 300,000 years ago, about the time the first *Homo neanderthalensis* emerged in Europe. The process would only be fully complete once anatomically modern humans emerged around 150,000 years later. Before syntax, one cannot speak of articulate human language. After the complete elaboration of syntax, humans spoke, and reasoned, like us. This was no sudden process. It evolved over many hundreds of thousands of years, beginning with *Homo erectus* and culminating (and still evolving) with *Homo sapiens*.

This theory of the importance of syntax in the history of human language, as championed by Noam Chomsky for over

40 years, is only one out of many competing theories. However, at present it appears to offer the best linguistic explanation for the observed phenomena. Most theories of language origins and development derive from palæoanthropological, palæoanatomical and neuroanalytical investigations that generally ignore the more immediate prerogatives of linguistic science. This theory of the role of syntax – perhaps the very marrow of modern articulate speech – in the history of human language deserves serious consideration, until such time as it may bow to a better one.

Between 100,000 and 80,000 years ago another ice wall intruded down over Europe. Again the Neandertals would have migrated south and south-east to the Middle East, where there are also traces of early *Homo sapiens* at least 90,000 years ago. Here the Neandertals' social activities, burials and hunting practices were indistinguishable from those of their *sapiens* neighbours. Indeed, there is every possibility that *neanderthalensis* and early *sapiens* interacted in some direct way; perhaps they even interbred. This would of course also have influenced their respective languages, resulting in some bilingualism (ability to speak two languages) between the species, isolated lexical (word) borrowings and perhaps phonological (sound system) contamination leading to limited systematic changes. But because of such sparse populations this contact would never have been as productive as that within one's own species using one's own territorial tongue.

The indistinguishability between the *neanderthalensis* and early *sapiens* cultures continued until around 50,000 years ago, when new technologies suddenly appeared among the *sapiens* – projectile weapons and finer blades for cutting. It appears some groups of *sapiens* had achieved an evolutionary 'jump' of some kind that allowed them and not the *neanderthalensis*, to evolve into modern humans. About this time, 'Cro-Magnon' *sapiens* began settling in Europe with their elaborate hearths, more efficient shelters and specially tailored clothing. Within about 20,000 years all Neandertals apparently were extinct, perhaps the victims of *Homo sapiens*'s encroachment and competition over food resources.[15]

Earlier it was believed that archaic *Homo sapiens* comprised the first hominids to emigrate from Africa. Research of only the past two decades has proven beyond doubt, however, that over a period of some 100,000 years *sapiens* replaced Neandertals in Europe and the Middle East and *erectus* in the Far East, two prominent hominid species who had long featured in these regions. Archaic forms of *sapiens* had already evolved by half a million years ago: powerfully built hominids with larger faces, smaller chins and protruding brow ridges. A new ice age 186,000 years ago created arid conditions in Africa and possibly compelled several human species there, including *sapiens*, to seek survival in smaller, more isolated groups. By 150,000 years ago anatomically modern humans, possessing all the physical features necessary for speech as we know it today, were emerging both there in Africa and perhaps also in the Middle East, where early contact with groups of Neandertals was likely occurring. By 120,000 years ago the ice wall covering Europe retreated, once more creating favourable conditions and modern *Homo sapiens*, identical to us, had emerged. The oldest bone fragments of modern *sapiens* date from this time; they are found in both southern Africa and Ethiopia and reveal distinctive traits of modern humankind: high flat foreheads – with barely visible brow ridges – and jutting jaws. Nowhere else have such early, clearly modern, *sapiens* fossils surfaced.

Many experts believe that *Homo sapiens* originated in Africa. The so-called 'Out of Africa' theory points to the evidence of mitochondrial DNA – the genetic material that only females can pass on – which indicates that modern humans have lived in Africa longer than anywhere else.[16] In addition, the theory recognizes that the oldest skeletal fossils with modern *sapiens* traits likewise hail from Africa. However, there is a competing opinion called the 'multiregional' theory that holds that modern humans evolved from *Homo erectus* predecessors in various regions: Native Australians, for example, would clearly preserve specific *erectus* characteristics.[17] Those who endorse this latter theory believe there was a constant exchange of genes among early populations. They discount the female-based mitochrondrial DNA evidence of the 'Out of Africa' theory, failing to see how it accounts for the role of the wandering, trading and breeding male through the millennia. However, the latest distributional comparison of mtDNA with the male Y chromosome among human populations has revealed that the migration rate for women thoughout history appears to be eight times greater than that for men.

Both theories influence our understanding of early human languages. If the 'Out of Africa' theory is correct, then all the world's present language families would originate in relatively recent African languages. If the 'multiregional' theory is correct, however, then these language families would be far more ancient and harbour a complexity of development stretching over a million years or more. There is also a compromise theory: that some areas, such as Western Europe, show a complete, or nearly complete, replacement of indigenous Neandertals by *sapiens*, whereas other places, such as the Far East, appear to indicate that some gene flow might have occurred between early hominid species. Perhaps one should consider this compromise theory when investigating macrofamilies of languages, for example (see illus. 2).

Recent genetic analyses have left little doubt that most Europeans, at least, are descended from the first modern hunting-gathering humans who migrated into Europe from the Middle East at the beginning of the Upper Palæolithic period, about 50,000 years ago. Genetic heredity has remained fairly constant in Europe since then.[18]

At the Klasies River Mouth site in South Africa stands a cave that sheltered *Homo sapiens* from 120,000 to 60,000 years ago. These modern humans could fell giant buffalos with spears. Their domestic activities were complex. Their red ochre 'crayons' may evidence colour used symbolically. The range and provenance of their tools indicate that particular tools were manufactured specifically for trade with neighbouring tribes. These early *sapiens* practised art and music and they ritually buried their dead with gifts. This was a small, elaborate human society living in permanent settlement. They harboured a knowledge of nature and hunting as rich and complex as our

Australopithecus *(4.1 million years ago)*	gestures, vocalizations (grunts, shrieks, sighs, etc.)

Homo habilis *(2.4 million years ago)*	gestures, vocalizations (grunts, shrieks, sighs, etc.)

Homo erectus *(2 million years ago)*	perhaps short utterances, including conditional propositions, by about 1 million years ago

(From erectus *came apparently two main divergences:)*

1. **Homo neanderthalensis** *(300,000 to 30,000 years ago)*	complex thought processes are possibly being enabled by complex sentences, allowing speech-based societies; but [i], [a] and [u] cannot be pronounced by this species
2. **Homo sapiens** *(300,000 years ago)*	complex thought processes are being enabled by complex sentences, allowing speech-based societies

modern humans *(150,000 years ago)*	all physical features necessary for speech as we know it today are present by about 150,000 years ago

2 A possible evolution of human language.

knowledge of modern society and technology. They would have used language much as we use it today.

By 40,000 to 35,000 years ago groups of *sapiens* had already arrived in northern Australia, where they were leaving decorations or symbols on rock shelter walls. As *sapiens* throughout the Old World were replacing and/or absorbing resident *erectus* and *neanderthalensis*, they simultaneously experienced a 'cultural explosion' commencing about this time and continuing up to 11,000 years ago: manufacturing artefacts that displayed themselves, animals, symbols and perhaps even the passage of time (lunar calendars) in bone, ivory, stone and wood; painting, etching or moulding walls of caves, flat stones, round bones and large boulders in a variety of breathtaking scenes or representations (Lascaux, Chauvet Cave); inventing new tools such as handles and hafts; and fashioning flutes, drums and stringed instruments. By now articulate speech – and the symbolic reasoning it allowed – was certainly being used in all the ways we are familiar with today and hominids were no longer merely the 'talking ape', but the 'symbolic ape'. It was brain, not brawn, that now mattered.

Humankind had put handles and hafts to Nature herself.

There was never an *Ursprache*, a 'primeval language'. Still, a capacity for language of some kind was present among the earliest hominids. Humans evolved from creatures without language and for this reason brain areas with other functions, such as gesturing, were called upon for the new task of speech. (The brain centres used in chimp vocalizations, it should be noted, are not those used in humans.) Language was superimposed and elaborated on top of these more primitive cerebral systems and, in addition, appears to be parasitic to them.

Human vocal language then evolved simultaneously with the human brain and developing speech organs over many hundreds of thousands of years. As the human brain enlarged its capacity, speech became more articulate as dependence on chemical and body signals simultaneously decreased. In turn, this required the evolution of specialized speech organs that demanded further brain capacity in order to accommodate the complexity of society this engendered. Cause and effect worked both ways. Each function fed the other in a closed, dynamic, synergistic system. Primitive thought and vocalizations evolved progressively into sophisticated thought and articulate speech at the same rate in evolutionary tandem. Modern human language appears to continue to evolve in this fashion, with primordial chemical and body signals now virtually reduced to subliminal perception.

The fundamental social system of all hominids, including our own, may indeed be an ape social system, but humans have uniquely elaborated vocal language and, with it, a culture based almost exclusively on this. Already nearly a million years ago with *Homo erectus*, primitive human speech enabled some form of social planning and organization in order to achieve vast cooperative projects such as sea crossings, something no group of great apes could accomplish. Later *erectus*, having perhaps evolved more sophisticated vocalizations, settled in more permanent villages with burgeoning technology and rituals and devised elaborate hunting strategems. Perhaps half a million years ago, symbolic thought and with it the beginning of articulate speech with more complex syntax and first language universals, were already being used by *Homo erectus*. This capacity was then inherited by and/or further evolved in – though in significantly different ways – *Homo neanderthalensis* and *Homo sapiens*. Modern human thought and language usage, as we know it today, was finally attained by *Homo sapiens* around 35,000 years ago, if not significantly earlier.

In the long process of evolving articulate speech there has always been an ebb and flow of human populations, the victims and beneficiaries of warfare and disease, accident and climate. Scores of thousands of languages and thousands of language families have come and gone without a trace. Frequent contact with neighbouring or other populations through trade, exogamy, migration, war and domination brought linguistic changes to larger and larger populations whose technological advances and new forms of transport in turn created their own dynamics. During periods of linguistic equilibrium that might have lasted for thousands of years, prototype languages would have formed through convergence of several different tongues. These periods then ended suddenly, creating families of languages with family trees.[19] It was perhaps this repeated process of pro-tracted linguistic equilibrium being, over eons, intermittently punctuated by abrupt change to create language families, that generated the languages we speak today.

By the time fully articulate speech had been achieved, indi-vidual bands of *Homo sapiens* were ruling autonomous territories with a radius of 30 to 40 kilometres, their immediate neigh-bours perhaps 40 to 60 kilometres distant. Group members traded and intermarried with these neighbours, exchanging with goods and daughters also words, expressions, stories and differing pronunciations. Close dialects, through long separa-tion, evolved over centuries into autonomous languages. Separate languages coalesced into hybrid languages which then altered lexicon and syntax, changed phonologies and yielded entirely to other dominant or prestige tongues. New language families, virtually unrecognizable from parent families or con-verging tongues, emerged through regional diffusion and internal adjustment. These then, through migration or some other cause, generated even larger language families as their speakers spread out or dominated other areas as a result of climate change, greed, or wanderlust, resulting in other popula-tions replacing their indigenous languages with that of the minority intruder.

By about 14,000 years ago *Homo sapiens*, the only hominid species which had survived evolution, had already differentiated thousands of languages grouped into hundreds of language fam-ilies from Scotland's Orkney Islands to Tasmania and from Alaska to Tierra del Fuego. Many modern humans in the Middle East and elsewhere were already by this time harvesting wild wheat, oats and barley using bone sickles fitted with flint blades.

Shortly after this, about 12,000 years ago, the climate again warmed. This increased the rainfall, which drove the last ice wall back north into the polar regions. Earth's oceans rose dra-matically, separating ancient peoples forever. Perhaps more significantly, the warming climate yielded a mutant grain form, a fertile hybrid of wild wheat crossed with a natural goat grass, producing emmer (*Triticum dicoccum*) with 28 chromosomes whose seeds scattered naturally in the wind. There followed a biological revolution. Modern humans in both the Old and

New Worlds, in half a dozen 'centres of origin', could now sow and harvest in one place. They began domesticating wheat and barley, sheep and goats for the first time and establishing permanent farming groups. Farming itself, within millennia, evolved from horticulture to agriculture to become the principal means of subsistence among many (but not all) human populations who produced surpluses, thrived and grew even larger. Social complexity increased. Humans remained settled for generations in one place. The first towns of mud brick arose. Regional languages became more influential and were recognized in foreign lands as the 'tongue' of a particular geographical area.

Human language was now bound to the land.

THREE

First Families

Only one generation ago, a leading American linguist earnestly proposed that Sanskrit, the ancient classical language of the Hindus of India, was genetically related to Aztec (classical Nahuatl), the language of the great empire of native Mexicans.[1] The evidence for this alleged affiliation was thought to lie in concordant sound changes in 'related' vocabulary items believed to derive from an ancient parent language spoken over 10,000 years ago, before the end of the last Ice Age. Today, however, one appreciates that this and similar claims about ancient language affiliations throughout the world defy both good science and common sense. The true history of languages is far more complex than anyone has hitherto imagined. One should be looking through the small end, not the large end, of the funnel to find the world's first families of languages. Yet even then, 'first' is merely a metaphor.

Language families are groups of languages that are genetically related. That is, sharing a common ancestor they display systematic correspondences in form and meaning not attributable to chance or borrowing. There are three reasons for linguistic similarity: genealogical sharing, areal diffusion and chance typological commonality. It is genealogical sharing alone that justifies 'family trees'. The number and quality of related features will vary according to the amount of time that has passed since divergence from the common ancestor.[2] The discipline of historical linguistics has provided certain techniques for 'reconstructing' languages (rather than simply inferring the history of languages). The application of these techniques has allowed the distinction of borrowed elements from inherited elements, the evidence of the age of linguistic features, and the identification of shared features from an ancient common source.[3] This process eventually allows a 'classification' of a language or entire language family based on similarities and dissimilarities in words and grammatical elements.

There are two kinds of linguistic classification: *typological* and *genetic* (or *genealogical*). A typological classification associates languages on the basis of distinctive features that can be categorized into defined types of linguistic phenomena. For example, a language might be *isolating*, like Mandarin Chinese, which is a root language. Isolating languages are those that tend to have, per word, only one morpheme – a language's smallest meaningful unit, like 'the' or 'book'. However, a language might be *fusional* instead, where many morphemes can be found in one word but the boundaries between them are unclear. This is so in Latin, which uses various word endings: *corpus*, which is 'body' in Latin, can also appear as *corporis*, *corporī* and *corpore* depending on the word's use in a sentence. This is called 'inflection' and fusional languages are also known as *inflectional* languages. A third type of language is *agglutinative*, in which a word may possibly contain many individual morphemes that can be either free (that is, stand on their own, like English 'drive') or bound (they can never stand alone, like the '-r' in 'driver'). Turkish is an agglutinative language in which, as in all agglutinative languages, word bases and word additions are kept distinct from one another so that all boundaries between morphemes are easily identifiable. Unfortunately, typological classifications such as these cannot provide direct historical information. With typological classification it is the relational, not the substantial, similarity between languages that is significant.

A genetic classification attempts to connect languages by virtue of their origins and relationships. Related languages are compared with regard to the interrelationships of subgroups and languages within a family, like French and Italian within the Romance language family or Germanic and Romance within the higher level Indo-European family of languages. In this way, genetic classification, particularly when based on grammatical forms and paradigms and not vocabulary, is able to provide direct historical information. For this reason it is the most productive approach to understanding the more recent history of human language.

Some languages, because of unique geographical or techno-logical circumstances, never generate daughter languages, but their speakers increase in population so that a language family comprises a single language, yielding a 'family language'. Geography has allowed Egyptian to become an example of this and its daughters are merely diachronic (temporal); English displays the same potential because of global communication via modern technology. Other languages expand – that is, generate daughter languages – under favourable conditions then shrink (remain with few daughters) under unfavourable conditions. This has happened to the Celtic family of languages.

Though it commonly happens that, under favourable circumstances, a language might generate eight to fifteen surviving daughter languages within 2,000 years – as occurred, for example, with West Germanic, Romance and East Polynesian – the qualification 'favourable' is relative. There is no justification to propose this observed phenomenon as a general rule for measuring the time depths of language families. That is, it is not axiomatic that a larger family with around 100 daughters (such as Indo-European) would be about 6,000 years old or that a superfamily with 1,000 daughters or more (the supposed 'Niger-Congo' or Austronesian) would be 10,000 years old. Too many uncertainties are involved, too few control-ling parameters and too many contradictory phenomena. Indeed, if one seeks primordial sources for the world's languages these might just as well lie in small, vestigial isolates (unique, unclassifiable tongues like Basque) on the peripheries of today's superfamilies that, until relatively recent intrusion, perhaps once figured among their region's most widely spoken languages.

For this and other reasons palæolinguists are no longer attempting to discover a chimerical 'first language' but instead to understand the complexity of the multitudes of ancient languages that once existed. An ancient pattern of language survives on each of the world's continents, one that is greatly obscured by a profound time depth. A recent innovative study has concentrated on the analysis of broader features of language groupings rather than on the evolution of individual languages.[4] Here, distributions and statistical frequencies of particular features of a sample of 174 languages were identified within entire continents. The study concluded that there appears to have been a three-stage spread of *Homo sapiens* since our African emigration of over 100,000 years ago. No linguistic features at all survive that original emigration (if one accepts that there was a 'single, original emigration'). The second emigration was that of *Homo sapiens* into the Americas from 60,000 to 30,000 years ago; it was then that the Sahul (Tasmanian, Australian, Papuan) languages also entered the Australian region. Finally, in the post-glacial era, large complex societies emerged, creating ever greater units of economic and political power that then basically destroyed human linguistic diversity.

However, over such a long period as 100,000 years the similarities that once might have obtained between close languages and language families have been wholly obliterated by constant change.[5] Proto-languages, like Proto Sino-Tibetan, are probably no older than 10,000 years and certainly no younger than 6,000 years. Very little is truly known of even quite recent language families. Palæolinguists command an impressive knowledge of Indo-European, Chinese and Semitic languages because of written documents from a relatively early period. The early history of other language families, such as Austronesian and the supposed 'Niger-Congo', must be retrieved through linguistic reconstruction, a relatively imprecise and artificial medium, as it 'recreates' what might never have existed in reality. It is to be regretted that most proto-family (or macro-family) studies, regardless of family orientation, simply extend the theoretical 'family tree' model of language history into higher level trees, creating relationships that might never have obtained.

At the end of the last Ice Age, with warming climate and rising oceans, human populations – then approximately ten million – were once again on the move, initiating a long period of social and linguistic change (illus. 3). Isolated attempts at primitive farming soon increased this figure exponentially. It was the very earliest period about which one can speculate on language affiliation. It was the era of the 'first families'.

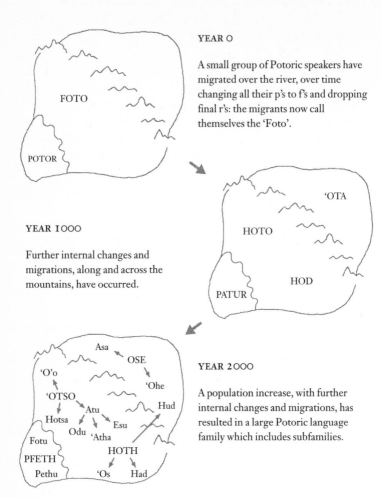

YEAR 0

A small group of Potoric speakers have migrated over the river, over time changing all their p's to f's and dropping final r's: the migrants now call themselves the 'Foto'.

YEAR 1000

Further internal changes and migrations, along and across the mountains, have occurred.

YEAR 2000

A population increase, with further internal changes and migrations, has resulted in a large Potoric language family which includes subfamilies.

3 How language families can emerge (with an imaginary people called the 'Potor').

Only after the Second World War was it possible for linguists to attempt the first exhaustive classification of indigenous African languages.[6] Since then, substantial advances have followed.[7] Identified by some as one of the world's 'superfamily' of languages, the supposed 'Niger-Congo' family, which is a statistical grouping of common features, is said to comprise over a thousand autonomous tongues, fairly evenly divided between two large subfamilies that are perhaps slightly more worthy of being called 'superfamilies' (if such a thing exists): Atlantic-Congo and Volta-Congo. As it stands at present, 'Niger-Congo' is simply too remote and nebulous to be accepted as a proved language family.

Unrelated to the nominal 'Niger-Congo' family is Africa's Nilo-Saharan family, each of whose eleven subfamilies contain between two and 96 individual languages. The 35 languages of the third, unrelated, Khoisan family have all but two of these in South Africa. Any of these larger groupings of languages – 'Niger-Congo', Nilo-Saharan and Khoisan – might well have represented an autonomous proto-language as early as 10,000 years ago, if any of these indeed ever existed as a real entity in the first place or merely reflect the convergence or coming together of diffused linguistic features.

The human history of Africa is so profound, showing evolving species of *Homo sapiens* for nearly half a million years, that one can expect nearly all the ancient language families of Africa to have come and gone without the faintest trace. Only a very small percentage of history's total of African tongues remains and these are the descendants of only the most recent creations. There are many unclassified African languages, such as Anlo in Togo, Bete in Nigeria, Imeraguen in Mauritania and about sixteen others, each of which might also comprise the relic tongue of what once had been a larger family many thousands of years ago.

Africa's luxuriant and fertile northern regions of 10,000 years ago – long before the relatively recent desertification – suggests a former population surfeit from which many ancient languages took their source. So far, 371 separate Afro-Asiatic languages have been identified, in six separate families: Berber (29 languages), Chadic (192), Cushitic (47), Egyptian (1), Omotic of Ethiopia (28) and Semitic (73) (illus. 4). The surprising number of Chadic languages in comparison to the other, much smaller families possibly points to the origin of this important and very early superfamily that, before the great migrations at the end of the last Ice Age, occupied those regions of central North Africa which desert now claims in great swaths.

4 The Afro-Asiatic language families.

One of the better known Afro-Asiatic languages, Egyptian, a 'family language' with written records dating back some 5,400 years, because of its unique geographical circumstances never generated multiple synchronic (contemporaneous) languages, but only single diachronic (temporal) ones. Like Egyptian, the Semitic family of languages possibly diverged from Proto Afro-Asiatic at a very early date, perhaps as early as 8,000 years ago. Semitic was the source of many of the most important cultural languages in history. It further divided at an early date into an East Semitic family (represented only by the Akkadian language of the Babylonians, preserved in cuneiform inscriptions from nearly 4,500 years ago) and a West Semitic family that eventually developed into Aramaic-Canaanite (Phoenician, Hebrew) and Arabic-Ethiopic. Recent theories linking Semitic to the Indo-European languages at a very early date have not found general acceptance among linguists.[8] For many thousands of years the Berber languages dominated most of the southern Mediterranean coastline, enriching powerful and influential societies with links to ancient Egypt, the Levant and the Ægean, such as the people of the Libyan Plateau and those of Putaya closest to ancient Crete.

Afro-Asiatic's East Semitic language family, in its dynamic eastward expansion nearly 5,000 years ago, supplanted an even older tongue in the ancient Middle East, that of the Sumerians. Spoken over 6,000 years ago in lower Mesopotamia (today's south-eastern Iraq) and written as early as 5,100 years ago, Sumerian is seemingly unrelated to any other tongue. It appears to have intruded into the territory of a more civilized people whose names for cities and professions the Sumerians borrowed. Recent arguments for a hypothetical 'Sumerian, Ural-Altaic and Magyar superfamily' fail to convince most linguists.

ASIAN LANGUAGES

Asia, where an early *Homo* species may have been evolving as early as two million years ago whom *Homo erectus*, then *Homo sapiens*, later replaced or absorbed, today presents, like Africa, one of Earth's most complex linguistic landscapes. Because various major language families claim Asia as their immediate or ultimate source, one may assume that several Asian language families were exerting influence already during the last Ice Age. A few of these crossed the Bering Strait land bridge perhaps as early as 30,000 years ago (some say 60,000 years ago) to become the first tongues of the Americas. Thousands of years later, as Earth's climate warmed, descendants of these same languages then migrated to all corners of Asia and beyond. They are known today as the Sino-Tibetan, Altaic, Uralic, Causasian and Palæo-Asiatic families of languages.

The Proto Sino-Tibetan language generated one of the most important language families in humankind's history. Very early on, perhaps only two or three thousand years after the last glaciation, Proto Sino-Tibetan differentiated into three major subfamilies: Chinese, Yenisei-Ostyak and Tibeto-Burman. The Chinese subfamily now consists of nine mutually unintelligible languages, with many major dialects. Its principal language, Mandarin Chinese (with four major dialects), based on the speech of Beijing, is today spoken by more people *as a first language* than any other tongue on Earth.[9] (Mandarin's pre-eminence does not reflect an ancient situation but is the result of Chinese speakers migrating to the Yangtze Delta less than 5,000 years ago, where rice cultivation generated a population explosion unprecedented in history.) Archaic Chinese was a medium for writing already over 3,000 years ago. The Yenisei-Ostyak subfamily includes languages today spoken in northern Siberia, apparently the ancient homeland of the entire Sino-Tibetan family. The ancient Tibeto-Burman subfamily eventually differentiated into the two sub-subfamilies of languages of Tibet and Burma.

Around 8,500 years ago the domestication of rice by pre-Chinese speakers in the Yangtze Delta allowed the elaboration of cultures there that eventually generated the four major – and perhaps anciently related – south-east Asian families of Tai-Kadai, Miao-Yao, Austro-Asiatic (mostly Mon-Khmer) and Austronesian (see below). By around 5,000 years ago (the dates are uncertain) these languages had spread across south-east Asia to serve the many diversified ethnic communities from northern Thailand to the islands of Hainan and Taiwan.[10]

The Altaic 'family', consisting of the Mongol languages and the Manchu-Tungus languages (that is, the Turkic tongues), is a recent classification based primarily on typological, not genetic, criteria. The classification remains speculative. All Turkic, Mongolian and Tungusic similarities are now generally regarded to be the result of areal diffusions, not of commonly shared inheritances. Turkic languages emerged in central Asia only around 4,000 years ago, or slightly earlier. They perhaps derive directly from a Palæo-Asiatic language of Siberia or from a common ancestor shared with the Palæo-Asiatic language family. (Several Turkic languages are still spoken today in southern Siberia.) Even more speculative than the Altaic classification is the theory that the Finno-Ugric languages are somehow genetically related to Altaic, which proto-family is then sometimes termed 'Ural-Altaic'.

One is on more solid ground with the Proto-Uralic speakers. Around 6,000 years ago these were apparently occupying an area of north-eastern Europe.[11] Early on they differentiated into two major language families, Samoyed and Finno-Ugric. The Samoyeds of far eastern Siberia, possibly a Lappish family, were the first to break away from the Uralic family, perhaps as early as 5,000 years ago. A common shared language around 4,000 years ago, Finno-Ugric thereafter divided into two separate families: Finnic (the source of the Balto-Finnic, Lappish, Volga-Finnic, Permian and Ugrian language families) and Ugric (Magyar, Vogul and Ostyak).[12] Today, the many daughter languages of the Uralic family are usually small in numbers of speakers, with the exception of Finnish (four million) and Magyar (Hungarian, thirteen million).

Western Asia's approximately 40 Caucasian languages of the Caucasus Mountains and their vast abutting plains apparently share a great antiquity (that is, they do not reveal any replacement). At a very early period, perhaps 10,000 years ago, the Caucasian family was differentiating into three major subfamilies as a possible result of one of the first post-glacial 'folk migrations', into South Caucasian, of which Georgian is the single most widely spoken of all the Caucasian languages (five million speakers); into West Caucasian; and into the very large East Caucasian family with its presently eight sub-subfamilies occupying what was perhaps the original homeland of Proto-Caucasian speakers.

The Palæo-Asiatic (or Hyperborean) family of languages of eastern Siberia are little understood. However, there can be little doubt that they have existed as an autonomous grouping of languages for at least 6,000 years. Today they are spoken by relatively small numbers. Though some linguists have attempted to link Palæo-Asiatic languages to New World languages, their claims lack convincing evidence.

The indigenous language of Japan, called Ainu, is an isolate whose origin is apparently so ancient that it cannot be linked to any known language or reconstructed language family. An altogether different language, Japanese, the tongue that in the last few thousand years has encroached on Ainu (marginalizing Ainu to Japan's northern island of Hokkaido), has, together with Korean, sometimes been affiliated with the highly speculative 'Ural-Altaic' family of languages; however, the affiliation lacks convincing evidence. Both Japanese and Korean obviously arrived from the Asian continent at an extremely early date. Japanese shares a common ancestor with the related Luchuan languages (Okinawan) of the Ryukyu Islands south of Japan.

AMERICAN LANGUAGES

Cautious scientific acceptance of the possibility of a *Homo sapiens* presence in the Americas as early as 30,000 years ago has emerged only within the last decade. Accepting such an early threshold in the New World might explain a linguistic landscape that apparently vies in complexity with that of Africa, Asia and Europe. Many hypotheses have been put forward about the relationship of New World languages to languages in other parts of the globe. However, all but one of these 'affiliations' have been rejected as groundless: only the proposed connection between America's Eskimo-Aleut languages and Asia's Luoravetlan languages of extreme eastern Siberia, perhaps reflecting a subsequent 'recent' migration, appears to merit guarded consideration.[13] Before seeking external relationships, one should appreciate that some 150 American language *fami-*

lies cannot be related even one to the other.[14]

Such linguistic convolution implies little possibility that a formal classification of the American languages will ever shed light on the region's earliest settlement; for this, one must turn to other disciplines. Indeed, it is now believed that there might have been multiple migrations into the Americas across the north-west land bridges. If true, then one might be tempted to accept the existence there of multiple strata (language layerings) that interacted and evolved together over many tens of thousands of years, creating a diachronically and synchronically complex population of related and unrelated languages. For want of written documents from earlier millennia, what information the historical linguist can provide for this region must come from the reconstruction of surviving American languages. This permits a disappointingly shallow classification similarly reaching back to no earlier than 10,000 years, at best.

For North American languages, a 'consensus classification' achieved in 1964 accepted seven large language families which might be derived from common languages spoken among autonomous groups there at the end of the last Ice Age: American Arctic-Palæosiberian (with two language families), Na-Dene (one family, two isolates), Macro-Algonquian (two, seven), Macro-Siouan (three, two), Hokan (ten, seven), Penutian (nine, six) and Aztec-Tanoan (two families, no isolates). There are also a surprising number of language families (such as Salish) and individual isolates (Keres) with no apparent affiliation to any of the above larger families. Comparative analysis (reconstructing a proto-language by comparing daughter languages) has hitherto failed to find any evidence that these North American languages are descended from a common ancestor.[15] Indeed, all identified larger families appear to be wholly unrelated to one another, probably as a result of the profound time depth (which current linguistic techniques cannot penetrate) and/or multiple settlements (that is, unrelated families arriving in the New World one after the other).

A similar situation obtains in Mesoamerica (Central America) where one has identified many autonomous families and isolates. Among the more important families are Otomanguean and Mayan. Otomanguean is one of the largest language families of Mesoamerica, with eight subfamilies. Mayan, which must have existed as an autonomous tongue over 4,000 years ago, includes the small Huastecan family and the very large Yucatan-Core family with many subfamilies and sub-subfamilies. There are also more than 100 extinct and unclassified languages or dialects in Mesoamerica mentioned in historical sources but otherwise unknown.

The threshold of human settlement in South America has similarly telescoped in recent years. The Monte Verde site in southern Chile is now generally – but not universally – accepted to be 12,500 years old. Archæologists have also dated villages along South America's Pacific coast to be at least 20,000 years old and one site in central Brazil indicates occupation as long ago as 50,000 years; however, both dates are still controversial. Mitochondrial DNA analysis now suggests an Amerind lineage 30,000 years old (in contrast, the Na-Dene lineage of North America's Northwest appears to be only 9,500 years old). These dates are of course far earlier than anything modern linguistic techniques can reconstruct.[16]

All of South America now presents a very ancient and complicated linguistic landscape dating back perhaps tens of thousands of years, with possible multiple incursions from the north-west (Panama) and north-east (Caribbean) before sea levels rose. Seventy-five unrelated language phyla or superfamilies have been proposed for South America, some of which also occur in parts of Mesoamerica and the Caribbean. Among these are Chibchan (the 'language bridge' between Mesoamerica and South America), Maipurean (the New World's largest family, with around 65 autonomous languages), Tucanoan, Quechuan, Panoan, Tacanan, Guaykuruan, Jean, Tupían stock and Cariban. South America currently offers one of Earth's most difficult linguistic challenges.

SAHUL LANGUAGES (TASMANIAN, AUSTRALIAN AND PAPUAN)

Before the oceans rose at the end of the last glaciation, Tasmania, Australia and New Guinea formed the ancient Sahul continent.

Though recent evidence suggests a possible human presence in Sahul between 60,000 and 50,000 years ago, most experts still agree that firm proof of humans there is no older than 35,000 to 40,000 years. A recent linguistic analysis has suggested that all of Sahul comprised one early stratum and that a subsequent colonization established a second stratum whose residual features are to be found in the languages of the north-west, the assumed point of entry.[17] However, the extreme time depth of human involvement in Sahul makes it highly unlikely that any features from a period of initial settlement survive; recognized features must date from long after *sapiens* intrusion. The language history of the area must be pieced together through an inductive approach using modern surviving languages. Again, historical reconstruction limits the linguistic threshold to only several thousand years before the present era, at best.

At the time of European arrival in the late eighteenth century, around 5,000 to 8,000 Tasmanians, felt to be somehow 'racially different' from Native Australians, were occupying the island of Tasmania south of Australia's eastern coastline.[18] Apparently two autonomous Tasmanian languages once existed: North Tasmanian and South Tasmanian. Both appear to be wholly unrelated to any of the mainland Australian languages or reconstructed language families. Perhaps Tasmanian speakers comprised the descendants of a very early Sahul population who had been driven to the continent's periphery and then stranded there 12,000 years ago when Bass Strait filled, separating Tasmania from Australia. However, the poor quality of the Tasmanian linguistic material at linguists' disposal, all of which predates the last speaker's death in 1877, hampers a rigid reconstruction.[19]

At the time of British intrusion in Australia in 1788, there were around 260 distinct languages spoken in Australia proper and on the islands of Torres Strait north of Australia. Since then, over 100 have become extinct and a further 100 are now dying; only around twenty are still being learnt by Native Australian children. Unlike the indigenous American, Asian and African linguistic situations, the Australian languages display a remarkable uniformity, particularly with their phonemic (significant sound) systems, which fact unfortunately hampers a comparative approach to classification since necessary distinguishing features are lacking. It appears that the uncharacteristic homogeneity of Australian languages can be ascribed to the continent's virtual isolation since the end of the last Ice Age. These languages might have also experienced a remarkably long period of linguistic equilibrium, punctuated only periodically by sudden change due to external (migration, invasion, social change and so forth) or internal (systemic pressures, self-organized criticality) factors. Indeed, it was the unusual Australian profile that first prompted the 'punctuated equilibrium' model of linguistic history.[20]

Borrowing a term from evolutionary biology, this recent model proposes that long periods of social equilibrium in the past experienced diffusion of linguistic features in a given area, causing different languages of that area to converge on a common prototype language (illus. 5). However, occasionally this state of protracted equilibrium would be 'punctuated' or disturbed by a sudden change caused by one or more of those external or internal factors mentioned above. This could then increase the number of peoples and split them and their languages, creating 'family trees' of languages.

Though many linguists have assumed the existence of an early Proto-Australian language, such a proto-language has never been satisfactorily established by a formal application of the comparative method (probably because of the weakness of the method itself, with its reliance on 'family trees' and thus on punctuated change alone). Some argue that Proto-Australian never existed as a real language, but represents a superficial coincidence of features artificially consolidated by modern linguistic techniques. Then again, something approximating a putative Proto-Australian might have gradually emerged out of the aggregate of languages spoken by *Homo sapiens* who interacted in some unknown way in Sunda and/or north-western Sahul about 35,000 years ago. The earliest *sapiens* languages of the area then spread out over the entire continent and were spoken for perhaps tens of thousands of years with changes and convergences coming from occasional areal diffusions and internal adjustments.

The present Australian languages do not comfortably

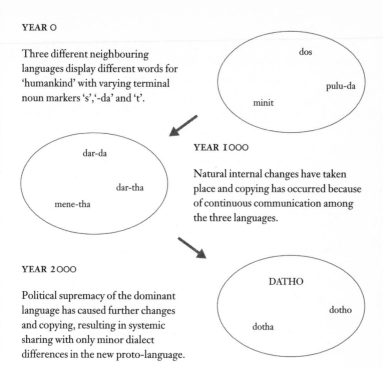

Three different neighbouring languages display different words for 'humankind' with varying terminal noun markers 's','-da' and 't'.

dos

pulu-da

minit

dar-da

dar-tha

mene-tha

YEAR 1000

Natural internal changes have taken place and copying has occurred because of continuous communication among the three languages.

YEAR 2000

Political supremacy of the dominant language has caused further changes and copying, resulting in systemic sharing with only minor dialect differences in the new proto-language.

DATHO

dotho

dotha

5 During a period of equilibrium, different languages can converge into one proto-language through diffusion.

divide into 'family trees' as other languages do.[21] For example, the 29 subfamilies of one large Australian family are phonologically (phonology is the science of speech sounds and their system) less differentiated than only two subfamilies in one larger American family. This fact is what principally urges the recognition of an erstwhile Proto-Australian, one with an extremely profound time depth. Many speakers of any given Australian language can understand their immediate neighbours' dialects, but in consideration of all the dialects of that language the density of the cognates (words related by origin) is as low as what should obtain between wholly different languages.[22] For this reason, linguists have here suggested the term 'family-like language'.

The Australian languages also display very similar, often almost identical, structures in all their dialects (with still as little as 45 per cent shared vocabulary between the dialect extremes). Such dialect chains are amazingly long, up to 1,500 kilometres. However, it is still virtually impossible to prove that this particular trait derives from a shared parent Australian language, or Proto-Australian. This latter language, if it did once exist as a real tongue, might have been a migrant form of language that imposed itself on an earlier language or languages so completely that the earlier one(s) can no longer be recognized today. Or it might have been Australia's only language. Only in Australia's regional vocabularies do there remain perhaps vestiges of earlier language(s).[23] Then again, these might be recent convergences derived ultimately from Proto-Australian, which might have experienced cyclic evolution stretching as long as 35,000 years without significant foreign intrusion until 1788.

Isolated from Sahul since the filling of Torres Strait around 8,000 years ago, New Guinea, Earth's second largest island, houses the world's richest treasury of languages, more than 700 (plus around 200 Austronesian tongues), within one confined geographical area.[24] Though one would expect genetic connections with Australian languages, none with reliable systematic phonological and morphological correspondences has been found. Contrary to earlier belief, many of New Guinea's 'Papuan' (that is, 'non-Austronesian') languages appear to be spoken by relatively populous communities, sometimes numbering more than 100,000 speakers.[25]

After Austronesian, Papuan languages comprise the second largest linguistic division in the Pacific and south-east Asia. Papuan is spoken on nearly all of New Guinea (except some coasts); northern Halmahera in the Moluccas; eastern Indonesia (Alor, Pantar, parts of Timor); parts of New Britain and New Ireland; and parts of Bougainville and other Solomon Islands down to the Santa Cruz group. Of the supposed 741 Papuan languages identified by the 1980s, 507 are alleged to belong to one 'superfamily' of languages, the so-called Trans-New Guinea Phylum.[26] This is a higher level (more ancient) grouping that is said to include some 80 per cent of all Papuan speakers. However, others have identified only around 60 small language families. Much comparative work in Papuan has been based on the statistical analysis of words and is thus generally unreliable, while little comparative historical linguistic research has been done. Indeed, 'Papuan' is all too often just a catchword for all the non-Austronesian languages of the area whose precise genetic affiliation is unclear.

AUSTRONESIAN LANGUAGES

The rising ocean levels at the end of the last glaciation also indirectly generated the relatively recent Austronesian superfamily of languages – now extending from Madagascar in the Indian Ocean to Easter Island in the South Pacific – that holds the greatest number of member tongues, some 1,200 or around 30 per cent of all the world's languages.[27] Spoken today by some 270 million people, the Austronesian family includes nearly all the languages of the East Indies, Micronesia and Polynesia. Surprisingly, only two per cent (25 languages in Malaysia, Indonesia and Brunei) of the total number of today's Austronesian languages account for 87 per cent of all Austronesian speakers.

It is possible that Pre-Proto Austronesian speakers, perhaps rice cultivators in the Yangtze Delta, belonged to a subgroup of an extended Sino-Tibetan language family that was spoken there some 8,000 years ago. The evidence for this lies in the monosyllabic and tonal reconstructions of Proto-Austronesian, which appear to resemble those of many of the languages and language families of China and South-east Asia.[28] Displaced by intruding Sino-Tibetan speakers from the north, Proto-Austronesian speakers possibly arrived at the island of Taiwan from South-east China between 6,000 and 5,000 years ago.[29] Taiwan then remained exclusively inhabited by Austronesian speakers until the Chinese invaded in the seventeenth century AD, driving the Austronesians into the mountainous interior; 200,000 Austronesian speakers remain there today, only one per cent of Taiwan's population.

Primeval language convolution on the Indian subcontinent resembles that of Africa, Asia and South America. Already at a very early date many major language families, whose origins now lie obscured by the passage of time, were struggling for supremacy. On the other hand, archæologists have identified a remarkable continuity in ancient Indian culture that stretches from 8000 to 1000 BC. It is generally accepted that Dravidian – with no identifiable cognates among the world's languages – was India's most widely distributed, indigenous language family when Indo-European speakers first intruded from the north-west over 3,000 years ago. (India's extremely populous Indo-Iranian languages are Indo-European.) The highly advanced Indus Valley culture of 4,000 years ago may well have been elaborated, for example, by Proto-Dravidian speakers. The Dravidian super-family, today spoken by approximately 175 million people, is the world's fourth largest and includes 24 major subfamilies.[30] Though a few Dravidian languages survive in parts of northern India – in eastern Baluchistan (central Pakistan), for example, the Dravidian language Brahui is still spoken today – the principal Dravidian languages are now located in southern India (Telugu, Tamil, Kanarese and Malayalam).

Classification of the other indigenous languages of India is difficult. These may well represent relics of once large families subsequently marginalized over many thousands of years, first by Dravidian, then by Indo-European. Similar to Basque in Europe, the Burushaski language of India's north-west, for example, has no identifiable cognate. The very populous Munda, Mon-Khmer and Annam-Muong language families of eastern India all belong to the Austro-Asiatic family that long ago intruded into Indian territory from South-east Asia.

EUROPEAN LANGUAGES

There have evidently been many language families in Europe, too, where various human species have thrived for hundreds of thousands of years. Nearly all of these families have disappeared without a trace. A few names of the more recent pre-Indo-Europeans (it is assumed) survive in early writings, such as the Picts or Cruithne of Scotland (who might, however, have been early Celts), the Ligurians of southern France and the western Alps, the Etruscans of Italy and the Basques of northern Spain and south-western France. The latter claim a special place in Europe's prehistory.

Named in Roman reports 2,000 years ago, the Basques genetically represent a Palæolithic type that apparently had once been more widespread in western Europe, seemingly related to the Roman-era Aquitanians of south-western Gaul. Evidently elbowed to the geographic periphery of the Pyrenees by intruding Gaulish-speaking Celts, the Basques speak a tongue – Euskara – unrelated to any known living language, though its vocabulary is layered with many Celtic, Gothic and Italic borrowings. (Earlier linguists inferred a link through ancient Ligurian to western Asia's Caucasian languages.)

Today, most experts accept that Euskara's speakers occupied, or linguistically evolved within, the Basque region before first contact with unrelated Indo-European, in this case Celtic, languages. Though some scholars have proposed that Basques and their Euskara language might be direct descendants of original *Homo sapiens* settlers of Europe 50,000 years ago, this proposal seems far-fetched, at least in regard to language (the genetic question remains open; see below). Basques, or their language, might well have preceded the first Celtic intruders by only a few thousand years. Basques appear to be genetically more distinct from their Spanish neighbours than from their French neighbours since their genetic profile gradually diffuses into that of the Garonne region (ancient Aquitania). The ten major dialects of Euskara are currently spoken by about 700,000 people, most of them in northern Spain.

Nearly three millennia ago, Basque speakers' territories were invaded by Celts speaking Gaulish, a now extinct Indo-European tongue. Indo-European is Earth's linguistic superfamily – history's most successful – and includes all but a handful of those languages that are today spoken in Europe and its far-flung former colonies, from the Americas to New

Zealand. (English, for example, is an Indo-European language of the Germanic subfamily and West Germanic sub-subfamily.) It has generally been assumed that horseback warriors from Eastern Europe had conquered all of Europe and supplanted the indigenous tongues with their own Proto Indo-European language. This interpretation was challenged in the 1980s by a theory that had Indo-Europeans arriving in Europe at the end of the last Ice Age 10,000 years ago from the Middle East – not as warriors but as ploughing, sowing, harvesting farmers.[31] According to the new theory, these new migrants entering Europe at a gradual rate of about one kilometre a year absorbed the resident hunter-gatherer populations. Their 'superior' language first dominated, then suppressed, all local tongues as farming slowly replaced hunting and gathering.

However, both geneticists and linguists, in turn, have challenged this theory. Geneticists point out that the human genetic profile in Europe has not significantly altered in 50,000 years: perhaps farming techniques, even new languages, were introduced from the Middle East as early as 10,000 years ago, but resident Europeans themselves were not displaced by another people. Linguists reject that there could have been such a gradual language replacement; there is also no linguistic evidence that it was the Indo-Europeans who introduced agriculture into Europe at such an early date – this might well have been achieved by a pre-Indo-European people, with the Indo-Europeans of the Corded Ware culture arriving many thousands of years later, around 3500 BC, not from the Middle East but from Eastern Europe.[32]

The science of historical linguistics argues for the original homeland of the Indo-Europeans to have been the geographical centre of the area from which their languages expanded – Eastern Europe. This would also explain apparent and extremely early affinities with the Finno-Ugric and Samoyed languages of the Uralic family.[33] If these affinities are substantial (a formal comparison is still outstanding), there is then the possibility that Indo-European and Uralic might claim a common ancestor language, or represent the motley convergence of two or more different but contiguous languages, that was spoken in the far eastern ranges of Europe around 7,000 years ago.

The Corded Ware people, perhaps the first Indo-Europeans to enter Central Europe some 5,500 years ago, would have represented those very early, loose groupings of Celto-Italic, Germanic and perhaps Balto-Slavic peoples who followed over subsequent millennia. Each individual Indo-European language then proceeded to *evolve* on its own soil: it was no 'invader' but an indigene.

Outgrowths of a historical mechanism that is sometimes difficult to understand, the indigenous European tongues known today arose only as a result of many forces. Linguistically, Modern Greek, French and English have emerged in much the same way as Proto-Greek, Italic and Germanic had earlier emerged, evolving out of older tribal aggregates through a myriad of language-specific processes. The genetic profile of modern Europeans reveals that the languages of the minority Indo-European intruders succeeded almost everywhere in replacing the majority residents' indigenous tongues, but for the Basques' territory and the northern regions of Scandinavia and the Baltic. Indo-European then differentiated, that is, it generated daughter languages, atop multifarious, dynamic substrata or underlying languages, a process which has ultimately yielded the extremely rich and culturally significant superfamily of languages that Indo-European has become over the last 5,500 years.

Documented in written records for nearly 4,000 of these years, Indo-European today comprises one of the world's most prosperous language families (illus. 6).[34] English alone, which is only one of Indo-European's more than 100 daughter languages in eight modern subfamilies (Celtic, Germanic, Romance, Albanian, Greek, Balto-Slavic, Armenian and Indo-Iranian), can presently count more first- and second-language speakers than Mandarin Chinese, hitherto the linguistic record-holder. In the latter half of the twentieth century English became the dominant language of world communication and the closest humankind has come to a world language. Indo-European also comprises the most studied family of languages on Earth and, in the eighteenth and nineteenth centuries, served, principally through Sanskrit, as the fountain-head of the modern science of linguistics.[35]

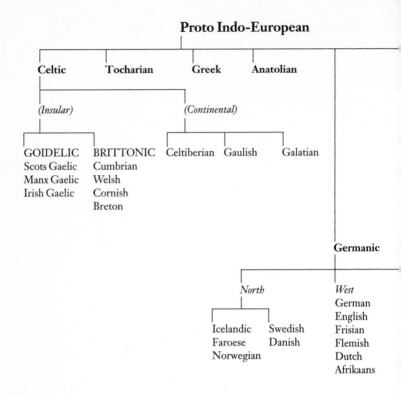

6 The 'family tree' of Indo-European languages (abridged).

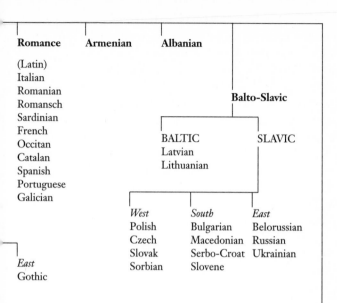

Romance   **Armenian**   **Albanian**

(Latin)
Italian
Romanian
Romansch
Sardinian
French
Occitan
Catalan
Spanish
Portuguese
Galician

Balto-Slavic

BALTIC   SLAVIC
Latvian
Lithuanian

East
Gothic

West	*South*	*East*
Polish	Bulgarian	Belorussian
Czech	Macedonian	Russian
Slovak	Serbo-Croat	Ukrainian
Sorbian	Slovene	

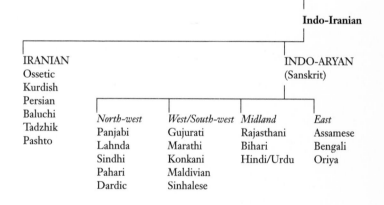

Indo-Iranian

IRANIAN   INDO-ARYAN
Ossetic   (Sanskrit)
Kurdish
Persian
Baluchi
Tadzhik
Pashto

North-west	*West/South-west*	*Midland*	*East*
Panjabi	Gujurati	Rajasthani	Assamese
Lahnda	Marathi	Bihari	Bengali
Sindhi	Konkani	Hindi/Urdu	Oriya
Pahari	Maldivian		
Dardic	Sinhalese		

The further back one probes linguistically, the less one is able to reconstruct an authentic language. This is because the comparative method of linguistic reconstruction does not allow the same sort of 'time travel' of other sciences. Palæolinguistics is limited to a large corpus of shared items that then should enable lexical (word) and phonological (significant sound system) comparisons between languages. When this corpus of items gets too small – as happens over a long period of physical separation between related tribes – then systematic sound correspondences between languages just fade away.[36] Reconstructions beyond a certain point in time dissolve into idle speculation for want of solid comparative data: 'It is neither sensible nor provident to look for a family tree of family trees'.[37] This temporal point is about 10,000 years ago for very broad proto-language family affiliations and is mostly speculation, but only about 6,000 years ago or less for specific proto-languages such as Proto Indo-European. In view of humankind's profound antiquity, this is very recent.

Nevertheless, the end of the last Ice Age 10,000 years ago was a major turning point in the history of humankind. For one, it was an era of greatest linguistic diversity. Isolated pockets of primitive society had hitherto only occasionally interacted. This natural isolation had engendered vast numbers of small, autonomous, linguistic groupings whose normal state was perhaps one of equilibrium and modest, gradual changes, often through areal diffusion. The enormous rise in human populations that followed the last glaciation, in perhaps paradoxical fashion actually reduced humankind's linguistic diversity, because the population increase in time established not merely greater language families but also single languages (such as Mandarin Chinese) with unprecedented numbers of speakers.

Increasing economic and political power in human society as a rule generates ever larger homogeneous linguistic units which then suppress all smaller ones. This synergistic system grows exponentially until, in the end, only a very limited number of languages and language families survive. This is the linguistic situation in the world today, with a rapidly decreasing number of languages in spite of a population surfeit. Perhaps for this reason, too, it is crucial for us to understand the teeming linguascape of 10,000 years ago, probably the absolute boundary of linguistic reconstruction: it was the yawning funnel through which the ancestors of all surviving languages once passed.

Recent genetic analyses have revealed that, over centuries and millennia, it is generally languages and not peoples that are replaced. That is, new languages are readily absorbed by relatively stable populations. In this way, for example, the pre-Celts of the British Isles and Ireland adopted the Celts' minority languages when these Indo-Europeans intruded. Their descendants, many centuries later, similarly adopted the minority language of the invading West Germans ('Anglo-Saxons'), while the islanders' genetic profile remained relatively unchanged. This is a phenomenon that has occurred innumerable times around the globe. Throughout history, human societies have donned new languages like new cloaks. The linguistic metamorphosis always went unnoticed – until there was writing.

FOUR

Written Language

'A scribe whose hand matches the mouth, he is indeed a scribe', wrote an anonymous Sumerian on clay some 4,000 years ago and in so doing captured the very essence of writing.[1] Writing did not gradually 'evolve' from mute pictures. It began immediately as the graphic expression of actual human speech and has remained so. Even the earliest Egyptian hieroglyph from around 3400 BC that immortalized a jackal, would have immediately evoked in its reader's mind the Egyptian word for 'jackal'.

No single person 'invented' writing. Writing first emerged, in a broad swath from Egypt to the Indus Valley, apparently as a result of improving an ancient system of tallies and labels. A tradesman or official improved a tally or label by pictorially depicting the commodity that was being counted, measured or weighed in order to lessen ambiguity. Though all early glyphs (short for 'hieroglyphs') comprised simple pictures, even the most rudimentary of these stood for a phonetic or sound value taken directly from language.

The most basic model of written language acknowledges three general classes of scripts, with many transitional variants and combinations (mixed scripts):[2]

* A *logographic* script permits a glyph to represent a single morpheme (the smallest meaningful linguistic unit, such as the three morphemes in English *mean* + *ing* + *ful*) or an entire word ('jackal' as in the early Egyptian hieroglyphic script).

* A *syllabic* script comprises glyphs that have only syllabo-phonetic value (for example, *ko-no-so* for 'Knossos' as in the scripts of the Bronze Age Ægean).

86

- An *alphabetic* script allows glyphs called 'letters' to stand for individual vowels and consonants (*a, b, c* as in the Latin alphabet).

Over time, most historical scripts reflect a shift in emphasis of class, whereby the earlier semantic or sense content is gradually superseded by the phonetic or sound content: in this way, logographic systems have tended to become syllabic systems. In contrast, the alphabetic system has remained unique: once it was developed – beginning in the Levant and completed in Greece – alphabetic writing was subsequently adopted by hundreds of languages. Today, the alphabetic writing system is the only one used to write previously scriptless languages.

It is possible that the idea of writing emerged only once in human history, to be imitated thereafter by many societies. Until quite recently, it was believed by most scholars that this emergence occurred solely in southern Mesopotamia (today's south-eastern Iraq).[3] However, new archæological evidence urges the consideration that primitive writing developed over a large territory stretching from Egypt to the Indus Valley. Through 'stimulus diffusion' – the transmission of an idea or custom from one people to another – the idea of the usefulness and mechanics of writing, wherever it began, then inspired neighbours to create their own similar writing systems, albeit graphically and phonetically unique.[4] In some cultures written language acquired veneration, as with the Hebrews of Canaan, ancient Germans and Easter Islanders. In such cases the graphic art of writing and not necessarily its transmitted message, was felt to be something apart from everyday existence, a transcendental communication to be practised only by special scribes or priests. Throughout history, the very act of writing has often been deemed a magical process.

One of the founders of modern anthropology, a Darwinist, promulgated that society's evolution from 'barbarism' to 'civilization' was enabled first and foremost by literacy, the ability to read written language.[5] One might do better, it is now felt, to view writing as civilized society's principal lubricant: writing did not enable social development, but it did greatly facilitate social change. One might also choose to avoid identifying 'stages' in the use of writing. The three classes of writing – logographic, syllabic and alphabetic (and their transitional and mixed usages) – are each maximized by a particular language, society and era. Writing systems experience fine-tuning as languages them-selves change over time, or a neighbouring language's writing system is borrowed and radically altered to fit a different lan-guage. The three classes are not quality grades, nor are they stages in a model of writing evolution; they are simply different forms of writing which are sometimes used to accommodate new and different needs as they arise.[6]

Languages may 'evolve', that is, develop in a way that is free from wilful human intervention, but writing systems are pur-posefully changed by human agents to achieve any number of specific goals. The most common goal is the best graphic repro-duction of the writer's spoken language. Over centuries and millennia, constant small changes to a writing system will result in enormous differences in a script's written appearance and use.[7] Even after more than 2,000 years, today's Latin alphabet, which has descended from the earliest Egyptian hieroglyphs, is still experiencing, in many different languages simultaneously, the addition of new system-external signs – or, because of new technologies, the semantic expansion of old signs – that each educated reader must learn, such as %, ¥, ™, © and, most recently, the Internet signage @ and //.

In those societies in which literacy is limited to a select few, it appears that writing has little effect on spoken language.[8] But in societies in which literacy is widespread, the impact of writing is profound. Writing preserves spoken language, it levels, stan-dardizes, prescribes, enriches and generates many other language-oriented processes with far-reaching social implica-tions. Human society as we know it today cannot exist without writing. The acquisition of literacy has become, in our modern world, second in importance only to the possession of language itself. The inspired elaboration of writing has made itself, in barely more than 5,000 years, almost as indispensable to humankind as the languages it transmits.

Scores of writing systems have come and gone in human his-tory. They and the dozens in use today throughout the world need not detain us in this history of language. (The curious

reader is recommended to any number of excellent surveys.[9])
Worthy of closer inspection are those scripts that give voice to
Earth's earliest cultures, those that have engendered entire fam-
ilies of scripts and those that command today. Surprisingly, only
three main script traditions have effectively guided the course of
written language: that of Egypt and Sumer, here termed Afro-
Asiatic writing; that of China, or Asiatic writing; and that of
Mesoamerica.

AFRO-ASIATIC WRITING

The peoples of Afro-Asia are perhaps the only ones in history to
have elaborated writing without external inspiration.
Everywhere else in the world, writing served the prerogatives of
priests and propagandists, implying a cultural loan to obtain
prestige and power. Only in the lands from Egypt to the Indus
Valley did writing emerge from a mundane need: bookkeeping.

Clay tokens dating from 8000 BC from Mesopotamia, the
'Land Between the Rivers' of the Tigris and Euphrates, may
have been the very first precursors of phonetic writing.[10]
Amounts of grain and numbers of animals were tallied in the
region's earliest farming settlements using clay shapes like disks
and cones. After the incursion into the area by the Sumerians,
who adopted the city and professional names and tallying
system of local peoples, new shapes and even markings
impressed with reed styli were developed to include more information for tallying jars of oil and wine and units of land. Once
the Sumerians had devised 'envelopes' of hollow clay balls to
hold the various tally tokens, other tokens reproducing the
envelopes' contents were impressed into its outer surface and
'read' as a label. In time, the Sumerians' tally markers inside the
envelope became superfluous, since the outside impression
already communicated both commodity and tally.

It appears that the Egyptians and the Harappans of the Indus
Valley, both of whom actively traded with the Sumerians, at a
very early date adopted this or a similar method of tallying with
the use of identifiable picture-symbols to represent spoken
sounds: one saw a recognizable object and simply pronounced

the name for it aloud. Such a symbol is called a pictogram and a script using pictograms is a *pictographic* script. The Egyptians, for one, then refined this process by reducing the pictures to morphemes and purely phonetic signs to better reproduce the Egyptian language. In the end a serviceable *logographic* writing system was born, one now fully capable of transmitting grammatical sentences of spoken language. It was writing as we know it.

Recent discoveries at Abydos, the most ancient 'power centre' of Upper Egypt, have revealed that the Egyptians there were using a more refined logographic or hieroglyphic script as early as 3400 BC. During this early Gerzean or Naqada II period, before the union of local provinces, the rulers of Upper Egypt were gradually consolidating their power base, creating a more efficient central administration in order to achieve their bold plans to unify Upper and Lower Egypt into one kingdom. The core of any administration is, as ever, information control. With the new logographic script that could capture and hold the royal edict and enable controlled bookkeeping with its obvious economic advantages, the powerbrokers of Upper Egypt had their vehicle to advance the process of political centralization. It is possible that Egypt's hieroglyphic writing emerged as an immediate result of the social dynamic that led to the unification of Upper and Lower Egypt. The new writing was also perfectly suited to the structure of Egypt's particular Afro-Asiatic language – indeed, far better than any of our modern alphabets would have been. This might also explain why the Egyptians' logographic writing system survived almost unchanged in its basic character for over 36 centuries, longer than any other writing system in humankind's history.[11]

There are three forms of ancient Egyptian writing. Most important are the *hieroglyphs* (a later Greek misnomer for 'sacred carving') of principally monumental or ritualistic usage. The two cursive scripts (a cursive script flows freely with joined characters), *hieratic* and the much later *demotic*, were written commonly with ink on papyrus.[12] However, the three scripts differ only in external appearance. All three are essentially one script.[13] The hieroglyphic script consisted originally of around 2,500 glyphs, but only some 500 of these were in regular use.

These glyphs were the graphic reproduction of the object to be named: the glyph of a 'hand' was pronounced *drt* and that of a 'lotus' *ssn*. (Egyptians did not usually designate vowel sounds, only consonants.) Other hieroglyphs are only suggestive: *wnm* 'eat', for example, is a seated man with hand to mouth. Such glyphs can be objects, actions or even abstractions. They can also be used homophonically, using one word to mean another of like sound: the word *db* 'finger' was also used to represent *db* '10,000'. Some 26 glyphs came to represent only one consonant, another 84 two consonants. A further 24 glyphs were specific syllables (syllabograms).[14] Around 100 determinatives – unpronounced glyphs that 'determine' or identify the class the respective glyph belongs to – slotted themselves after the phonetic (sound) glyphs. A single bar below a glyph meant the glyph is a logogram; two bars below it meant two of the depicted object; and three bars meant there were three or more (illus. 7).

The Egyptian hieroglyphs appear to have already assumed their standard shapes and sound values long before the First Dynasty, around 5,400 years ago, in time yielding a mixed writing system of several hundred logograms, syllabograms and determinatives. Only in this way could one write things other than specific, easily identifiable objects. For example, one said *par* for 'house' and 'to exit' but wrote only *pr* for both, which later scribes used also for words having nothing to do with 'house' or 'to exit', often attaching determinatives to identify which specific word was meant. Though in time 26 single-consonant glyphs emerged, they never developed into an alphabet. However, in the second millennium BC they did perhaps inspire the proto-alphabetic syllabaries (sets of symbols representing syllables) of the Levant and, ultimately, our own alphabet.[15]

Egyptian hieroglyphs were most often written with ink on papyrus, leather and ostraca (inscribed fragments of pottery). This enabled a cursive script – the one later called hieratic – to develop by the end of the Second Dynasty, around 2600 BC, in order to facilitate writing the accounts of the central government. The script's initial pictorial features had been stylized to non-recognizability, just as was occurring at the same time with the wedge-shaped Sumerian cuneiform in the Middle East. Though hieroglyphs were preserved by edict and tradition,

'Illumine his face, open his eyes'

The sounds *s* and *ḥd* are prompted by the hook sign and long-handled mace, giving *sḥd* 'illumine'. The sun sign repeats this meaning as a determinative. The basket is a masculine suffix signifying 'you'. Therefore: 'May you illumine'.

The face is 'face' and the sound *ḥr*. The rod sign tells the reader, 'the reading here is the object you see'.

The horned viper is the masculine suffix *-f*, meaning 'he', 'him' or 'his'.

The hare is *wn* and also the word for 'open'. This is supported by the wavy sign, read as *n*.

The two following determinatives are a door lying on its side (so it is 'open' too) and a forearm grasping a stick (suggesting 'effort').

Again, the basket is a masculine suffix signifying 'you'. It belongs to the foregoing four signs to provide the reading, 'may you open'.

Two 'eyes' mean just this, reproducing the word *irty*.

Again, the horned viper is 'his' (relating to the two eyes above), while the two diagonal signs point to the duality of the eyes.

7 How Egyptian hieroglyphs work: on King Amunhotep II's sarcophagus, the image of goddess Isis invokes this benediction to earth god Geb.

cursive or flowing writing developed in a separate custom that allowed continuous change. Different characters emerged, depending on whether the cursive was used for official, personal, profane or religious purposes.[16] By the Twenty-Fifth Dynasty in the seventh century BC an everyday form of cursive was being used, called the demotic; it relied heavily on abbreviated expression and was used for all administrative and commercial transactions. With the introduction of Christianity in the third century AD, the three Egyptian scripts were replaced by a much later descendant of Egypt's hieroglyphs, the Greek alphabetic script, which, along with the Coptic alphabet, was then used to write the Egyptian language.

By around 3100 BC, perhaps through inspiration from their Egyptian trading partners, the Sumerians had already replaced their external token labels with simple impressed tablets that used logographic markings indicating units, measures and weights.[17] Sumerian is a monosyllabic language with many homonyms, that is, words of the same sound with different meanings, like the English homonyms *to*, *too* and *two*. This creates ambiguities when writing in a logographic script, where a glyph stands for a single morpheme or a complete word. The Sumerians devised a way to avoid confusion, again perhaps borrowing an idea from the Egyptians: they devised purely phonetic glyphs to help identify the logograms. These phonetic glyphs were particularized, again as the Egyptians were doing, using the *rebus* principle (by which pictures represent parts of the word): for example, the English word 'betray' would be 'written' with the pictures of a *bee* and a *tray*. (The rebus principle has been used throughout the world many times since.) Because there are so many homonyms in the Sumerian language, however, this phonetic writing was felt to be insufficient. So the Sumerians used determinatives, too, again like the Egyptians. For example, the names of all Sumerian gods and goddesses were written with an accompanying asterisk *. The Sumerian writing system could reproduce grammatical elements graphically only once it developed syllabic values from the logograms, after the earlier Egyptian method. Only then did it become a truly useful script, capable of being used also by speakers of other languages.

By 2500 BC, a very sophisticated writing technique had developed in Sumer that vied with Egypt's hieroglyphs in its simple efficacy: the Sumerians used a stylus possessing a blunt triangular tip that could easily be handled to form cuneiform or wedge-shaped impressions on soft clay in quick succession.[18] Glyphs were no longer easily recognizable objects that would immediately evoke a word in the Sumerian language, but standardized and abstract shapes made up of successive impressions with the stylus. This greatly increased the system's ability to form individual words. Within the next 500 years a working corpus of around 600 glyphs was created, capable of expressing everything in the Sumerian language and with it the world's earliest documented literature was impressed onto clay.

It was no longer only the Sumerian language that was read in cuneiform. Beginning around 2600 BC, East Semitic Akkadians intruded who began assimilating the non-Semitic Sumerian culture and, by 2400 BC, Sumerian cuneiform writing as well.[19] With these the Akkadians then developed their glorious Babylonian culture. (It was the Akkadians who gave the name 'Sumer' to the region.) Though the Sumerians themselves were wholly absorbed by the Akkadians by around 1800 BC, their language survived in the Akkadians' reading of Sumerian cuneiforms. Akkadians also read the same glyphs in the Akkadian language, too, awarding to each glyph two different readings.[20] Because of the Akkadians' powerful Babylonian empire, various neighbours over the following centuries adopted the Sumerian-Akkadian cuneiforms for their own wholly different languages, with respective alterations and additions in order to better reproduce their differing phonologies.[21] When the Indo-European Hittites adopted the cuneiform script around 1600 BC, their scribes added a new Hittite value to the already present Sumerian and Akkadian values for each glyph. Each Hittite cuneiform glyph could theoretically be read, then, three different ways. However, the Hittites' facile use of determinatives greatly reduced any potential ambiguity.

By 1400 BC, cuneiform writing was the international script of diplomacy and trade. Even mighty Egypt used cuneiform in its diplomatic correspondence to its north-eastern neighbours. Great cuneiform libraries were amassed by powerful Semitic and Hittite rulers: Ashurbanipal of Assyria (669–633 BC) possessed a cuneiform library at Nineveh that has thus far yielded nearly 25,000 inscribed clay tablets. Cuneiform's expansion slowed, then halted. In the first few centuries BC, cuneiform's use contracted to Babylonia alone, where it continued to be written in the astronomical schools until AD 50, when cuneiform writing finally succumbed to the much more influential Semitic consonantal scripts.

An early offshoot of Sumerian logographic writing may have been the still undeciphered script of the Indus Valley civilization, in what is today eastern Pakistan. Around 4,600 years ago, the Indus Valley's first urban society emerged with two heavily populated cities laid out in grids, with paved roads and water engineering: Harappa in the north and Mohenjo-daro in the south. Both exerted influence over a region larger than ancient Egypt.[22] The Indus Valley people developed their own unique type of writing on carved copper tablets and steatite (soapstone) stamp-seals. A proto-form of this writing, apparently dating from 3500 BC, appears on ceramic shards from Harappa. Characteristic Harappan seals have been found in Mesopotamian cities in archæological contexts dating from 2500 BC. Several thousands of such seals have been found in the Indus Valley itself, commonly square or rectangular objects that depict intricately carved figures of animals, mythical beasts, costumed people and so forth. However, the script is not contained in these depictions, but in the five or so glyphs that usually appear alongside them. The total number of autonomous glyphs in the Indus Valley script's inventory of thousands of illustrated seals is approximately 400, many of which, however, are unclear and non-standardized. Since this is far too many glyphs for a syllabic or alphabetic script, one assumes that they express some sort of logographic script, perhaps identifying an owner by name.[23] Though it has been proposed that the script reproduces an early Dravidian language,[24] there is no firm evidence for this. The Indus Valley civilization declined around 1900 BC, for unknown reasons.

The Egyptian hieroglyphic system, which included 24 syllables as well, perhaps generated the earliest West Semitic script of 22 syllables, based on the acrophonic or initial consonant principle.[25] The West Semitic syllabary then generated the scripts of Arabic, Mongol, Manchu, Syrian, Aramaic and Pahlavi.[26] It also inspired Indic Brahmi, which then in turn generated Devanāgarī – the script used for Sanskrit and for various modern languages of India – as well as several other scripts of southern Asia. All these remained syllabic scripts, like their source.

In the early second millennium BC the West Semitic syllabic

script of the cosmopolitan Canaanite culture, with its integrated system of international economies and diplomacy, also inspired the several syllabic scripts of the Indo-European Greeks, evidently through Cyprus. The Greeks had occupied the area of modern Greece in the third millennium BC and then, several centuries later, now dominating the region, had commenced active trade with the far richer Canaanites of the Levant. The Greeks borrowed from the Levant only the *idea* of syllabic writing; their elaborated glyphs and phonetic values were wholly Ægean in shape and sound, based on the rebus principle and using a very early form of the Greek language. (The traditional theory that the region's pre-Greeks independently elaborated the first Ægean scripts now appears to be untenable.)

Among the several syllabic scripts used for many centuries by the Minoans and Mycenæans of Crete, the Ægean islands and the Greek mainland was the famous hieroglyphic script of Crete (with variants) and its stylized simplifications Linear A and Linear B. The more than 4,000 fragments of these that survive constitute Europe's earliest literature. The Greek syllabic scripts were evidently abandoned in the last few centuries of the second millennium BC with the introduction of the eminently more suitable proto-alphabet, again from the Levant. The island of Cyprus, on the Greek periphery, maintained until the second century BC an archaic syllabic script reserved for special use.[27]

Evidence for the world's oldest alphabetic script – one adorning the Gezer Jars from the area of modern Israel – dates from the sixteenth century BC.[28] This proto-alphabet, used in Canaan as pictographs, was written 200 years later alongside the cuneiform alphabet that served simultaneously in Ugarit (now Ra's Shamrah, Syria) and other important Levantine cities. Ugarit's scribes had maintained the writing material and technique of the earlier cuneiform, but had invented their own alphabetic glyphs and values.

Around 1300 BC, the Phoenician scribes of Byblos elaborated a highly simplified syllabary using glyphs derived from the acrophonic or 'initial consonant' principle. Semitic Phoenicians never found vowel representation necessary in their syllabary; among other non-linguistic reasons for not using the Egyptian script, for them it sufficed to acknowledge that a syllabic script was better suited to the Phoenician language than Egypt's logographic script. (Semitic languages prioritize consonants before vowels in word formation.) This new Levantine syllabary, a proto-alphabet that was used in various forms by trading centres in the Late Bronze Age, lasted only until around 1200 BC when, together with the cuneiform alphabet, it succumbed to the consonantal alphabet that had developed from the pictographic alphabet of Bronze Age Canaan.[29]

The Greeks, still regular trading partners, adopted this new consonantal alphabet as well. However, they soon discovered that while it may efficiently represent Semitic languages its lack of vowels caused too much ambiguity for an Indo-European language like Greek, in which vowels are important grammatical and sense-bearing components. They realized something had to be done to create an alphabet that was readable for both the writer and reader of Greek. This 'something' effected the greatest development since the emergence of writing itself: the Greeks introduced vowels into the Levantine consonantal alphabet, thereby completing a whole new class of writing. The Greek alphabetic script has, since this time, essentially remained the same but for external appearances: nearly 3,000 years.

The Greeks' achievement was disarmingly simple and stunningly effective (illus. 8). With the Semitic consonantal glyph ' from Hebrew 'aleph 'ox' – whereby the initial consonant ' represents a Semitic glottal stop (as in English uh-uh), a phoneme unknown in Greek – the Greeks used only the glyph's a value without the glottal stop, creating with it a pure vowel sign. They then borrowed another initial consonant (Semitic yōdh for ι) and invented two new 'letters' (glyphs in an alphabet), until they had signs for all the short pure vowels they needed to show in Greek: α (AH), ε (EH), ι (EE) and o (OH). The Greeks then tailored this new 'alphabet', a word composed of Greek's first two letters αλφα and βητα, to even more faithfully reproduce the Greek language as it was actually spoken. First, η was borrowed from the Semitic hēth glyph to distinguish the long ε from the short ε. In similar fashion, Ω was devised – an o with its bottom opened up – to distinguish the long o from the short o. The four special Greek sounds υ (upsilon), φ (phi), χ (chi) and ψ (psi) were all

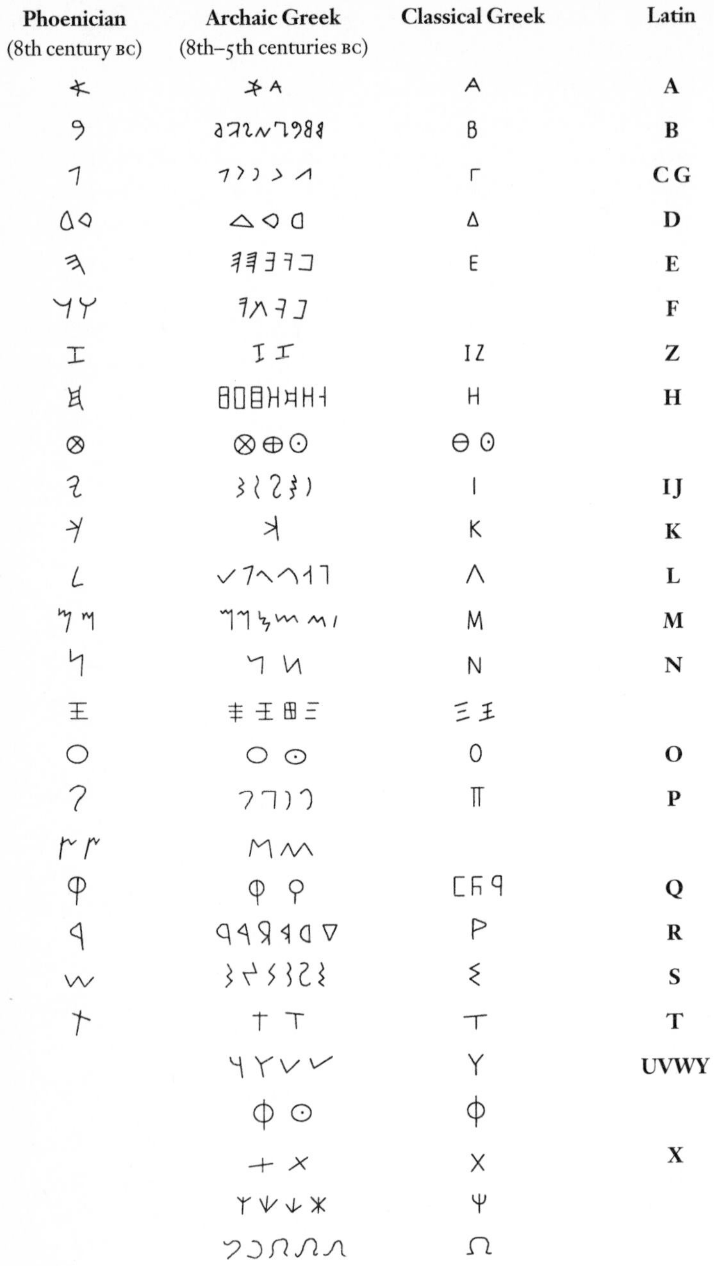

Phoenician (8th century BC)	Archaic Greek (8th–5th centuries BC)	Classical Greek	Latin
⋆	⋆ A	A	A
9	ᴅ𝟩ᴌᴎ⏋98𝟪	B	B
⌐	⌐⟩⟩⟩⋏	Γ	C G
△◁	△◁◁	Δ	D
⇉	∃⇉∃⇂⊐	E	E
⅄Ⴘ	⅂⅃⅂Ⴘ		F
I	I I	IZ	Z
⌶	BΘ⊟Hⵂⵂ	H	H
⊗	⊗⊕⊙	Θ Ο	
Ϩ	ϟ⟨Ϩ⟩⟩	I	I J
⅄	⅄	K	K
⌐	✓⅄⌐⋏⅄⅂	Λ	L
⅄ ᴍ	ᴍ⅄ϟ↖ᴎ ʌʌ⥝	M	M
⅄	⅄ И	N	N
Ⴌ	⌶ Ⴌ⊞⊟	⊟⌶	
○	○ ⊙	Ο	O
ϒ	ϒ⟩⌐⟩	Π	P
⌐ ⌐	Mᴍ		
Φ	Φ Ϙ	⊏Ϩ9	Q
�	9Ϥ8Ϥ◁Ϙ▽	P	R
⩘	ϟϟ⩘ϟ⟨Ϩϟ	Ϩ	S
⳱	⳱ ⏉	⏉	T
	⅄ϒ∨⌵	Y	UVWY
	Φ ⊙	Φ	
	⼗ ⤬	X	X
	ϒ∨↓⤬	Ψ	
	⊃⊃Ω⋂Ω	Ω	

8 The development of the Greek and Latin alphabets.

awarded an individual letter, too, perhaps taken from older Cyprian values.

At the end of this process the ingenious Greek scribes possessed a small, workable alphabet of letters for both individual consonants and vowels. All they had to do to write their language was to combine the consonants and vowels together in spoken sequence to form entire words, the same method we use today. Nowhere else in the world was this invention of a complete vocalic and consonantal alphabet ever independently repeated. Perhaps more significantly, no writing system has ever refined anything more eminently useful for the majority – but not all – of the world's languages.[30]

All the scripts of Western and Eastern Europe derive from the Greek alphabet, including the script of this book. On encountering the Greek alphabet, preliterate Europeans either borrowed only the idea of writing itself from the Greeks, or adopted the Greek alphabet with or without change. The early German tribes, for example, simply borrowed the idea of writing in order to elaborate their own unique system of *runes*. This consisted of 24 signs, in three series of eight, used for short inscriptions, most often at burials. The very earliest Germanic text, from the first century AD, is written in runes. Only once the most northerly Germanic tribes had converted to Christianity and adopted the Latin alphabet by the tenth century, did rune usage entirely cease. Similarly, early Irish and Welsh, having encountered alphabetic writing, developed their own script, called *ogham*. This consisted of lines or notches incised in post corners; one to five dots, or one to five lines, providing five vowel signs and fifteen consonant signs that run either left or right or both directions at once. The introduction of Christianity saw ogham also succumbing to the Latin alphabet.

The Etruscans of the first millennium BC used Greek letters to write their own language. Today this script, still undeciphered (the script is known but the language is unknown), allows one to read Etruscan but not to understand it. In the fourth century AD, Germanic Goths elaborated their *Gothic* script based on Greek, which was soon defunct. In the ninth century AD, Slavic peoples used the Greek alphabet of Constantinople to construct two Slavic scripts: *Cyrillic*, based on Greek capitals and adopted in

Russia (today's Russian script, used by several hundred million people), subsequently served many other Slavic and even non-Slavic languages; and *Glagolithic*, perhaps derived from Greek small letters by St Cyril, apostle of the Slavs, survives today only in Croatia's Roman Catholic liturgy.

By far the most important adaptation of the Greek alphabet was that by the Romans who, around 600 BC, encountered Greek writing on Italian soil through the neighbouring Etruscans. The Romans hardly changed the Greek original. Most notably they voiced the C, that in Latin stands for the sound [k] and wrote it as G. Rome's subsequent military and economic power saw written Latin used throughout the western world, also for languages of non-Latin origin such as the several Celtic and Germanic languages.

Final alphabetic modifications were effected around AD 800, when the need for a clear, classically based script was felt by Charlemagne's learned advisors. The letter V was doubled to create W for the sound [w]; U was invented to distinguish the vowel [u] from the consonant V; and J was innovated to distinguish the consonantal function of the letter I. But today's alphabet is essentially little different from that used by the Romans 2,000 years ago. (An ancient Roman would have little difficulty roughly pronouncing the sounds of this book.) By the third millennium AD the Latin alphabet has become Earth's most important writing system.

There have been fascinating offshoots of this venerable tradition. In North America around 1820, Sequoyah, leader of the Cherokees, modified the shape of the Latin alphabet to create 85 special syllabic – not alphabetic – signs so as to reproduce Cherokee phonology. Even today, Sequoyah's Cherokee script can be read in Cherokee religious publications and newspapers. From 1905–9, Woleai-speaking Caroline Islanders in the South Pacific remodelled European missionaries' Latin alphabet to similarly create a special syllabic script capable of expressing their language. Two further indigenous expansions of the Latin alphabet are Duala Bukere's Vai syllabic script of West Africa from 1834 and King Nshoya's decreed Bamum script of Central Cameroon from 1900.

Apart from Celebes's Macassar-Buginese scripts and the

$$A_1 + B > C$$

manu ma'u	*ika*		*ra'ā*
manu mau	*ika*		*ra'ā*
bird all	*fish*		*sun*

(Te) **manu mau** *[phallus: ki 'ai ki roto ki] (te)* **ika***: (ka pū te)* **ra'ā**

'All the birds copulated with the fish: there issued forth the sun'

9 Reading Easter Island's *rongorongo* script.

Philippines' Bisaya scripts – daughters of writing systems introduced from India – the Pacific remained without writing until
the end of the eighteenth century. Indeed, writing was unnecessary in ancient Pacific societies, since elaborate states had never
developed there that required bookkeeping and oral literature
and a prodigious memory fulfilled all of these societies' requirements in that vein, including long genealogical recitations.
Then, one of the world's most intriguing scripts was elaborated
on isolated Easter Island in the far eastern South Pacific.[31]
Apparently borrowing the idea of writing, linearity and a left-to-
right script direction from Spanish visitors in 1770, the
indigenous Polynesians of Easter Island wrote their famous
rongorongo with approximately 120 basic logograms – birds,
fishes, deities, plants, geometrics and so forth – that accept
assorted semasiograms (glyphs indicating ideas directly without
language) as attachments, resulting in a loose mixed script of
main glyphs, fusions, attachments and compoundings. Writing

had not suddenly become 'necessary' on primitive Easter Island. The *mana*, or 'socio-spiritual power', of the writing that the alien visitors had displayed, with their great ships, their flintlocks and cannons, was exploited to re-establish the waning authority of the island's ruling class, the chief and his priests. Most, but not all, of *rongorongo*'s 25 preserved inscriptions, all incised in wood, appear to comprise simple 'telegram-style' $A_I + B > C$ procreations in their hundreds, such as 'All the **birds** *copulated* [with the] **fish**: [there issued forth the] **sun**' (illus. 9).

ASIATIC WRITING

Perhaps inspired by Western scripts, Chinese writing began in the second millennium BC with simple standardized depictions of objects on bones, bamboo sticks, wooden tablets and very rarely silk, whose names were to be spoken aloud. As a rule, one wrote from top to bottom in columns running from right to left. In time, depictions became more stylized. This allowed faster, more efficient writing. Also, the picture-related writing could be used over a larger area by more speakers, of the same language and of different languages, too.

The ingenuity of Chinese writing lies in its combinatorial possibilities, which were already fully developed by the end of the second millennium BC.[32] Two primary or *wen* glyphs (originally pictograms), like 'tree' and 'sun', create a new derived or *dze* glyph – 'east', the sun rising behind a tree. 'Love' is the compound of 'female' and 'child'. 'Brightness' is the 'sun' and 'moon' written together. Other glyphs are more symbolic: 'above' and 'below' are horizontal lines with respective perpendiculars either above or below (illus. 10).

The *wen* and *dze* originally comprised around 2,500 glyphs. These could also be used phonetically in order to furnish a sound that no longer had to be linked to a definite physical object. In the second half of the first millennium BC one of around 625 determinatives (identifying signs) was commonly attached to the 'phonetic' in order to show which object was meant with a particular phonetic's sound.

The oldest known form of Chinese writing is the 'Old

木 'tree' plus 日 'sun' creates 相 'east'

女 'female' plus 子 'child' creates 好 'love'

日 'sun' plus 月 'moon' creates 明 'brightness'

上 'above' and 下 'below'

10 Chinese writing.

Script', whose younger stage is the 'Great Seal Script'. On unification of the first empire under Xin Shi Huang Di in the third
century BC, Xin's Imperial Chancellery script prevailed, the
'Small Seal Script'. Since then, no fundamental change in the
script has occurred, only smaller formal alterations. The greatest of these came around 200 BC with the decreased use of the
wooden stylus and increased use of the hair brush, necessitating
a new technique that resulted in the 'Curial Script'. In the
fourth century AD, this further developed into the æsthetically
more pleasing 'Standard Script' used in official correspondence
and printing. For daily use, less precise and more abbreviated
cursives emerged.

Because of the numerous phonological changes in the
Chinese language over the past millennia, the original values of
many Chinese glyphs are no longer transparent. Nonetheless, a
glyph's total value, both semantic and phonetic, is easily recognizable because of the determinative glyph that is usually
attached to the 'phonetic' glyph. In this way, when one sees the
Chinese glyph *ma* one immediately knows whether one is reading the 'leech-*ma*', 'agate-*ma*', 'board-*ma*', 'scold-*ma*' or
'weight-*ma*'. Most Chinese glyphs today consist of one identifying element and one phonetic. Though there may well have
once existed as many as 50,000 individual glyphs, only about
4,000 are now commonly employed, logograms that make use
of 214 determinatives (WOOD, FIRE, WATER and so forth). Like

all logographic scripts, Chinese writing is highly phonetic (sound-related) with a strong semantic (sense) component, facilitating memorization. The innate simplicity of the Chinese writing system, which is perfectly adapted to the underlying tonal, monosyllabic and uninflected (that is, no change in word endings) languages it reproduces, has assured its survival in virtually unchanged fashion for over 3,000 years. The script is today read by well over a billion people.

Among the several Asian peoples who adopted the Chinese writing system, the Japanese introduced perhaps the most fascinating changes. Having displaced Japan's original Ainu people and possessing no writing of their own, in the first few centuries AD Japanese scholars learned Chinese writing on the mainland and later introduced it at the Japanese court in order to write Japanese political and religious texts. Japanese culture soon became permeated with Chinese monosyllabic words, producing large numbers of homonyms (words pronounced alike but different in meaning, such as English *pool* 'pond' and *pool* 'a game'). One Chinese glyph or *kanji* came to have several different pronunciations, both Sino-Japanese and indigenous Japanese. Chinese writing was ill-suited to the polysyllabic (not monosyllabic, like Chinese), inflected (word endings changing to show grammar) Japanese language that was so different from the Chinese the script was meant to convey. For the first few centuries, reading Japanese in the Chinese script was a slow, laborious, confusing process.

For this reason, over 1,000 years ago Japanese scribes selected several dozen Chinese glyphs for their sounds only and reduced these graphically to their essentials in order to provide five vowels (*a, i, u, e, o*) and 41 consonant-vowel (*ka, ki, ku* and so forth) syllables.[33] With this, they fashioned a 46-glyph syllabary from which emerged eventually the two separate syllabic *kana* scripts of Japan, each now with 48 glyphs. The more important of the two, *hiragana*, was developed already in the eighth or ninth century and commonly supplies the grammatical word endings attached to the Chinese *kanji* root (roots are nearly always written with the Chinese glyph); provides the syntactic or sentence-sequence markers; and often, in miniscule writing, glosses obscure *kanji* to help the reader. The second, *katakana*, was developed around the twelfth century as a simplified version of the *hiragana* and is primarily used to write foreign, onomatopoeic (imitating the sound of what is meant) and other words phonetically.

Today, one makes use of all three Japanese scripts – logographic *kanji* and syllabic *hiragana* and *katakana* – concurrently when writing a Japanese text, complying with loose rules of standardized usage within restricted domains. Often a *kanji* will have an original Chinese meaning and pronunciation as well as one, two, or even three Japanese meanings and pronunciations. For these reasons Japanese is perhaps the world's most complicated writing system, resembling Mesoamerican in its complexity.

Korean followed first a similar, then a wholly different path. Chinese writing was used exclusively in Korea until AD 692, when Korean *ido* glyphs were elaborated to provide indigenous Korean word endings in Chinese-written texts, in much the same way as the *hiragana* syllables are used in Japanese. However, once the Koreans encountered the Western alphabet in the fifteenth century they created a Korean alphabet called Hangul, first with 28, later only 25 letters. In contrast to Japanese, Hangul is claimed to be the world's simplest script.

MESOAMERICAN WRITING

Only a small handful of Native American peoples ever used writing and this was solely in Mesoamerica.[34] Its origin is unknown. Some scholars have claimed an indigenous origin, with the writing as perhaps a 'natural reflex' of the region's attainment to a high level of civilization. However, writing as a 'natural reflex' of civilization appears to exist nowhere else on Earth. The idea of graphic art reproducing human speech seems to have emerged only once in human history – over 5,000 years ago among an Afro-Asiatic people – and to have been carried from there to all other parts of the globe. (This is the so-called 'monogenetic theory' of writing that perhaps best explains the origin of the world's scripts, according to the cumulative weight of evidence currently available.) With the several Mesoamerican scripts one might actually be dealing with a single, very long, writing tradition that first began, perhaps through inspiration from abroad, with the powerful Olmecs of southern Mexico in the first half of the first millennium BC, flourished with the incredible Maya during the first millennium AD, then ended about 1,000 years ago. The minor scripts of the Mixtecs and Aztecs of the same region appear to comprise simple later developments of the rich Maya script tradition.

In southern Mexico during the first half of the first millennium BC a unique Olmec (1200 to 500 BC) hieroglyphic system emerged.[35] Few fragments remain of this writing, but by 600 BC Olmec scribes in Oaxaca and parts of Chiapas and Veracruz were carving intricate hieroglyphs on stone, probably recording rulers' names and their conquests – themes that predominated in Mesoamerican inscriptions until the arrival of Europeans more than 2,000 years later. Occasionally these are accompanied by numbers. Integral to all Mesoamerican writing and therefore implying a single tradition, number glyphs were associated with the calendar, one of the most complex and socially pervasive calendars ever devised anywhere. The Olmec inscriptions may have inspired the better documented Epi-Olmec script of the same area (150 BC to AD 450). In turn, the Epi-Olmec script is perhaps related to Maya writing, with both sharing a common source. However, the pedigree of the Mesoamerican scripts remains unclear.

All Mesoamerican writing was logographic, whereby glyphs stand for objects, ideas or sounds (from the names for objects).[36] There was also a syllabary of purely phonetic values used in a mixed system with the other glyphs. The inference is either of an extremely long indigenous writing development predating the first millennium BC, or of a borrowed writing system that had already developed over a long period abroad. The most sophisticated and best known writing system of Mesoamerica, the Maya script, contains around 800 glyphs in total. However, many of these glyphs represent royal names used only once; only 200 to 300 of these glyphs were in regular use. More than 150 Maya glyphs represent syllables, almost all of the consonant-vowel type. The script displays *polyvalence*, whereby one glyph comprises several values, such as sound and determinative; *homophony*, whereby the same sound is used by several different glyphs; and also *polyphony*, whereby one glyph has several sounds. This means that one glyph can also possess dual functions, both logographic (representing a morpheme or the entire name of an object) and syllabic (representing the first syllable of the name of the depicted object, to be pronounced separately).

In their codices or manuscript books the Maya wrote with ink and hair brush (like the Chinese of the third century BC) on pages of beaten bark (like Chinese paper of the second century AD) sized with stucco, recording glyphs in vertical columns reading top to bottom (like Chinese writing) and left to right in pairs.[37] Individual glyphic blocks combine two or more glyphs (like Chinese writing). To write the name of the Maya ruler Pacal, for example, one would, among other possibilities, depict a *pacal* 'shield' with the glyphs for 'lord' written above and attach to the right the syllabic glyphs *pa-ca-la* to 'spell' it out (like the Chinese 'phonetic').

During the Classic Maya period (AD 250 to 900), the average intelligent Mayan man and woman could probably read the date, names and events on a colourfully painted stela (inscribed stone pillar). Writing would have had an immediate and profound effect on the local population and language. Not only stelæ, but great public monuments, similarly inscribed and painted in bright colours, proclaimed the glorious lives and genealogies of powerful Maya rulers – hardly 'factual history' in the modern sense, but more of a propagandistic tool to uphold leadership, proclaim pre-eminence and justify tribute, as one finds among writing's manifold roles in many parts of the world.[38] Ceramics were decorated with glyphs, too, identifying chocolate containers, funerary vessels and other objects.

And then there were those thousands of thick bark codices that once graced the royal libraries of the Maya. In the wake of the wholesale destruction of Mayan literature following Spanish intrusion in the sixteenth century, only four Maya codices miraculously survived, Post-Classic productions comprising ritual and astronomical tables. 'Even the burning of the library of Alexandria', the American Maya expert Michael Coe has lamented, 'did not obliterate a civilization's heritage as completely as this'.

The Egyptian-Semitic branch of Afro-Asiatic writing experienced the greatest adaptation of any of the world's writing systems, from pictograms to logograms to syllabograms to letters of the alphabet – depending on who needed what, according to the demands of their respective era and language. The history of Sumerian cuneiform and Chinese logographic writing progressed in similar fashion but, because of the requirements of their languages, experienced greatest 'sophistication' or linguistic complexity only in the syllabic writing of their daughters Old Persian and Japanese. A need for alphabetic writing was never felt with these languages. Throughout history, each language has found and/or adapted the script to which its phonology is best suited. Scripts do not 'evolve': they are purposefully changed by human agents to improve the quality of speech reproduction (sound) and semantic transmission (sense).

Originally, inventive writing began with pictograms, where the name of the depicted object was meant to prompt a pronunciation. On this adequate foundation a logographic system, in which glyphs stand for objects, ideas or sounds (from the names for objects), eventually arose to reproduce human speech more faithfully and efficiently. In time, however, logographic scripts appear to generate new needs and when this occurs syllabic solutions are always found. These can emerge language-internally, when the logographic script fails to reproduce the evolving language, as with Egypt's later addition of syllabic glyphs; and they also can emerge language-externally, when the logographic script is borrowed by an unrelated language, as with Japanese *kana*.

The greatest changes in writing systems seem to occur with speakers of other languages who borrow and adapt an ill-fitting system. Among the West Semitic speakers of the Levant, syllabic glyphs were themselves modified into consonantal symbols that better reproduced the consonantally-oriented Semitic languages of the area. This was then the catalyst for the Greeks' greatest contribution to world culture: a pure alphabet with signs for both vowels and consonants. The most efficient form of written communication ever devised (for most, but not all languages), the Greek alphabet has been adopted and imitated throughout the world for hundreds, if not thousands, of languages, particularly in the nineteenth and twentieth centuries of our era. Today, any preliterate language in need of a script is automatically assigned alphabetic writing.

With pre-writing, the so-called pictographic 'script', an object's depiction triggers the memory of a vocalic utterance. With the first class of actual writing, logographic writing, the picture again triggers the memory of a vocalic utterance, but here the utterance alone – not what the object portrays – conveys the message. With the second class of writing, syllabic writing, this utterance is then reduced only to its first syllable and its position within a defined, limited syllabary of sounds. With the last class of writing, alphabetic writing, the picture is a letter that is no longer related to an object at all but reproduces only one of two different types of sounds, either a vowel or a consonant; this is then read sequentially in combination with other similarly reproduced sounds. In all classes, graphic art remains inextricably linked to human speech. That is to say, *there is no writing that can convey the full range of human thought that is not phonetic.*

It is also through writing that one can best follow a language's history.[39] Internal linguistic reconstruction (working within one language to retrieve older forms) and comparative linguistic reconstruction (comparing two or more related languages to achieve the same) yield precise but unproven hypotheses about earlier language stages. But ancient documents – writings – display these stages. This allows the linguist not only to view a language's earlier forms but also to appreciate the exact types of changes that can occur in languages over centuries and millennia. In this way the science of linguistics was born. What is more, borrowed words and place names in ancient documents often preserve otherwise unattested languages, like Rhætian and Gaulish in Greek and Latin accounts of early Europe from over 2,000 years ago, revealing prehistoric linguistic landscapes otherwise lost forever.[40] Even modern spellings, like English 'light', can be miniature time capsules, pointing out vestigial features, historical origins and the dynamics of relatively recent change: in this case, English's loss of an ancient Indo-European sound that is still preserved on the Continent in *light*'s German cognate *Licht*.

Just as there is no such thing as a 'primitive language', there is no such thing as a 'primitive script'. Each script adequately fulfils the duties assigned to it for a given period in time. If one sees 'primitive' features in a script, then one is judging from a time perspective. In a similar vein, there is no 'passive script': writing affects speech as much as speech affects writing; one comes to appreciate this when reading ancient letters.[41] Literacy has always had a profound impact on spoken language. Educated, literate speakers are usually their society's leaders. They habitually pattern their speech after formal, written language, eventually to be imitated by other members of society. Since its beginnings, speech's 'signature' has also been speech's model.

This has awarded writing an exceptional influence in society – greater than most people realize – particularly in modern literate societies which have enshrined the written word. Written speech slows the process of language change by levelling, standardizing and preserving forms and usages that would otherwise disappear through natural attrition. The reading of past literature enriches any living vocabulary. Written speech can also prescribe spoken language usage for centuries (the *King James Bible* of 1611, the *Talmud*, the *Koran*); it can define art forms (Shakespeare's plays and the *Nō* theatre of Japan); it can constitute the medium of entire technologies (programming languages), replacing spoken language.

However, all writing systems, no matter how revered or innovative, are imperfect and conventional. Nearly all are an approximation, not an exact reproduction, of human speech. In English, the single letter *a* can represent as many as six different sounds (depending on dialect): *an*, *was*, *pa*, *date*, *all* and *hat*; or, because of English spelling's archaism, it stands for no sound at all, as in *bean*, *beau* and *beauty*. Ambiguity, the doubt or uncertainty in meaning arising from indistinctness or obscurity, occurs often with syllabic and alphabetic scripts.

English in particular fails to reproduce its suprasegmentals – that is, pitch (Yes?/Yes!), length (British English cot/cart), stress (désert/desért), juncture (Van Dyck/vanned Ike) and tone (eee!/duh . . .) – because it uses an inadequate alphabetic script. Writers of English try to correct the problem with unsystematic punctuation, space between words, capital letters and other things, but it must be admitted that a precise reproduction of English as spoken cannot be written with the standard English alphabet. Take stress, for example, which English does not mark. When we read *desert*, do we mean 'wilderness' or 'to abandon'? Is *attribute* 'an inherent characteristic' or 'to designate'? Here the English alphabet simply breaks down. Only context will reveal the sense and, with it, the desired stress. Chinese logographic writing, on the other hand, with its combination of determinative (identifying the word's class) and phonetic (sounding out the word), does not know this problem.

Ideally, an alphabetic script should perhaps represent all phonemic utterances – a language's smallest significant sounds. However, only the linguists' special symbols can reproduce fairly exact pronunciations, but these are too ponderous for popular use. Popular alphabetic scripts in use throughout the world constitute convenient approximations, with many ambiguities and enormous differences in pronunciation between different dialects and between different languages using the same alphabetic script. Though the demonstrable efficacy of a simple alphabetic script has assured its adoption throughout most of the world, logographic writing such as Chinese and Japanese still continues to be practised by a significant portion of humanity, who find it eminently preferable for their respective language.

However imperfect, writing is now an indispensable expression of living speech. Speech also responds dynamically to writing. Both speech and writing exist in a synergistic relationship, each now linked inextricably to the other, in much the same way that primitive thought was linked to the vocalizations of early hominids and this continues to change and advance humankind with multidimensional magic. At the beginning of the twenty-first century, the hand no longer merely 'matches the mouth' but, through computer programming languages, is creating whole new worlds and giving voice to humanity's electronic future.

FIVE

Lineages

Like Africa's Bantu languages and the Pacific's Polynesian languages, most of the world's tongues possess no written pedigree. These must reveal their histories through comparative reconstruction. Modern linguistic techniques honed on languages with long written histories, such as the Celtic, Germanic, Italic and Chinese languages, have enabled comparative reconstructions to attain to a level where one can now, despite a lack of written records for most languages, better understand where languages came from and how and when they differentiated from related tongues.

Nevertheless, reconstructed proto-languages are too regular and homogeneous to be real. Only modern constructed languages, such as Esperanto, can compare with the regularity of reconstructed proto-languages, showing us how far from reality the reconstruction lies. Linguistic reconstruction always yields only a partial approximation, never a complete natural 'language'.

All language growth, decline and change is the result both of time and of a society's strength or weakness. While all languages mutate, strong societies' languages thrive and weak societies' languages perish, that is, they are replaced by a foreign tongue. Extinct languages have always been as much the victim as those who spoke them; perhaps even more so, as people everywhere have more willingly yielded their tongues than their lives. For 50,000 years the genetic profile of Europeans hardly changed, while wave after wave of new languages washed over them. Prestige or dominant dialects and languages are adopted, unavailing or dangerous dialects and languages are forsaken. This has happened throughout history, it is happening right now and it will shape the course of all languages to come until only one dominant language is left on Earth. Hundreds of minor languages are currently being replaced by Bahasa Indonesia, Mandarin Chinese, English and Spanish and a depressingly small number of other languages. Future centuries will certainly not enjoy the enormous linguistic diversity that Earth's past has known.

The history of human languages is the story of language change. Certain generalizations appear to obtain with regard to the way languages relate and change over time in every part of the world and in every epoch:[1]

• A language family's homeland – that is, the region where the parent language was spoken – is usually, but not always, one region of the area where its daughter languages have been, or are currently being, spoken.

• The earliest differentiations in a parent language usually, but not always, occur near the homeland. For this reason, one will commonly find highest linguistic diversity near the homeland and lowest linguistic diversity at its periphery.

• A historical relationship between languages is established once one identifies systematic similarities too great to be attributable to chance.

• Sister languages display shared innovations from the parent language and this parent or proto-language might in fact be a linguistic area where two or more separate languages combined.

• A small diversity among sister languages usually, but not always, implies a shorter common development apart from the parent tongue.

• A great diversity among sister languages usually, but not always, implies a longer period of separation from the parent tongue.

There are four basic types of linguistic change:

Phonological change, or systematic sound change, is effected by the speakers of all the world's languages much more readily than any other type of linguistic change. This is why the Londoner Chaucer's English *hūs* and *mūs* 600 years later are pronounced in London 'house' and 'mouse' (Middle High German *hûs* and *mûs* are today Modern German *Haus* and *Maus*, too).

Morphological change is a systematic modification in the form of words, something that occurs much less frequently than phonological change. For example, 400 years ago Shakespeare used 'goeth' and 'didst' in those contexts in which we use 'goes' and 'did' today.

Syntactic change systematically reorders the words in phrases or sentences. Today's 'court martial' and 'Attorney-General', for example, are fossilized mediæval Norman French borrowings for what the English syntactic system – under pressure from its Germanic substrate – otherwise should have reversed, already several hundred years ago, to 'martial court' and 'General Attorney'.

Semantic change alters the commonly accepted meaning of a word. For example, Old English *cniht* was a very common word for 'boy' or 'youth', but by Middle English times *kniht*, with the *k* still pronounced, was 'a military servant of the king' and later 'a feudal tenant responsible for military duty to the king'. Today's 'knight' (the *k* is no longer pronounced) is 'a person raised to an honourable rank by a king or queen or otherwise qualified person', a word now with extremely limited domain, perhaps soon to become extinct.

Each of these processes is the result of any number of well-known linguistic operations – assimilation, dissimilation, lenition (a softening of articulation), excrescence (adding a sound or letter), apocope (cutting off the last sound or syllable), syncope (cutting off a middle letter or syllable), analogy, metathesis (transposition of a sound or letter), borrowing, levelling, expansion, reduction and many more. The interested reader may wish to consult historical linguistic textbooks for details of such operations. (See Bibliography.)

All these processes and operations took place in the following representative lineages.

The Celts were among the first Indo-Europeans to migrate from the eastern homeland west across Europe around 5,500 years ago.[2] Sharing early relations with the Italic people, Celts were already at a very early date inhabiting wide regions of central and western Europe. Their former presence there is attested by place names such as Bohemia; by river names such as Danube, Rhine and Rhône; and by city names such as Vienna and Paris. Around 2,600 years ago, the Celts were again on the move, occupying the Iberian Peninsula and the British Isles. In the fourth century BC they intruded into what had been the Etruscan regions of northern Italy and nearly took Rome. A century later they settled as far as Ankara in what is today Turkey, where St Paul addressed them as 'Galatians'.[3]

In the last few centuries BC three Celtic languages dominated the European mainland and Asia Minor. *Gaulish* speakers of eastern Gaul were eventually overwhelmed by German speakers in the first few centuries AD; by then the Romans' Latin had already replaced the Gaulish of France and northern Italy. (Gaulish remained in Brittany for two or more centuries until replaced by a Celtic back-migration from south-western England.) The *Celtiberian* language of Spain and *Galatian* of Asia Minor similarly succumbed to Rome's might.[4]

Only the Celtic languages of the British Isles survived (illus. 11). Today they are classified into two groups according to their interpretation of the Proto Indo-European phoneme /k^w/. The *q*-Celts or Goidelic people (Gælic-speaking Irish, Manx, Scots) preserved /k^w/, so this is why, for example, Proto Indo-European *k^{w}etuores* 'four', with subsequent changes, is Irish *ceathair*, Manx *kiare* and Scots Gælic *ceithir*. The *p*-Celts or Brythonic people (Brittonic-speaking Welsh, Cornish, Bretons) changed the /k^w/ to /p/ and so 'four' is Welsh *pedwar*, Cornish *peswar* and Breton *pevar*.

The original Gælic (Goidelic) speakers were the Irish, probably the first Celts to arrive in the British Isles around 600 BC. The *Irish* language generated several major dialects by the Old Irish period (AD 700-950); none of these had developed into daughter

11 Range of the Celtic languages today.

languages by the Middle Irish period (950-1400), perhaps because of Norman English conquest. Subsequent suppression of Irish by the English followed in the Modern Irish period (1400 to the present), particularly in the seventeenth and eighteenth centuries when English replaced nearly all Irish dialects. On the establishment of the Republic of Eire in the twentieth century, the south-west Irish dialect of Munster was selected to serve as the new national language in place of 'foreign' English. However, economic, social and historical pressures have so far frustrated its success. Today, Irish is spoken as a first language mainly by a few thousand generally economically disadvantaged residents of the island's far west, north-west and outer isles who are presently encouraging their children to speak English as first language, chiefly for economic reasons.

Around the fifth century AD, Gælic-speaking Irish colonists sailed east to settle the Isle of Man and Scotland, assimilating the indigenous Cruitne (Picts). On Man their tongue eventually became the autonomous *Manx* language, whose 'last native speaker' allegedly died in 1974. In Scotland, the Irish colonists' language also evolved, on a Cruitne substratum, and later became known as *Scots Gælic*.

The Brittonic (Brythonic) Celts, or Britons, followed the Irish into the British Isles in the first few centuries BC. Their tongue remained so similar to continental Gaulish, however, that a 'Gallo-Brittonic language' is acknowledged as the lingua franca of the Celts of France and Britain up to the time of the Roman invasion, when Latin and German speakers intruded. Invading Germanic tribes, particularly in the fifth century AD, then pressed the Britons to Britain's peripheries: southern Scotland, Wales, Devon and Cornwall.

For more than two centuries Britons also escaped the Saxon trespass by migrating back to the continent, south to Brittany in France. Their descendants, the Bretons, now number around half a million, but few speak *Breton* today. Young Bretons have recently shown a renewed interest in learning their ancestral language, which is not recognized as an official tongue by the French government.

The Celtic language with the greatest number of active speakers is *Welsh*. What J. R. R. Tolkien has deemed 'the senior language of the men of Britain' was spoken in 1991 by 510,920 or 18.7 per cent of the population of Wales over the age of three.[5] Welsh has survived with great difficulty. Roman occupation introduced many Latin words. Irish settlers later encroached on Welsh territory, introducing Gælic words up to the seventh century towards the end of the Early Welsh period (to around 850). The influence of English increased in the Old Welsh period (850 to 1100). During the Middle Welsh era (1100 to 1500), England's Norman French nobles conquered Wales, resulting in many borrowed French words; however, the Welsh language prevailed. Only in the Modern Welsh period (1500 to the present) – and principally because of Henry VIII's Act of Union incorporating Wales into England – did Welsh use decline, as English became the language of Wales's courts and office-bearers. Still, Welsh survived.

It was above all the advance of English that had divided the Brittonic speakers: Cumbric was spoken in southern Scotland and north-west England; Welsh in Wales; and Cornish in south-west Britain. The Anglo-Saxons called all speakers of these tongues *Wealas* or 'non-German', the origin of English 'Welsh'. Welsh and Cumbric Britons were now calling themselves *Combrogi*, 'fellow countrymen', marking a new sense of ethnic identity. Today's Welsh are *Cymry* (pronounced CÚM-REE) and their language *Cymraeg* (CUM-RÁH-EGG). Cumbric survived under increasing pressure until the collapse of the kingdom of Strathclyde in about 1018. In Cornwall, the Celtic kingdom fell to the English around 878; since then, the use of the Cornish language steadily declined until its extinction in the nineteenth century. Like Manx, it is now being artificially revived.

Indo-European's most important and widely distributed language family 2,300 years ago, the Celtic family today – first because of the Romans and Germans, later because of national consolidation (England, France) – constitutes one of Indo-European's smallest families, confined to western France and the peripheries of the British Isles. With the exception of the official Munster dialect of Ireland, the Celtic languages belong among those 'non-state' tongues that are at the mercy of dominant metropolitan languages, suffering the fate of Catalan (Spain, France, Italy), Galician (Spain), Occitan (Spain, France, Italy), Romany (most European countries) and many other European speech communities who number over *twenty million* speakers of languages not their nation's official tongue. Until quite recently, it was feared that the Celtic languages might disappear altogether. Socio-political dynamics and a rediscovered sense of pride among Celts have caused a new resurgence of interest in Irish, revived Manx, Scots Gælic, Welsh, revived Cornish and Breton and allowed the number of their speakers to grow as ever greater political autonomy is granted them in the new unified Europe.

By the first millennium BC, most of the Italian peninsula, with the exception of the non-Indo-European Etruscans and Rhætians in the north and north-west; the Messapic tribes of Illyrian descent from across the Adriatic; and the independent Greek colonies of the south, was speaking an Italic language belonging to one of three subfamilies: *Picene, Osco-Umbrian* and *Latinian.*[6]

Having differentiated in the second millennium BC, if not earlier, the *Southern Picene* language of middle Italy's eastern coast appears to have been closely related to the Osco-Umbrian family, although it also shared features with Venetic and the Balkan languages. Its speakers fell to Rome in 268 BC.

Osco-Umbrian (Sabellian) included Oscan, Umbrian and Volscian (and their minor dialects).[7] Like the *p*-Celts, all Osco-Umbrian speakers had replaced Indo-European /k^w/ with /p/, so Proto Indo-European k^w*i(s)* 'who?' became Oscan *pis*, while Proto Indo-European *penk^{w}e* 'five' became, with subsequent changes, Umbrian *pompe*. Preserving many Proto Indo-European vowels without change, Oscan was the most powerful and widely distributed of the subfamily; it survives in some 200 inscriptions mostly from the last two centuries BC. Umbrian is chiefly known through the famous Iguvine Tablets, the most significant non-Latin texts of ancient Italy: seven bronze inscriptions from perhaps the first century BC that contain rules about auspices, penance, offerings and prayers. The central Italian Osco-Umbrian dialects – Sabine, Æquian, Hernican, Marsian and others – very early succumbed to Rome's dominant Latin. The Volscians of south-east Latium – central Italy bordering on the Tyrrhenian Sea – spoke an autonomous language closely related to Umbrian.

Its early history unclear, *Venetic* was spoken by the Veneti of the Adriatic coast between the Po and Aquileia.[8] Their language survives in some 300 inscriptions, mainly from Esta and Làgole di Calazio in today's Venetia. Many characteristics suggest Venetic's affiliation to the various Italic languages, particularly to Latin. Venetic might represent, then, a vestige of the first

Italic incursion into the peninsula in the third millennium BC.

The Latinian languages *Faliscan* and *Latin* are probably among the oldest Italic tongues spoken on the peninsula, displaying an archaic Indo-European phonology and a greatly modified vocabulary, perhaps prompted by a pre-Indo-European contact population. Faliscan was the language of the ancient Italic tribe whose capital was Falerii (modern Cività Castellana north of Rome), as of the eighth century BC under Etruscan influence. It was then destroyed in 241 BC by the Romans, rendering Faliscan extinct even before the Oscan-Umbrian languages.

Latin emerged in Latium in the first millennium BC as Rome rose to power and subsequently suppressed all other Italic languages of the peninsula.[9] At first simply the local dialect of the village of Rome, in time Latin became one of history's great languages. Only around 240 BC did Latin literature commence in earnest, which then empowered and enriched the expanding Roman Empire. Latin's history follows the developmental stages: pre-literary Latin up to 240 BC; Old Latin, 240 to 100 BC; Classical Latin (the preserved literary Latin), 100 BC to AD 14; Silver Age, AD 14 to around 120; Archaic Latin, 120 to 200; Vulgar Latin of late antiquity, 200 to 600; Middle Latin, 600 to the fourteenth century; and, since then, Modern Latin.

Classical Latin was the everyday speech of Julius Cæsar, Augustus and Virgil. Soon 'petrified' as the written medium of the expanding Empire's administration and culture, it eventually became the written and spoken medium of the Christian Church and all education in the West. It survived into the eighteenth century as the primary language of education and into the twentieth as the language of Roman Catholic liturgy. Neglected for many decades, Classical Latin in Europe and North America is now experiencing a dynamic resurgence as a second or additional language.

Spoken Vulgar Latin continued to evolve on foreign substrates throughout the Roman Empire. This created the Romance family of languages.[10] Each daughter language was spoken in proto-forms for many centuries before finally being entrusted to parchment: *French* in the ninth century; *Italian* in the tenth century; *Provençal* of southern France a century later;

the three Ibero-Romance languages *Spanish*, *Portuguese* and *Catalan* in the twelfth century; and *Romanian* in the sixteenth century. The minor Romance languages include *Walloon* of southern Belgium, *Rhæto-Romanic* (Romansch, Ladin) of the Swiss valleys, *Sardinian*, the recently extinct *Dalmatian*, *Haitian Creole* and *Judæo-Spanish*, the language of Spain's expelled Jews that is now facing imminent extinction.[11]

All Romance languages except Romanian have continuously borrowed from Classical Latin. For this and other reasons there is much greater mutual intelligibility today between speakers of Italic languages than between speakers of Germanic languages. Though the Vulgar Latin-speaking population of North-west Africa was overwhelmed by Arabic speakers by around AD 700, Spanish, Portuguese, French and Italian colonists much later took the Italic languages to other parts of Africa and even further afield to the Americas, Asia and Western Pacific where they thrived. Italic languages are for this reason second only to Germanic (English) in current worldwide distribution.

French emerged from Vulgar Latin on a Gaulish substrate, retaining several Celtic pronunciations: *ct* as *cht* (as in Scottish *Loch*) which later became *it* (in this way Latin *factum* became French *fait*); and Latin *u* as the high *ü* like in French *tu*. Just when Gaul's Latinization was perfected under Romano-German tutelage, new Germanic tribes invaded, with the Franks eventually dominating most of Northern Gaul. The combined German influence greatly affected the phonology of the Vulgar Latin spoken there. (Southern Gaul did not share in this process; its Vulgar Latin developed into the autonomous Provençal language.) French's developmental stages are Old French (842 to 1350), Middle French (1350 to 1605) and Modern French (1605 to the present).[12] Since the twelfth century, French has been one of the world's great cultural languages, its rich literature affecting the course of many other, even non-Indo-European, languages and literatures.[13]

Spanish emerged from the Vulgar Latin spoken on the Celtic substrate of the Iberian Peninsula.[14] Old Spanish (1100 to 1450) is today partially preserved in the speech of the few remaining speakers of Judæo-Spanish (just as Yiddish partially preserves Middle High German). Modern Spanish (1450 to the present) has been dominated by the Castilian dialect which sets the standard for the written language, or *castellano*. Spanish has retained many Vulgar Latin features lost in the other Romance languages. However, because of Spain's long Muslim occupation (713 to 1492) its language has acquired many Arabic words. In more recent times, American Spanish dialects have borrowed many Native American words. Spanish is now, after English, the world's second most widely distributed language.[15]

Italian is the evolved form of the Vulgar Latin spoken on the original soil of the Italic peoples.[16] Because of its indigenous character Italian has retained the greatest number of original Latin features – that is, it has not experienced the various substrates or invasions that so altered other Romance languages. Specific grammatical innovations such as plural formation (*-i/-e/-a* endings) differentiate Italian from the West Romance languages (*-s/-es*), so that Italian is formally aligned, with Romanian, to East Romance. Unique among the Romance languages – indeed rare in the world – is the almost unchanged phonology of Italian over many centuries: any educated Italian today can easily read his or her mediæval poets without special training. For this reason, Italian's history is not categorized into the Old, Middle and Modern periods that one finds with most European languages. Italian's protracted political disunity also promoted a separate dialectal development that has led, like with German, to local dialect literatures of great strength: Southern and Middle Italian (with Sicilian); Tuscan (with Corsan dialects) and Roman-Umbrian; and Upper Italian or the Gallo-Italian group of dialects. Today, the Italian dialects of the main Tuscan cities (Florence, Siena, Arezzo) and of Rome constitute the national standard, or the *lingua toscana in bocca romana*.

GERMANIC LANGUAGES

By the third millennium BC, an Indo-European people who had followed the Celts out of eastern Europe were occupying what is today southern Sweden, Denmark and northern and north-eastern Germany. This was the Germanic people, their language characterized foremost by a radical systematic reinterpretation of the Indo-European consonants (the First Sound Shift) and by other specific innovations. A thousand years later, isolated Germanic tribes migrated east to the Weichsel, south to the Danube and west to the Rhine, driving out or absorbing indigenous Celts. By this time there were two major Germanic tribes, identified by their interpretation of specific Proto Indo-European sounds: North Germanic (Gotho-Norse) speakers had changed these sounds; West Germanic speakers preserved them. During the first millennium BC, West Germanic speakers, growing in numbers, began driving neighbouring Celts further south and west. By the first few centuries BC, Scandinavians, Baltic Germans, North Sea Germans, Elba Germans and West Germans were each living in small, differentiated communities.[17]

Apart from early Greek and Roman accounts that confuse Germanic tribes with Celts, the hitherto oldest linguistic evidence of a Germanic presence is the short inscription on the Negau Helmet from the Steiermark (south-eastern Austria) that is dated to the beginning of the Christian era. At this time eastern North Germanic speakers, better known as 'Goths', were repeating what Celtic speakers had done centuries earlier: migrating to Spain (even to Africa), Gaul, Italy, the Balkan peninsula, the Black Sea and Asia Minor. Gothic's most significant document remains the Visigoth Bishop Wulfila's (AD 311–83) translation of the Bible that survived in an Ostrogothic manuscript transcribed in Greek letters over a century after the bishop's death. Since Gothic preserves many older Germanic linguistic forms, it is of considerable use for historical linguistic comparisons. Among other North Germanic languages whose speakers were forging history in Western Europe in the first few centuries AD were Burgundian, Vandalic, Gepidic, Rugian, Sciran and others that succumbed in the first millennium AD to the local Vulgar Latin. Crimean Gothic, spoken along the Black Sea, survived into the sixteenth century.[18]

North Germanic's original Norse language is preserved in a number of runic inscriptions found in almost all regions of Scandinavia, some dating as early as the fourth century AD. The inscriptions display an archaic language that retains the vowels of unstressed syllables (*horna* 'horn'), a feature later lost. This Norse tongue had probably already differentiated into East Norse (later to comprise Swedish, Danish and Gutnish) and West Norse (Norwegian, Faroese and Icelandic) by the middle of the first millennium AD; however, active intercommunication in the following centuries kept the two groups from losing mutual intelligibility.[19] Norse had a great impact on Old English at the end of the first millennium AD. Shortly after this, Old Icelandic enriched world literature with its Edda songs, sagas and poems and histories of the Skalds or bards. Scandinavia preserved linguistic unity much longer than any other Germanic community. For this reason, its languages can today be regarded more as dialects of the Scandinavian language than as separate tongues.

The High German 'Second' Sound Shift divided West Germanic tribes into two separate groups: speakers of High German in the interior and speakers of Low German in the north and north-west coastal area.[20] As early as the seventh and eighth centuries AD mediæval scribes were using the Latin alphabet to record a variety of things in Old High German. The Rhenish Franconian of Charlemagne's court predominated. Later in the Middle Ages, political influence shifted to Upper Germany, where two main dialects were spoken: Alemannic in the west and Bavarian in the east. By the sixteenth century, the Church reformers, led by Martin Luther, were making use of Central Germany's new political weight to broadcast their publications; from their Central German dialect emerged Modern High German, today Germany's standard language.[21]

High German became one of Earth's great cultural languages. German poets, playwrights and novelists are still prominent in world literature. In the nineteenth century, German was the primary language of science and scholarship. German is rich in dialects, from Plattdeutsch in the north to Southern Tyrolean in Italy's northernmost Alpine valleys. Mediæval German phonology can still be heard today in parts of the Alps. A relic mediæval German dialect, Yiddish or Jewish, has for many centuries been preserved by a special community; it is still spoken today, primarily in New York and Israel.

A Low German language, mediæval Low Franconian survives in the Netherlands as Dutch; its southern dialect is Flemish, one of Belgium's three official languages (Flemish, Walloon and German). The Dutch that was taken in the seventeenth century to South Africa has since developed into an autonomous language, Afrikaans, but is now being replaced by English, South Africa's former colonial language, under the new indigenous regime.

In the fifth century AD, many communities of Low Germans living along the North Sea – Angles, Saxons and Jutes from Denmark – migrated to Britain's east and south, joining Upper German descendants of Rome's Romano-Germanic troops. Their linguistic fusion created a new language that would one day overtake the world: English. Old Saxon was first written on English soil in the seventh century; the Anglian poem *Beowulf*, the Germanic peoples' oldest and greatest saga, was probably composed in England's north a little before AD 750. Old English (AD 700 to 1100) comprised three main dialects, with many variants and foreign influences: Kentish in the south (Kent and Surrey), Saxon in the central southern territory (Sussex to Middlesex) and Anglian north of this (Essex to Northumbria). Almost replaced by French after the Norman invasion of 1066, Middle English (1100 to 1500) covered four main dialects heavily influenced by French and Latin: these were Southern, West Midland, East Midland and Northern. Chaucer wrote his *Canterbury Tales* in the London dialect that bordered on both Southern and East Midland English. This London dialect, because of political centralization, eventually became Britain's standard language.

Beginning in the seventeenth century, the English language followed the lead of Dutch and was taken to North America, the East Indies, the West Indies, parts of Africa and India. As the influence of Dutch waned, that of English grew. The colonization of Australia, New Zealand and many parts of the Pacific followed in the eighteenth and nineteenth centuries. This global expansion has resulted in the creation of International Standard English, the world's primary language of bilingual speakers. In numbers of first-language speakers, English is second only to Mandarin Chinese. The international growth of English has been unparalleled in world history. With the advent of International Standard English, a veritable world language has nearly been achieved for the first time.[22]

Most early commonalities that the Germanic languages once possessed have been displaced by the large number of extreme idiosyncrasies that have since emerged in the surviving tongues: English's Italic vocabulary and loss of inflection (word endings showing grammar, as in 'whom'), German's convoluted sentence structure (with the verb often at the end), Scandinavian's suffixing of definite articles (Icelandic *bók* 'book', but *bókin* 'the book') and many more innovations. The Germanic languages' diversity is the antithesis of Italic homogeneity.

BANTU LANGUAGES

Africa's Bantu family of languages comprehends today some 550 tongues – a massive number when compared to Indo-European which has a little over 100. A daughter family of the Benue-Congo branch of the supposed 'Niger-Congo' superfamily of languages, Bantu serves an immense geographical area.[23] Nearly all the peoples of Central Africa, from the lower Cross River in the west to southern Somalia in the east, speak related languages loosely grouped under the name Bantu ('people'). Limited originally to the region of the Bight of Benin before AD 1000, only in the last millennium have the Bantu languages achieved the enormous distribution they now enjoy – although in the seventeenth century the Dutch reached the Cape of Good Hope before the Bantu. Also, the large degree of linguistic resemblance between Bantu languages reveals a protracted proximity.

Four of the major 'Niger-Congo' languages are Bantu: Rwanda, Makua, Xhosa and Zulu. Swahili is the Bantu language of Africa's eastern coast and Zanzibar which, many centuries ago, borrowed a great deal of Arabic vocabulary in order to be used, with Bantu grammar, as a lingua franca. In the nineteenth century, Arab slave dealers used Swahili as a trade language as far inland as the Congo.[24]

The Bantu languages were recognized as belonging to one family more than a century ago. Since then, reconstruction of

Bantu phonology (system of significant sounds) and morphology (systematic word formation) has followed. However, frequent borrowing among related Bantu languages (that is, areal diffusion and convergence) has made the description of Bantu's pedigree extremely difficult.[25]

A recent study has relied on the method of lexicostatistics – the comparison of 100 (or 200) items of basic or culturally neutral words among related languages – to effect a general and highly speculative, outline of Bantu's 'family tree'.[26] Lexicostatistics holds that core vocabulary always behaves differently from non-core; that word replacement occurs at a constant rate; and that a lexicon or list of words alone can provide information on genetic relationships. The origin of the Bantu family, according to this study, is claimed to lie in the Benue Valley of today's Nigeria. Here, around 5,000 years ago, Bantu divided into West Bantu and East Bantu. The West Bantu languages developed east of the Cross River in western Cameroon, it is claimed. Commencing around 1560 BC, West Bantu languages gradually expanded over all Central Africa, perhaps with the bearers of new farming techniques. West Bantu diverged into a succession of daughter languages which each differentiated at different times from the 'main body' (a relative term) of West Bantu speakers, a process quite different from the general fragmentation of the Germanic languages.

First to 'depart' were the Nen-Yambassa speakers, according to this interpretation. After them, the Myene-Tsogo departed, followed by Bioko. In around 1120 BC the Aka-Mbati, the northern Zaire languages, differentiated from the south-western languages and dispersed. About two centuries later, the 'main body' of West Bantu speakers split in two to establish two separate families of languages: South-west Bantu and Savanna, including the Kongo languages and the Gabon-Congo languages. Around 580 BC the Buan-Soan languages differentiated, whereupon Buan split internally a century and a half later. Around AD 170, the Biran languages diverged from Buan as the easternmost assemblage of this subgroup. The initial expansion of West Bantu ceased once the southern Maniema group of languages had differentiated from its West Bantu neighbour on the Savanna by around AD 330. Only as of the second millennium

AD did the Bantu languages then rapidly expand east and south to Africa's extremities, replacing many of the indigenous tongues they encountered along the way.

This pedigree of West Bantu tongues has recently been proposed, in the absence of written language, on the basis of a lexicostatistical comparative reconstruction which acknowledges that, as with all linguistic change, certain innovations must come before others.[27] To this pedigree, further statistical estimates have been attached which study vocabulary to determine the relationship between particular languages and their development over time. This is called glottochronology and is as speculative a linguistic method as lexicostatistics. Its formula is based on the observed fact in languages with a long written history that all basic vocabulary changes or is replaced at a constant rate. The formula should allow any given lexicostatistical percentage (calculated by comparing selected basic words among similar languages) to be expressed in terms of specific years, according to the proponents of glottochronology.

However, rates of vocabulary replacement are not constant. This may be because, as one new theory proposes, languages also experience long periods of equilibrium. During such a period, changes might come about through diffusion, internal adjustments of the language, or language convergence. This period might then be followed by a sudden 'punctuation' or disturbance that leads to the creation of so-called 'family trees'. Consequently, all glottochronological dates for Bantu remain subjective speculation.

Only phonological comparisons (based on the system of sounds in a language) providing relative chronologies for related linguistic developments hold an unassailable validity in this field of research, though they cannot provide absolute dates. None the less, one can say with reasonable certainty that, by the beginning of the Christian era, West Bantu speakers were occupying most of western Central Africa. Over a millennium later, the Bantu began their great migrations that eventually led them to the southern tip of the African continent by the end of the seventeenth century.

CHINESE LANGUAGES

Chinese or Sinitic is the most easterly and important subfamily
of the larger Sino-Tibetan family of languages.[28] Its members
are isolating languages – that is, their 'word' is generally a morpheme (the smallest meaningful unit of a language), with word
order and/or special particles showing grammatical relationships. Unlike the Celtic, Germanic and Italic languages which
only recently became isolating, Chinese has preserved its isolating status in all stages of its history. Probably less than 5,000
years ago, the first Sino-Tibetan speakers entered the Yellow
River Valley to settle there permanently. Whom they met there
– whose language then helped to create what came to be
Chinese – remains unknown. It appears that a large part of the
Chinese vocabulary, but not its grammar, may have been borrowed from these earlier inhabitants.

During the Zhou Dynasty (1050 to 220 BC), Chinese was
spoken in a much more restricted area than at present. Its heart-
land was the Yellow River Plain. But already in the first
millennium BC its domain expanded to the peripheries. Over
centuries the conquest of ethnic neighbours imposed the
Chinese language on those territories where one hears it today –
similar to Latin in the west. Before the sixth century AD Old
Chinese was spoken. Middle Chinese designates the language
between the sixth and tenth centuries. Old Mandarin was heard
from the tenth century to the middle of the fourteenth century
(the beginning of the Ming Dynasty), Middle Mandarin from
the fourteenth to the nineteenth centuries and Modern
Mandarin from the beginning of the nineteenth century to the
present.

Apart from the fact that Sinitic's daughter, Mandarin
Chinese, is spoken by more people as a first language than any
other tongue on Earth, Chinese is one of the world's very few
contemporary languages (or language family) whose history is
documented in writing in an unbroken tradition reaching back
to the middle of the second millennium BC. At this time, during
the Shang Dynasty (around 1700 to 1100 BC), divinatory texts
on shell and bone were written in a language obviously related

to that which was more copiously documented in the succeeding Zhou Dynasty. There is no doubt that this language of the Zhou Dynasty generated all later stages of Chinese, including the Chinese languages spoken today.

Because of Chinese's logographic writing system (that is, non-alphabetic), the reconstruction of the pronunciation of even Middle Chinese logograms has been difficult, as the phonetic (sound) element is unclear. The reconstruction process has been aided by early Chinese rhyming dictionaries, which can help to reconstruct word endings and by comparing borrowings into Korean and Japanese which then identify word beginnings. Historical linguistic reconstruction has demonstrated that before the second century BC Old Chinese used consonantal clusters at the beginning of a word, but their precise nature is still unknown. In time these were reduced to single consonants, resulting in morphemes of the Chinese languages being words of one syllable. (Consonantal clusters survive at the end of words in a few Chinese languages.) Also, it has been suggested that the Old Chinese vowel system contained as few as two vowels, which is improbable, or as many as fourteen. In addition, it is clear that very early Chinese was an inflected language – that is, grammar was shown through word changes – and that the distinctions effected by inflections, once these inflections were lost, were preserved through the introduction or expansion of different word tones, another method to mark the special function or meaning of words. Experts are still in the process of reconstructing Old Chinese.

During the Zhou Dynasty the written Chinese language, like Classical Latin, probably did not differ too greatly from normal educated speech. However, in the later Han Dynasty (206 BC to AD 220) the spoken language no longer followed the written language and the gap between the two widened in succeeding centuries. Again like Latin in the West, written Chinese did not reflect the vernacular languages that were emerging. There had always been regional dialects in Chinese, even at a very early date. But these did not develop into separate languages until near the end of the first millennium BC, or nearly 1,000 years earlier than the emergence of the Romance languages out of Vulgar Latin.

Middle Chinese differed greatly from Old Chinese. By this time, initial consonantal clusters had totally disappeared. Also, the Middle Chinese tonal system now counted four word tones in each of the higher and lower registers, as is still spoken in China's southern languages. (In contrast, today's Beijing Mandarin, spoken in the north, recognizes only four word tones in all.) Between Middle Chinese and Modern Mandarin there occurred a great reduction in the number of phonemes – a phoneme being the smallest significant sound in a language that distinguishes one word (or part of a word) from another – such as the two phonemes that distinguish English *bin* and *pin*. This left as residue many homophones, or words having the same sound, and the Beijing language now contains the least number of phonemes. This reduction in the number of phonemes necessitated in all Chinese languages the formation of new word compositions, primarily compounds of synonyms (words with the same or nearly the same meaning). For this reason, today's Chinese 'word' is usually no longer monosyllabic (of one syllable) but bi- or even polysyllabic (of two syllables or more).

Today, the eight major Chinese languages constitute a family of mutually unintelligible tongues, each displaying several principal dialects. Though Old Chinese may now be as different from the contemporary Mandarin Chinese of Beijing as Classical Latin is from the French of Paris, there none the less remains a strong sense of linguistic unity among all Chinese speakers. This is the result of three factors: a logographic script that does not reflect different languages or diachronic changes; a written language based on a standard dialect that prevented competition from other dialects; and the almost unparalleled political unity of the Chinese people throughout history. Today's written Chinese language is a direct continuation of the standard language in the literary vernacular of Middle Chinese.

However, in the spoken – not the written – language the originally verbal or pronominal (relating to pronouns) meaning of many of the grammatical particles used to clarify syntactic relationships in a sentence have been weakened in Modern Chinese to the role of grammatical affixes or word attachments. Modern Chinese is now tending towards polysyllabicism, using words of several syllables and even towards agglutination – the formation of derivative or compound words by joining together single-meaning constituents.

The north's *Mandarin Chinese* claims three principal dialects: Northern Mandarin (Yellow River Basin and Manchurian), South-eastern Mandarin and South-western Mandarin. Throughout most of China's history there has been a standard language, comprising both the written and the spoken language. A common spoken medium or lingua franca was necessary for trade, bureaucracy and political consolidation by a severe central government. Present-day Mandarin Chinese emerged from the lingua franca used in the foreign dynasties of Liao (AD 916 to 1125), Jin (1115 to 1234) and Yuan (1271 to 1368), all three of which maintained their capitals in the general area of Beijing. Serving all of northern China and beyond, or some two-thirds of Chinese speakers, Mandarin is spoken by approximately one billion people. The Northern Mandarin dialect of the capital Beijing is the basis for the Common Chinese Vernacular heralded since the beginning of the twentieth century and the Chinese that most Western dictionaries follow.

Today's seven major southern Chinese languages are generally more conservative in phonology and tone system than the northern dialects. *Min Nan* dialects are spoken in the south-east, generally in Zhejiang, Fujian and the islands of Hainan and Taiwan. *Min Pei* dialects are found in north-west Fujian. In Shanxi and south-west Hebei, *Gan* dialects can be heard. *Wu* idioms are spoken in the Yangtse Delta, including Shanghai and other parts of Anhui, Jiangsu and Zhejian. The *Yüeh* or Cantonese dialects of the south are heard mainly in Guangdong, southern Guangxi, Macau and also Hong Kong. *Hakka* is a widespread language, whose dialects are spoken foremost between Fujian and Guangxi. *Hsiang*, known also as Hunan, is spoken in the central southern Hunan region of China.

For many centuries Koreans, Japanese and Vietnamese used literary Chinese as their everyday medium of written expression. Even today, these three peoples continue to use Chinese roots to create new words in their vocabularies. For this and other reasons, Chinese can well be called the 'Latin of East

Asia'. Because of numerous recent migrations – perhaps small in scope when compared to those of English and Spanish speakers – Chinese can be heard throughout the world in most large cities. The influence of the Chinese family of languages will no doubt remain considerable throughout most of the twenty-first century.

POLYNESIAN LANGUAGES

Polynesian, too, claims a venerable pedigree.[29] Around 6,000 years ago its parent Austronesian superfamily of languages generated a Proto-Oceanic family that included, on one hand, the Austronesian languages of New Guinea, the Bismarck Archipelago, the Solomon Islands, New Caledonia and other islands in the West Pacific and on the other, the Proto-Eastern Oceanic family of languages. The latter comprised the western languages of the North and Central New Hebrides, Nuclear Micronesia and Rotuma and the eastern Proto-Central Pacific languages that eventually became Proto-Fijian in the west and Proto-Polynesian, by around 1500 BC, in the central eastern part of the Fiji-Tonga-Samoa crescent.

Polynesian languages are among the most conservative in the world. Polynesian vowels, vocabulary and grammar have remained extraordinarily stable over the past 3,500 years, to a degree perhaps seen nowhere else on Earth. One might ascribe this to the extreme reductionism (simplification) already present in the Proto-Polynesian basis – few consonants, simple monosyllabic and bisyllabic vocabulary, frequent reduplication (word doubling, like *hulahula*) and a very limited number of particles in order to show grammar. After this, the changes that occurred in Polynesian languages are generally one-stage consonantal shifts, such as *k* to ', the glottal stop; *ng* to *n* or '; and *t* to *k*, that are almost dialectal in nature, allowing near-intelligibility across Polynesia. The remarkable conservatism and homogeneity of the Polynesian languages is probably also the result of continuous active trading between most island groups until only several hundred years ago.

Unlike most other language families, Polynesian contains no

member language whose inclusion is controversial. However, the delineation between language and dialect is often unclear, owing to the large number of similar languages sharing a nearly identical vocabulary except for minor, easily identifiable phonological substitutions. For example, 'house' is Samoan *fale*, Tahitian *fare*, Rapanui (Easter Island) *hare*, Māori *whare* and Hawaiian *hale*. There are around 36 Polynesian languages spoken today, from the Solomon Islands in the western Pacific to Easter Island in the distant south-eastern Pacific, that are all descended from a single original community who, around 3,500 years ago, were developing in their new isolation, with only sporadic contact with the homeland, a unique culture and language that millennia later Westerners would call 'Polynesian' from Greek *poly* 'many' and *nēsos* 'island'.

After differentiation from its sister Proto-Fijian, Proto-Polynesian had experienced a protracted period of isolated development, probably on Tonga.[30] Throughout Polynesia's history the common cause of linguistic differentiation continued to be the removal of speakers from one island or archipelago to another. The linguistic continuity of the settling population was assured, because small numbers of subsequent visitors would not have imposed their language on a large island population. On Tonga in the second millennium BC, the proto-language then split into two separate families: Proto-Tongic (which eventually generated Tongan and Niuean) and the Proto-Nuclear Polynesian family of languages which probably had its origin in the settlement of Samoa. Around 2,000 years ago Proto-Nuclear Polynesian speakers migrated to the North-west Marquesas Islands where they succeeded in establishing a permanent settlement. It was in the North-west Marquesas, over many centuries and with only sporadic trade with the homeland, that a new language evolved – Proto-East Polynesian.

Meanwhile, back in Samoa, the ancestral language continued to develop as well, eventually becoming Proto-Samoic-Outlier. In time, this generated the Samoan language as well as the individual tongues spoken by groups who had left to settle other islands, particularly in the first millennium AD. Since these latter languages diverged from evolving Samoan at different epochs, they became in their isolated island homes such tongues as Tokelauan, Tūvalu, East Uvean, East Futunan, Niuafo'ou, Pukapukan and around fifteen more languages, some of these belonging to special subgroups of so-called 'Outliers', or Polynesian-speaking communities west of the 'Polynesian Triangle' of New Zealand-Hawai'i-Easter Island.[31]

Early in the first millennium AD Proto-East Polynesian speakers in the North-west Marquesas migrated to Easter Island, perhaps by way of the Tuamotu Islands, Mangareva and Pitcairn; their language evolved into today's Rapanui language. The South-east Marquesas Islands were subsequently settled at the same time as a Proto-Central Eastern Polynesian language was evolving there. Perhaps in the fourth century AD, one group of Marquesans left for Hawai'i, where their language over many centuries eventually became Hawaiian. A century or so later another group of Marquesans left for Tahiti, where their language established its own subgroup – Tahitic – which then spread to the Tuamotus, the Austral Islands, the Kermadec Islands and the Cook Islands. Around 700 AD a group of Māori-speaking Cook Islanders brought their Tahitic tongue to New Zealand.

Once the great Polynesian migrations were over by AD1000, when nearly every inhabitable island of the Pacific had been settled, North-west Marquesan and South-east Marquesan differed more and more in their phonology and vocabulary until by the eighteenth century they had become separate languages. The same process had occurred elsewhere among East Polynesian speakers, as in the Austral Islands south of Tahiti, though in most cases – the Tuamotus, Cook Islands and New Zealand – these differentiated languages are called 'dialects', though they may differ from one another more than Danish does from Swedish.

In the nineteenth century, European and American intrusion into the Pacific caused up to 96 per cent population loss through calamitous pandemics and slave raids, with concomitant cultural ruin, language levelling, dialect loss and language contamination and replacement: English (Hawai'i, New Zealand, Samoa, Cook Islands), French (Tahiti, Tuamotus, Marquesas, Australs, Mangareva) and Spanish (Easter Island).

Only monarchic Tonga and more remote smaller islands were spared the onslaught.

Now, most Polynesian Islanders have wholly lost, or are currently losing, their ancestral language to a metropolitan Western tongue or, particularly in French Polynesia, are replacing it with the Tahitian lingua franca. Vigorous Polynesian languages characterize the large populations (Tongan, Samoan, Tahitian), tiny isolates (Kapingamarangi, Tikopian and several others) and also those once populous languages being revived at grass roots level with governmental support (Hawaiian, Māori). The rich oral literature of Polynesia – dance songs, holy chants, mythical histories, genealogies and much more – was all but lost in the nineteenth century. Only a small fraction of this literature was written down by Western scholars and a handful of educated Islanders. Easter Island alone possessed indigenous writing; however, this *rongorongo* was a European-inspired elaboration from the end of the eighteenth century.

These representative lineages – Celtic, Italic, Germanic, Bantu, Chinese and Polynesian – display the rich diversity and universality of language change. Celtic demonstrates how an important and widespread family of languages can be reduced to relative insignificance in only a few centuries. Italic shows how one small daughter language, Latin, can generate an enormous but homogeneous family of its own, the Romance languages, whose phonology and vocabulary then continue to profit from the parent tongue millennia later. For its diversity and fragmentation Germanic displays just the opposite development to Italic, with a single daughter tongue, English, heavily altered by Italic, eventually approaching the status of a world language. Bantu produced many daughter languages of few divisions in west Central Africa, then experienced in the past millennium an unparalleled expansion that allowed it to overwhelm most of eastern and southern Africa. Chinese is characterized foremost by its uniformity and consistency, as a result perhaps of severe social conformism and political centralization over several millennia. And Polynesian expanded to become prehistory's most widely distributed language family while qualifying at the same time as perhaps the world's most conservative, now generally in peril of succumbing to more powerful metropolitan tongues.

Large trends become evident over millennia. For example, many of these languages share the transition from a fusional type of language (synthecism) to an isolating type (analyticism); that is, the proto-language used word endings to show grammar but the daughter languages drop these endings and use a fixed word order with particles or prepositions instead. Nearly all linguistic change is cyclic, with periods switching between fusional, agglutinative and isolating statements of language and between head marking (verbal attachments), dependent marking (subject/object attachments) and rigid syntactic order in their sequencing of phrases and sentences. Over about 3,000 years, Egyptian evolved from fusional to agglutinative and back to fusional again. As all languages change, they tend to describe a similar typological circle.[32]

A hierarchy of change can be detected, whereby some linguistic elements change more readily than others. Phonological change is the most frequent type of linguistic change. Semantic change also occurs at a relatively rapid rate. Less frequent is morphological change, the systematic change in word formation and changes in grammatical forms, too, especially paradigms (like Latin *puer*, *puerī*, *puerō*, *puerum* and so forth). Also occurring seldom is syntactic change, the systematic change in a phrase's or sentence's word order. One of the most seldom changes of all is word stress. The accent or stress on a word tends to be a rather archaic feature that can help linguists to align daughter languages to a parent, or borrowed words to their foreign source. For example, French *Marcel*, with its stress on the final syllable, maintains the ancient penultimate stress of the original Latin *Marcellus* although, when becoming an isolating language, French lost the *-us* ending. The modern French ultimate stress is therefore in reality a historical penultimate stress. Recognizing such relics, linguists can ferret out any number of linguistic origins and relationships.

Another trend becomes evident over time. Paradoxically, the greater the human population, the fewer the languages. The isolated communities of prehistory presumably enjoyed enormous linguistic diversity. Rising populations since the beginning of urbanization have meant the depletion of this linguistic diversity. In particular, the rush to cities in the early nineteenth century as a result of the Industrial Revolution which created history's third great population surge (still continuing) generated nations that, with political centralization, required a standardized national tongue. Today's national tongues, the so-called metropolitan languages, are now eliminating hundreds of smaller languages throughout the world. As Earth's population of some six billion is estimated to double within the next 50 years, one can expect many of the world's smaller languages to disappear during this period.

A fine point concludes this review of linguistic lineages. One often hears such popular expressions as the '5,000 year-old Tamil language' or the '1,500 year-old English language'. Nothing could be further from the truth. No language on Earth is 'older' than any other: every currently spoken, natural – that is, neither revived nor invented – tongue shares exactly the same age.

SIX

Towards a Science of Language

'Linguistic science is a step in the self-realization of man', wrote the eminent American linguist Leonard Bloomfield at the beginning of the twentieth century.[1] The step traverses millennia. Long before written language, ancients divined human speech as a special gift of a god, a belief still held by many unrelated cultures. Serious organized study of language began in India and Greece in the first millennium BC and has continued, in an unbroken and mutually enriching tradition, up to the present day. Latin translations of Greek grammatical terms – noun, pronoun, verb, adverb, adjective, article, transitive, intransitive, inflection, declension, tense, case, gender, subject, object and many more – are still used to describe language in most Western cultures.

In ancient India, Sanskrit scholars excelled in phonetic (sound) and phonological (system of significant sounds) theory and in aspects of grammatical analysis. At the time, their work was much more scientific – that is, it exhibited the methods and principles of systematized knowledge – than anything of the kind in Europe. But little is known of the origin and early development of ancient Indian linguistics. In contrast, there is a continuity of development from ancient Greek beginnings to the present day. Greek linguistics passed to Rome. Rome's late Latin grammarians, who studied Latin's classes of words, their inflections and their functions and relations in the sentence, inspired mediæval scholars, whose work was reinterpreted by Renaissance grammarians. These then provided the initial foundation for the modern science of language that finally emerged in the nineteenth century. There is a consistent flow in European linguistics since the earliest Greek speculations on the subject; each generation has enjoyed a knowledge of and has profited from, the work of insightful antecedents (illus. 12). For this reason, the history of European linguistics can embody a history of linguistics in general. Nevertheless, one should not underestimate the influence of non-European linguists, since each scholar who has written seriously on language over the past two-and-a-half millennia has contributed to the knowledge of what language is, where it has come from and where it is going.

INDIA

The world's earliest known linguistic studies were effected in India between around 800 and 150 BC in an attempt to preserve the oral literature of India's much earlier Vedic period.[2] As in the West, Indian scholars have maintained linguistic continuity up to the present day. Indian phonetics and various grammatical topics, including profound treatises on phonology and semantics, up to the eighteenth century surpassed anything the West had achieved. Though not historically minded, Indian linguists predicated their studies on the observed phenomenon of language change over time.

Unlike ancient Greek linguistics, Indian tradition appeared already fully matured, the exquisite culmination of a protracted, but unrecorded, theoretical development. The first great work of Indian linguistics was Pāṇini's *Aṣṭādhyāyī* or 'Eight Books' of Sanskrit grammar, the earliest scientific work on any subject in any Indo-European language, written or orally transmitted sometime between 600 and 300 BC.[3] Indian writings on language can be grouped under the same general headings one finds in Western scholarship, though India's linguistic tradition precedes and supersedes Europe's, which was already treating in depth linguistic theory and semantics, phonetics and phonology and descriptive grammar. Measured against literary investigation and philosophical speculation, India's early linguists arrived at the cogent insight that language's relation to form and meaning owes more to arbitrary convention (passing along society's custom) than natural mimesis (copying nature's sounds). Their semantic study already viewed word meanings as observational creations, as well as inheritances.[4] India's first linguists took the remarkably modern view that entire sentences could comprise autonomous linguistic units. (Western linguists, long concentrating on the 'word' as language's elementary particle, first achieved this insight in the twentieth century.)

The age-old question of language's form versus substance – that is, actual utterance as opposed to the inherent system of features, categories and rules – had already been anticipated by India's earliest Sanskrit scholars, who developed the theory of the *dhvani-sphoṭa* relationship. Utterance was the *dhvani*; permanent linguistic substance, unuttered, was the *sphoṭa*. The *dhvani* thus drew from the *sphoṭa* 'as one draws water from a well'. In phonetics, already by 150 BC India's linguists had ordered phonetic description into phonological structures, with precise processes of articulation (the act or manner of giving utterance), consonant and vowel segments and segmentational synthesis. From this, it is evident that ancient Indian scholars intuited fully the principles of phonemics – to which parts of the *sphoṭa* theory approach – that Western scholars were able to describe adequately only in the twentieth century (see below).

India's linguists are perhaps best known for their grammatical analysis of Sanskrit, especially Pāṇini's *Aṣṭādhyāyī*, though the work fails to fully comprehend what one today understands under 'grammar'. Ancient Indian scholars appear to have been obsessed with grammar, seeking to state all rules in the most economical, prioritized set: one commentator noted that saving half the length of a short vowel while positing a rule of grammar was 'equal in importance to the birth of a son'. Word formation rules, applied in a strict set in aphoristic *sūtras* or 'threads', take precedence; in contrast, Sanskrit's phonetic and grammatical description is almost wholly assumed. Pāṇini's 'grammar' not only founded Indian linguistics but also, some 2,300 years later, contributed to the creation of those European comparative and historical language studies which co-authored the modern science of linguistics.

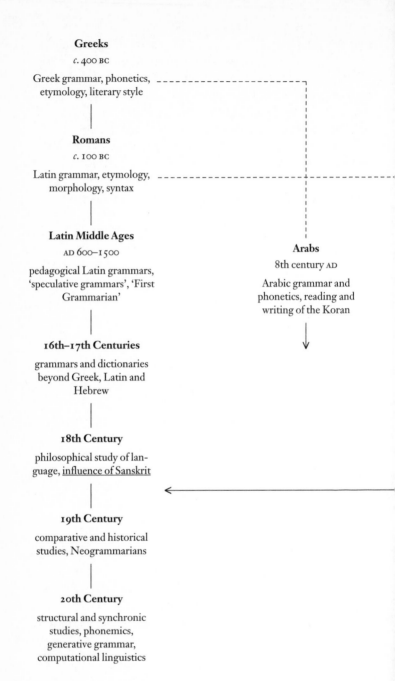

Greeks

c. 400 BC

Greek grammar, phonetics, etymology, literary style

Romans

c. 100 BC

Latin grammar, etymology, morphology, syntax

Latin Middle Ages

AD 600–1500

pedagogical Latin grammars, 'speculative grammars', 'First Grammarian'

Arabs

8th century AD

Arabic grammar and phonetics, reading and writing of the Koran

16th–17th Centuries

grammars and dictionaries beyond Greek, Latin and Hebrew

18th Century

philosophical study of language, <u>influence of Sanskrit</u>

19th Century

comparative and historical studies, Neogrammarians

20th Century

structural and synchronic studies, phonemics, generative grammar, computational linguistics

12 Brief overview of the development of linguistics.

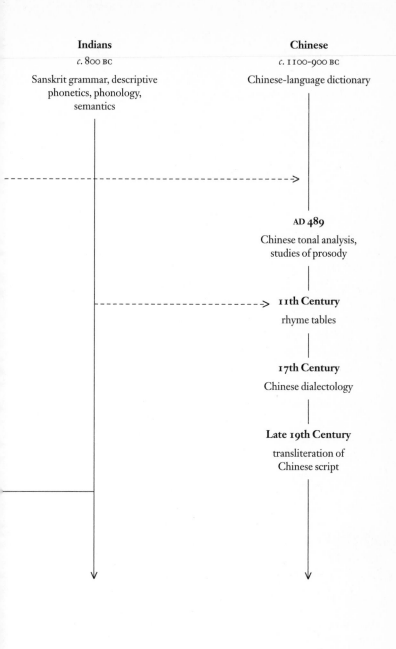

It is on a Greek plinth, however, that this science stands.[5] The earliest record of linguistic study in Greece dates from the beginning of the classical age in the fifth century BC. Greeks were not interested in the speech of *bárbaroi* or 'alien speakers'. But Greek dialects fascinated them, since Old Greek was as highly differentiated as today's Scandinavian languages yet its underlying unity was keenly sensed by all speakers. (At the beginning of the fifth century BC, the historian Herodotus wrote of 'the whole Greek community, being of one blood and one tongue'.)

Most, but not all, of these dialects were reduced to writing. Indeed, perhaps the Greeks' greatest cultural accomplishment, early in the first millennium BC if not before, had been the elaboration of an alphabetic script (see Chapter 4). The skill of reading and writing the Greek alphabet's letters (*grámmata*) was the *téchnē grammatikē* and one who mastered this was a *grammatikós* or 'grammarian'.[6] The study of letters was an integral part of *philosophía* or 'intellectual striving'. Rhetoricians in particular, such as Gorgias of Sicily in the fifth century BC, studied and wrote about language as a tool for improving oratorical skills.

Plato (427?–347 BC) was later credited as having 'first investigated the potentialities of grammar'. His *Cratylus* dialogue comprised a debate on language's origin and on the relationships between words and their meanings: it revealed that Naturalists believed words were onomatopoeic (the sound suggesting the meaning) and symbolic in their sounds, but Conventionalists held words to be arbitrarily mutable so that any linguistic change is mere convention.[7]

Aristotle (384–322 BC), antiquity's greatest intellect, wrote eclectically on language, developing his own opinion on the subject: 'Language is by convention, since no names arise naturally'. His understanding of language was unequivocal: 'Speech is the representation of the experiences of the mind'.

Separate works by the Stoics in the second century BC investigated individual aspects of language for the first time in

Western culture. The Stoics were the first to divide language study into phonetics, grammar and etymology (word history). The Greeks excelled in grammar and their study influenced the course of Western linguistics for more than 2,000 years.

As with mimesis (imitating nature) versus convention (society) in language's origin – the Stoics favouring mimesis, Aristotle convention – there was also a dichotomy of thought as to whether anomaly (irregularity) or analogy (regularity) was language's principal theme.[8] (While crossing the Alps on a military campaign in the first century BC, Julius Cæsar took time to reflect on the anomaly-analogy controversy in classical linguistics, such was its popularity.) Aristotle had held analogy to be the dominant feature in Greek morphology, or systematic word formation. To his credit, modern linguists now understand an economical description of Greek morphology to rest on the identification and regularization of formal analogies.

After the Stoics, Greek linguistic study concerned itself chiefly with correct pronunciation and literary style, along with creating accent marks to accurately reproduce spoken Greek in writing, and with producing the best texts of Homer's works. A few phonetic studies were written, but these were alphabetically oriented, assuming an invalid relationship between a text's letters and the discrete sounds of spoken language. (The true relationship between letters and sounds was not appreciated until modern times.) Greece's understanding of phonetics remained subjective and poetically interpretative and came nowhere near the descriptive adequacy of India's linguists.

However, the ancient Greeks' grammatical analysis was of a high standard and their system and nomenclature became exemplary. Based chiefly on written Attic Greek of the Athens area, Greek grammatical description assumed the word-and-paradigm model so familiar to generations of Latin students: *amō* 'I love', *amās* 'you love', *amat* 'he/she/it loves' and so forth. But classical morphology was no substitute for a theory of the morpheme (a language's smallest meaningful unit) and so Greek linguistics, 'stuck' at the higher 'word level' only, failed to advance to that stage of insight to which India had attained centuries earlier. Phonology, too, was mired in pronouncing letters of the alphabet, ensuring that Greek language study would remain principally a description of the written – not the spoken – tongue. Nevertheless the Greeks, particularly through the writings of Plato and Aristotle, created a linguistic nomenclature to describe observable features and processes of language for the first time in a European tongue and it was in this way that such eminently useful word tools as 'noun' and 'verb' came into currency.

The earliest explicit description of the Greek language, Dionysius Thrax's *Téchnē Grammatikē* of the early first century BC, provides what was for thirteen centuries regarded as the definitive text on the language, omitting only syntax (phrase and sentence order). Characteristic are Thrax's brevity, precision and neatness, as well as his exaggerated exposition of linguistic regularities, then the chief domain of grammar. In Egypt's Alexandria in the second century AD, Apollonius Dyscolus, whose later influence on Latin grammarians was enormous, compiled apparently the first comprehensive theory of Greek syntax. Essentially, he constructed his syntactic description on two pillars, the noun and the verb, and discovered grammar to lie in the relationship between the two and between these and the other word classes. In this, Apollonius prefigured the much later syntactic distinctions of subject and object and the concepts of government and dependency.

Greek linguistic studies in mediæval Constantinople, apart from notable exceptions such as Maximus Planudes's (*c.* 1260–1310) semantic investigation of the Greek cases (taken to Renaissance Europe, this later influenced case theory) comprised, in the main, literary commentaries of ancient texts and lacked the Hellenistic writers' profundity of thought.[9] By then, the dynamics of Greek scholarship had long since passed to the Romans, whose Latin language had become the vehicle for perpetuating Greek grammatical theory.

THE ROMANS

During the third and second centuries BC, Greece gradually yielded to Rome's supremacy. Ironically, with Rome's complete takeover of the Hellenistic world by the first century AD, the

Greek language did not bow to Latin, but Latin capitulated to Greek. Though the Germans and Celts in the west of the Roman Empire were forced to submit to Latin-speaking administrations, the eastern Empire, under Greek administration, remained firmly Greek-speaking, with Greek officials, Greek culture and Greek ideals, an ideological dichotomy that, within several centuries, led to the Empire's division. Greek literature comprised educated Rome's model and Greek language was the language of culture itself, just as Latin was to become for the European Middle Ages a millennium later.

As in other intellectual and artistic domains, Roman linguistics was the extension of Greek linguistics. There was no clear separation of thought between Greek and Latin language theory, but a continuation of the same dynamic within identical philosophical parameters, a process fostered in part by the relative similarity of the two Indo-European languages.[10] The prolific polymath Varro (116–27 BC) is the first critical Latin author to treat of linguistics whose writings have survived, though Romans must surely have compiled earlier works. His *De Lingua Latina* of originally 25 volumes – only books five to ten and some fragments of others remain – discusses lengthily the anomaly-analogy controversy in linguistics, but also provides original insights, not mere imitation of Greek mentors, into the nature and earlier stages of the Latin language. Varro's work, divided into etymology, morphology and syntax, with discerning treatment and copious Latin examples, vies with Greece's best. Though antiquity's ignorance of historical linguistics is pronounced here, too, whereby synchronic and diachronic considerations are unhappily interchangeable, Varro, when discussing variations in word form from a single root, achieved in his arguments for and against anomaly and analogy a compromise solution that recognized both in a language's formation of words and their associated meanings.

If his ideas did not derive from an earlier lost author, Varro was unusually innovative for his era. He distinguished between derived (as illustrated in the word 'derivation' from 'derive') and inflectional (as illustrated in the word 'derives') formation of words, finding the latter a natural variation but the former an unnatural and more restricted one. His morphological classification of Latin words was also highly original. Unlike the Greeks, Varro did not simply recognize case and tense as Latin's and Greek's main categories and establish the four classes – according to the way they inflect – of nouns (case inflection), verbs (tense inflection), participles (case and tense) and adverbs (neither case nor tense): he characterized the specific functions of each. Nouns named things. Verbs made statements. Participles joined elements (they shared the former two's syntax) and adverbs supported all these. Varro was obviously fascinated by the wide grammatical range of words based on a simple common root: *legō* 'I choose, read'; *lector* 'reader'; *legēns* 'reading, someone who is reading'; and *lectē* 'choicely'.

Varro was undoubtedly Rome's most original linguist. He towered over other Roman writers who only superficially discussed the topic, concentrated on literary matters, or blindly followed Thrax's *Téchnē*. After Varro, no further interest lay in the anomaly-analogy controversy. A notable successor was Quintilian in the first century AD who, in his twelve books of the *Institutio Oratoria*, repeated Thrax's claim that grammar comprised an indispensable tool in a liberal education and only superficially reviewed the Latin case system. Up to the sixth century AD, Roman linguistics constituted the adoption, analysis and application of Greek nomenclature and categories to the Latin tongue. The Alexandrian scholar Didymus, writing as early as the second half of the first century BC, had already 'demonstrated' that every feature of Greek grammar was to be found in Latin grammar, too.

Only in the late Latin period was a descriptive Latin grammar formalized, which then served as the foundation of all Western education in the centuries that followed.[11] The leading work of late Latin grammarians was Priscian's *Institutiones Grammaticæ*, written around AD 500 in Constantinople. In his thousand-page tome, Priscian reflected Constantinople's retrospection and Greek-based categorization of the already archaic language of classical literature, ignoring the evolving dynamics of the spoken tongue. Priscian's aim was clear: to trace Latin linguistics atop a Greek matrix, in particular Thrax's *Téchnē* and the works of Apollonius Dyscolus whom Priscian called 'the greatest authority on grammar'. Priscian's working model was the Greek word-and-paradigm and no significance was attached to any element below the level of the derived word. That is, Priscian saw *domus*, 'house', for example, as language's primary level and, like all Western antiquity, remained unaware that both *dom-* and *-us* were morphemes (smallest meaningful units) and that *d*, for example, was a phoneme (here contrasting with the *t* in Latin *tomus* 'cutting, chip'). Priscian achieved the most comprehensive description of Classical Latin, one which has served as the foundation of Latin language teaching up to the present day. The *Institutiones* was the most copied grammar of mediæval scriptoria. It furnished the stage for the linguists of the Middle Ages.

THE ARAB WORLD

Islam's cultural sophistication in the Near East, North Africa and Spain engendered a number of significant linguistic studies during the Middle Ages.[12] Some authors of these works were actually Spanish Jews, such as Ibn Barun, who compiled a comparative treatise of Arabic and Hebrew. However, most were Muslims who centred their research on the Koran which, since the seventh century AD, has been looked upon as the word of God mediated by the prophet Muhammed in the Arabic language and not admissible of translation, even among non-Arabic-speaking Muslims. The demands of Arabic teaching throughout the far-flung realms of Islam necessitated the establishment, over many centuries, of hundreds of Arabic schools which then elaborated rules of Arabic reading, writing and pronunciation.

Some Koran schools stressed the natural, diverse origin of Arabic as the representation of nature and generalized this to include all languages, much like the Naturalists in classical Greek linguistics. Then there were other schools, such as that at Basra in southern Iraq, in which Aristotle directly influenced the Arabic acknowledgement of the conventional arbitrariness and systematic regularity of language.[13] Nevertheless, the Arab world developed its own unique approach to language and so avoided Latin grammarians' wholesale adoption of Greek prototypes.

The non-Arab Persian Sībawaih of Basra, writing in the eighth century AD, consolidated all Arabic language instruction in his grammatical treatise *Al kitab* (*The Book*). Striking out from a firm foundation of preceding linguistic studies, Sībawaih defined classical Arabic as it is known today. His phonetic and anatomical description of sound production, each aspect of which is furnished with precise terminology, leads one to suspect an Indian inspiration, though this need not be the case. *Al kitab* is certainly, in its descriptive accuracy, superior to anything the Greeks and Romans had ever achieved.

Arabic linguistics never attained to such linguistic prominence again.

CHINA

Though the first Chinese-language dictionary was compiled as early as 1100–900 BC, Chinese preoccupation with language analysis centred on the most faithful reproduction of the spoken word through syllabo-phonetic glyphs.[14] In AD 489, Chinese tones were first identified in systematic fashion as components of uttered syllables, perhaps through the agency of Buddhist monks familiar with alphabetic writing. Further phonological analysis in the eleventh century came through Chinese rhyme tables that arranged initial syllables in vertical columns and final syllables in horizontal rows, allowing all potential medial, final and tonal features in Chinese to be highlighted, even if they did not occur in spoken language because of natural phonotactic ('sound-touching') restrictions. The influence of Sanskrit linguists is evident in the precise ordering of the rhyme tables' initial syllables according to articulation and in other characteristics.

This pseudo-prosodic (that is, having to do with prosody or the systematic study of versification) phonological analysis, befitting the type of script Chinese was written in, remained the basis of Chinese linguistic investigation throughout the Middle Ages and into the modern era. If Chinese scholars initially addressed classical Middle Chinese literature, then this later attached to the Mandarin of Beijing and to other Chinese languages. Noteworthy are the writings of the dialectologist Pan-lei, who journeyed throughout China in the seventeenth century describing the many languages and dialects he encountered.

Chinese linguistics never attained to that level of scholarly enquiry both the West and, above all, India had achieved already in the first millennium BC. Since the late nineteenth century, one of the principal topics in Chinese linguistics has been the question of the most efficient transliteration of the Chinese script in a Western alphabet.

THE LATIN MIDDLE AGES

Linguistic investigation during the Latin Middle Ages – a convenient if perhaps historically misleading name for the period in Europe between about AD 600 and 1500 – is characterized principally by its orientation: Church-based, it remained pedagogical. Because spoken and written Latin had survived Rome's collapse as the language of education in all Western countries regardless of local tongue, language study meant the study of Classical Latin grammar, particularly in the early Middle Ages.[15] Of the 'Seven Liberal Arts' that comprised this education, no fewer than three – grammar, dialectic (logic) and rhetoric – directly involved the study of the Latin language. Indeed, throughout the Middle Ages Latin grammar was regarded as the most important of the seven, the very foundation of a proper education. All Seven Liberal Arts were of course subordinate to theology.

In Latin grammatical studies, the two main authorities, Priscian and Donatus, were merely regurgitated with insignificant changes.[16] While Bible copying and Latin teaching dominated the monasteries, linguistically minded monks also commented or glossed, penned etymologies and compiled lexicons. Most notable for the latter was Isidore of Seville in Spain who, in the early seventh century, wrote the *Etymologiæ*, the '*Britannica*' of the Middle Ages. However, attempts at independent Latin grammars and conversation books, such as those by the Northumbrians Bede and Alcuin in the eighth century, also appeared from an early date onwards. The Irish in particular were among the first to apply Latin grammatical principles to the local vernacular, starting a tradition that thrived in Ireland for several centuries.[17]

During the period of philosophical scholasticism that began around 1100, with the advent of the first universities in Europe, Gothic architecture and courtly literature, linguistic studies still comprised doctrinal pedagogy. Yet several of them stand out: Alexandre de Villedieu's *Doctrinale*, a Latin manual of around 1200; Welsh and Irish grammars; and the *First Grammatical Treatise* by an extraordinary, unknown, twelfth-century Icelander called the 'First Grammarian'. While advocating a spelling reform so as to better reproduce the Icelandic language in writing, the Icelander included a rare phonetic and phonological analysis. Indeed, the 'First Grammarian' identified the underlying principles of phonemics, a language's internal system of significant sounds. His work, comprising the best the Middle Ages had to offer, lay ignored until the twentieth century.

Linguistic tradition, not innovation, flowered in the Middle Ages with 'speculative grammars', treatises titled *De Modis Significandi* (*On the Modes of Signifying*) that were written by many authors between around 1200 and 1350 who generally shared the same theoretical stance and linguistic conception.[18] These 'Modistæ' integrated Priscian's and Donatus's descriptions of Latin grammar into philosophical scholasticism. (Scholasticism is the school of thought incorporating Aristotelian philosophy into Catholic theology.) The Modistæ claimed that Latin's simple description no longer sufficed; a deeper theory and greater justification for elements and categories in Latin were needed. Philosophy was now added to the soup of grammar: 'It is not the grammarian but the philosopher who, carefully considering the specific nature of things, . . . discovers grammar'.

Out of this theoretical climate came the notion of a 'universal grammar' serving all languages. England's Roger Bacon (1214?–94), author of one of the earliest speculative grammars, wrote that 'Grammar is, in its substance, one and the same in all languages and varies in these only accidentally'. (Theoretical linguists have been seaching for a 'universal grammar' ever since.) Semantics was particularly addressed in an attempt to define the difference between a word's *significātiō* (meaning) and its *suppositiō* (relational substitution).

But the chief interest of the Modistæ was grammar itself and here they created an elaborate terminology to explain an integral and coherent system of philosophical grammar, turning away from Priscian in significant ways in order to provide an explanatory dimension to Priscian's merely descriptive analysis of Latin. The Modistæ's syntactic system, for example, achieved a much greater transparency in the function of specific word classes, allowing a more adequate definition of these. The Modistæ achieved a comprehensive and coherent theory of sentence structure and of syntactic analysis, too. This involved deeper structural levels than Priscian's inflected words. In their theory of language, the Modistæ believed that the human mind carried out processes of abstraction, consideration and communication in all languages alike – a theory that collapsed once non-Indo-European languages were encountered. While still far from today's formal grammar, the 'speculative grammars' of the Modistæ represent a bridge between antiquity and the modern age.

UP TO THE NINETEENTH CENTURY

Classical writers collected data and described Greek and Latin. Mediæval Modistæ speculated about Latin's use. But after the Middle Ages, European scholars studied non-European languages and read the works of non-European linguists and no longer allowed Greek and Latin to dominate linguistic study. Language itself became the object of investigation. Of course, some Arabic and Hebrew had been studied in the Middle Ages, particularly Hebrew for its significance to Christianity. In the Renaissance, however, Hebrew became a major object of investigation. The German Johannes Reuchlin's *De Rudimentis Hebraicis* of 1506 illustrated for European linguists Hebrew's radically different word-class system of declinable nouns and verbs and indeclinable particles. Grammars of other languages were also appearing at this time: Italian and Spanish in the fifteenth century; French, Polish and Old Church Slavonic in the sixteenth century. The first dictionaries were printed. The Bible was translated into vernacular languages and the relationship of the original Hebrew and Greek compared to these. Pronunciation and spelling became more standardized with emerging national literatures.

The new grammars of vernacular languages concentrated on orthography (spelling) to achieve maximum comprehension among peoples not yet united into nations. Particularly among the related Romance languages of Italian, Provençal, French, Catalan, Spanish and Portuguese it was now appreciated that these were not simple corruptions of Classical Latin, but autonomous tongues that differed in systematically describable ways. The vernaculars were breaking free of Latin altogether and being studied for their own merit as separate tongues whose grammars were equally worthy of consideration by scholars.

A precursor of modern structuralism, Frenchman Pierre Ramée (*c.* 1515–72) whose *Dialectique* was the first philosophical book in the French language ('Everything Aristotle said is wrong'), authored grammars of Greek, Latin and French and theorized about grammar in *Scholæ Grammaticæ*. Departing from preceding orientation, Ramée claimed that the ancient languages should adhere to classical usage but the modern languages to observed usage. In this way, Ramée's grammatical descriptions and classifications stress the relations between observed word forms, not classical ideals.

Grammars of Peruvian Quechua (1560), Basque (1587), Brazilian Guaraní (1639) and many other languages, including Chinese, also began appearing in print. One quickly came to appreciate how greatly the world's languages actually differed from Greek and Latin. The classics were now revered as ancient models, but no longer as living ideals. Vernaculars began replacing mediæval Latin as the language of education, a protracted process that was completed only in the nineteenth century in some European countries. Fittingly, Classical Latin was now enshrined and objectively described as well. Ramée himself introduced the new Latin letters *j* and *v* to stand for the exact semivowel pronunciations that are distinct from the vocalic pronunciations of Latin *i* and *u*. Printing furthered literacy and greater literacy meant an explosion in general knowledge and awareness, one similar only to the technological revolution of the twentieth century. Learned societies were formed, such as France's Académie Française in 1635 and Britain's Royal Society in 1662, that were often forums for and even 'watchdogs' of, linguistic research and issues.[19]

From the sixteenth to eighteenth centuries, linguistic science transcended purely language-oriented issues to allow itself to become a tool in the philosophical debate between empiricists and rationalists, each seeing language in a different way. Empiricists, rejecting mediæval scholasticism, stressed observed fact; rationalists did not trust what the senses perceived but, perhaps more traditionally, what human reason adduced. However, both believed the basis of philosophical reasoning to lie in mathematics and Newtonian science. All linguistic studies during this time were influenced by the empiricist-rationalist debate. From this came the first serious calls for a new, invented 'universal language' as the international medium of learning and trade.

An upshot of English empiricist linguistics was the first systematic description of English phonetics and the beginning of the formal analysis of an English grammar freed from Priscian's Latin dictate. The English school of phonetics was born that essentially founded the study of English phonetics and phonology. Though most English grammarians still forced English into the straitjacket of Priscian's Latin word classes, there were exceptions who dared to discard tradition in view of direct observation of actual English usage: William Holder's *Elements of Speech* (1669) approached articulatory diagnosis of the voice-voiceless distinction in consonants – that is, *b/p*, *d/t*, *g/k* and so forth – better than any Western scholar before him.

For its part, the rationalist movement produced philosophical grammars, in particular those owing their inspiration to the French Port Royal schools of 1637 to 1661 whose influence continued well into the eighteenth century. Because of the Port Royal schools' institutional distrust of pagan classicism, these rationalist grammars prolonged the scholastic grammars of the

Middle Ages by proposing a 'universal grammar', but as a general theory of grammar expressed in the vernacular, not as a Latin model or ideal. It was the Port Royal grammarians' aim to reveal the underlying unity of all grammars in communicating human thought. This they attempted to achieve, among other things, through a radical semantic reinterpretation of the nine classical word classes, such as seeing adverbs structurally as only abbreviated prepositional phrases. Port Royal grammarians even undertook to write a general grammar based on Greek, Latin, Hebrew and contemporary European languages, believing such a theoretical postulate to exist in reality.

In the eighteenth century, linguistic speculation addressed the origin and development of language in a more general philosophical way. The French philosophers Condillac and Rousseau saw language's origin as lying in the imitation of nature through gestures and cries; later abstractions and grammatical complexities would have developed from very simple 'tonal' beginnings. The German Johann Gottfried Herder argued that human language grew through successive stages of development and maturity together with human thought, each depending on the other; Herder believed the auditory sense first promoted language, with the other senses contributing their share later to form a 'simple vocabulary' as language matured. The Englishman James Harris, a disciple of Aristotelian philosophy who recognized with Herder the idiosyncrasies of individual languages, developed a linguistic theory based on the two universal 'principals' of nouns and verbs that Harris believed to underlie all grammars since the beginning of human speech.

The six-volume treatise *Of the Origin and Progress of Language* (1773–92) by Lord Monboddo (James Burnett) of Edinburgh also addressed historical development, positing human society as a prerequisite to linguistic creation and contending that contemporary 'primitive' languages reveal characteristics of humankind's 'one original language', such as a paucity of abstract vocabulary and of grammatical organization – that is, in the sense of Greek, Latin and Hebrew. (It is now appreciated that no living language is more 'primitive' than another, each being equally sufficient in all its immediate needs.) This is not 'linguistic arrogance', as many have claimed. It is linguistic probing, on the eve of the greatest breakthroughs in the long development towards a true science of language.

Near the end of the eighteenth century, as a result of an influx of new data, linguists adopted a more historical and less theoretical and philosophical approach towards language study, with typological comparisons of hitherto unknown languages. The encounter with ancient Sanskrit texts and the rich tradition of Sanskrit linguistics revolutionized and transformed Western study. The hallmark year was 1786 when Sir William Jones, a 42-year-old British judge with the East India Company, read a now legendary paper to the Royal Asiatic Society in Calcutta that identified Sanskrit's genetic relationship with the Greek, Latin, Gothic, Celtic and Old Persian languages.

The concept itself was not new; but Jones was the first to introduce two new notions: that languages could be *historically related* – 'sprung from some common source', as he put it – rather than products of each other (that is, Sanskrit to Greek to Latin); and that there existed *ancestral languages*, what linguists today call proto-languages. Jones's scholarship not only inaugurated the field of historical linguistics, but also opened up the over 2,500-year-old tradition of Sanskrit linguistics to Western scholars. The resulting blend of Sanskrit and Western traditions established modern linguistic science in the first half of the nineteenth century.

THE NINETEENTH CENTURY

At the beginning of the nineteenth century a true science of linguistics began to emerge. The nineteenth century is the era of comparative and historical linguistics – that is, seeking languages' similarities and differences and their historical relationships to one another and developing the scientific vocabulary and tools to achieve this. The historical investigation of the Indo-European languages dominated the nineteenth century and set the standard for the investigation of all other language families. This was the domain of principally German-speaking scholars who played the leading role in founding a new

linguistic science mirroring the contemporaneous contribu-
tions in the natural sciences, mathemathics, physics, medical
science, astronomy, history and other disciplines from the
German principalities, Austro-Hungary and Switzerland.

Already in the twelfth century, Iceland's 'First Grammarian'
had noted similarities in word forms of Icelandic and English.
In the early fourteenth century in his *De Vulgari Eloquentia*,
Italy's Dante Alighieri had described dialect and language differences as resulting from the passage of time and the
geographical dispersion of speakers of a single source language
(proto-language). However, for Dante, Hebrew was the first
language on Earth, Adam's gift from God in Eden. All language
differentiation came from the destruction of the Tower of Babel
as described in Genesis 11. Similar historical writings about language continued up to, and including, the nineteenth century,
with none daring to question the Biblical account.

Many scholars, such as the German Gottfried Wilhelm
Leibniz (1646–1716), had called for the preparation of grammars and dictionaries of the world's languages so as to provide a
greater store of information on which to base linguistic generalizations. Particularly in the eighteenth century, word lists were
compiled, usually including the Lord's Prayer, and language
surveys effected. The culmination of this frenzy of gathering
was the German Peter Simon Pallas's four-volume *Linguarum
Totius Orbis Vocabularia Comparativa* (St Petersburg, 1786–9)
that included 200 languages. The review of the compilation's
first volume by the German C. J. Kraus in 1787 provides possibly the first scientific discussion of comparative and historical
linguistics in a modern – that is, in a non-classical and non-
Biblical – framework.

In 1808 Friedrich Schlegel published a treatise on Sanskrit in
which he urged the study of languages' 'inner structures' (morphology or systematic word formation) in order to reveal
genetic relationships. In this seminal work Schlegel coined the
term *vergleichende Grammatik* or 'comparative grammar' to
embrace both comparative and historical linguistics.

Two scholars initiated the comparative and historical study
of the Indo-European family of languages: the Dane Rasmus
Rask (1787–1832) and the German Jacob Grimm (1785–1863,

one of the two Brothers Grimm). Rask was the first to compare systematically the word forms of several Indo-European languages and establish a pattern of etymological relationships. In 1818 he recognized, 'If there is found between two languages agreement in the forms of indispensable words to such an extent that rules of letter changes can be discovered for passing from one to the other, then there is a basic relationship between these languages'.

In his *Deutsche Grammatik (German Grammar)* in 1822, Grimm, who was familiar with Rask's work, described what came to be called 'Grimm's Law', identifying the replacement by Germanic languages of the consonant classes of three articulatory places and three types of release in view of other languages' phonology that does not reveal these same changes. Formulated and illustrated by Rask four years earlier, this provided the first and most important of the so-called 'sound laws' that eventually distilled the recognition of Indo-European and other language families. (Grimm himself did not see a linguistic law here, merely a 'sound shift' that was a 'general tendency'.)

Other scholars were effecting similar work, creating a new science in the process. Franz Bopp (1791–1867), who had been studying Sanskrit since 1812, published in his first study four years later a comparison of the verbal forms in Sanskrit, Greek, Latin and the Germanic languages with the intention of tracing the development of inflection (systematic word endings showing grammar). In his main contribution to the field published between 1833 and 1852, *Vergleichende Grammatik*, Bopp carried out this intent for all inflected forms. Following Rask, he also investigated the sound correspondences between the individual languages, eventually including Litauan, Armenian, Albanian and the Slavic and Celtic languages as members of the Indo-European family. Bopp is considered today as the father of the comparative historical study of Indo-European languages and the true founder of modern linguistic science.

One of the nineteenth century's most original linguistic thinkers was Wilhelm von Humboldt (1767–1835), writer, historian and one of Prussia's foremost statesmen. He published widely on language during his lifetime, stressing in his theory of language the inherent linguistic ability of all humankind. It is the human mind, claimed von Humboldt, that creates words and grammar, not external phenomena as the Greek and Latin philosophers had alleged. Every language on Earth is an individual creation of those who speak it, with the *innere Sprachform* – the internal structure of the language – imposing patterns and rules, some of which are language-specific but others common to all humankind (language universals). Each tongue is the reflex of past languages and each word in a language presupposes the entirety of its tongue within a semantic and grammatical framework. Differences between languages lie not merely in sounds but in complete *Weltansichten* – attitudes and understanding of the world.

Von Humboldt was the greatest theoretical linguist of the nineteenth century, exerting a tremendous influence particularly on the German-born American linguists of the early twentieth century and European linguists of the mid-twentieth century. At the beginning of the twenty-first century, von Humboldt's *innere Sprachform* provides universal linguistic theory with a framework for explaining how different ethnic communities, through language, can dwell in different mental realities and embrace different systems of thought. Von Humboldt's most immediate contribution to linguistic theory is perhaps his division of types of languages into isolating (Chinese), agglutinative (Turkish) and inflectional (Sanskrit), based on the 'word' as the dominant grammatical unit.

Other personalities rapidly furthered linguistic science. August Schleicher (1821–68) introduced a biological approach to language study in his reconstruction and grammatical description of the Proto Indo-European language. Best known for his *Stammbaumtheorie* or 'genealogical tree model', Schleicher grouped together surviving daughter languages; divided them into subfamilies like Germanic, Slavic, Celto-Italic and so forth on the basis of shared characteristics; then traced these back to the Indo-European parent language that Schleicher then attempted to piece back together, or 'reconstruct'. Despite its weaknesses – real languages do not 'split' or 'branch' from each other and only very few language families are actually amenable to the model (such as Indo-European, Polynesian and Semitic) – the genealogical tree model has proved to be one of the most important theoretical tools in historical linguistics. It also accommodated extremely well the Darwinian approach that was dominating the natural sciences by the end of the nineteenth century.

Linguistic science in the last quarter of the nineteenth century was characterized by the at first controversial *Junggrammatiker*, or adherents of Neogrammarian doctrine. Originating in Leipzig, Germany, under the tutelage of Hermann Osthoff (1847–1909) and Friedrich Karl Brugmann (1849-1919), the new theory proposed that, as mechanical processes, all sound changes occur under laws that allow no exceptions within the same dialect, so that the same sound, in the same environment, will always develop in the same fashion. This stance had been forced by the recognition of order lying behind the sets of formal correspondences between the Indo-European languages. The entire science of comparative and historical linguistics appeared to be predicated on the acceptance of regularity in the sound changes of human languages over time. If there is no regularity of sound change, the Neogrammarians were saying, then random variation ruled and there could be no true science of linguistics.

The work of the Neogrammarians transformed linguistic investigation into a scientific discipline whose methods were as exact as those of the burgeoning natural sciences. Speculation about language was discarded in order to address only data and the laws governing data. Much valuable work on language's structural conception, such as von Humboldt's, found no welcome in this new 'mechanization' of language. The Neogrammarians triumphed over all competing theorists and a long list of prominent linguists – Delbrück, Paul, Meyer-Lübke, Wright, Meillet, Boas, Sapir and Bloomfield – further developed, or were trained on, Neogrammarian principles and methods.

There was much justifiable critique of the Neogrammarians, too, especially by dialectologists who discovered great irregularity in languages in the local, non-generalized level of usage. France's leading dialectologist Jules Gilliéron (1854–1926) even stated that 'every word has its own history', which, in one way of thinking, is perfectly true. But each word belongs in a larger system and it was the greater system itself that the Neogrammarians were addressing. Twentieth-century linguistic science constituted in the main the modification of Neogrammarian doctrine, not its supersession.

THE TWENTIETH CENTURY

Twentieth-century linguistics heralded the expansion of Neogrammarian principles and methods to include non-Indo-European languages and the reaction to Neogrammarian doctrine by those practising not comparative and historical (diachronic) but structural and synchronic linguistics. If the Middle Ages had stressed pedagogical linguistics, the eighteenth century philosophical linguistics and the nineteenth century historical linguistics, up to the middle of the twentieth century descriptive linguistics prevailed – the study of a language's structure at a particular time, usually with exclusion of historical and comparative data.

The beginning of the twentieth century continued the nineteenth century's three major thrusts of traditional grammar, Sanskrit scholarship and adoption of other scientific disciplines' principles and methods. The greatest linguistic personality at the beginning of the century was the Swiss Ferdinand de Saussure (1857–1913), whose Geneva lectures changed the course of twentieth-century linguistics.[20] De Saussure defined the distinction between diachronic (temporally ordered, thus historical) and synchronic (self-contained at any epoch, thus descriptive) language studies, each possessing its own principles and methods. He distinguished further between *langue* (a speaker's linguistic competence) and *parole* (a speaker's actual utterances), with *langue* comprising the main object of linguistic investigation. And de Saussure demonstrated that *langue* was to be addressed synchronically within a system of lexical, grammatical and phonological elements all operating relative to each other: *langue* was like chessmen on a chessboard, he asserted. This structural approach to language signalled the birth of 'structural linguistics'.

De Saussure's most immediate effect lay in phonology. His

structural approach coincided with the latest thinking on phonetics – the study and systematic classification of the sounds
made in spoken utterance. Briton Henry Sweet (1845–1912)
had already in 1877 all but defined the concept of the phoneme,
the distinction evident in the contrasting English pair *bin/pin*.
The exact naming of the phenomenon of a *fonema* had come in
1894 in a work published by the Polish Baudouin de Courtenay,
who had distinguished between a simple phone (arbitrary
sound) and a phoneme (significant sound). Only once de
Saussure's lecture notes achieved international recognition at
the end of the First World War did the concept of a phoneme,
and the word itself, become part of linguistic canon.

In the 1920s and 1930s, the 'Prague Linguistic Circle' further developed the theory of the phoneme.[21] They saw the
phoneme as belonging to *langue*, to language's internally related
constituents, and treated it as a complex phonological unit.
Each phoneme, they believed, comprised a number of individual distinctive features whose sum characterized it as an
autonomous linguistic element; but each distinctive feature also
contrasted with its absence or with a different feature in at least
one other phoneme in the investigated language. Entire phonological systems could then be classified according to their
inventories of contrasting features in their constituent
phonemes. In this way, Welsh *p/b*, *ff/f*, *th/dd*, *t/d*, *ll/l* and *c/g*
(here written alphabetically, not phonetically), for example,
reveal a phonemic voiceless/voiced contrast. Such contrasts
were seen to contract, expand or even disappear in different
word positions, with various other phonemes affecting them, or
as a result of any number of phenomena. Even stress, length,
pitch, tone and juncture – the so-called 'supra-segmentals' –
were found to reveal distinctive features that bore significance
beyond the normal consonant-and-vowel segments. Because of
the work of the 'Prague Linguistic Circle' the phoneme
assumed a leading role in linguistic theory and today is implicit
in the description and analysis of any of the world's languages.

While Europe continued to produce a number of seminal
synchronic studies, the USA in the 1920s began to excel in
descriptive linguistics, too and would eventually dominate
linguistic science by the middle of the twentieth century.[22]

This was the achievement of three American-based linguists: the German Franz Boas (1858–1942), the German Edward Sapir (1884–1939) and Chicago-born Leonard Bloomfield (1887–1949). Both Boas and Sapir were products of their German background and era and von Humboldt's linguistic theories resonate in their writings. But America affected them, too, where anthropology uniquely comprised a fundamental part of linguistic study. The native languages of the USA and Canada came under scientific scrutiny at this time and Boas edited and co-authored the *Handbook of American-Indian Languages* (1911, 1938) in which he used the techniques of descriptive linguistics to address languages that had never been described in formal scientific terms. Generations of field linguists would rely on Boas's studied combination of theory and technique when approaching a hitherto undescribed language for the first time. Following German models, Boas redirected the course of Americanist anthropology during the period of the professionalization of science in the USA.

Sapir, who had studied under Boas, approached language through a broad perspective, seeing the workings of a variety of human endeavours permeating every aspect of speech. He was particularly interested in the typology of languages – the analysis of languages based on types (such as isolating, agglutinative, inflectional and so forth) – and believed a valid typology could be achieved through determining general grammatical and morphological characteristics of a wide variety of languages, as opposed to the reliance of Sapir's contemporaries mainly on semantics and psychology. Sapir's *Language* (1921) remains the best general introduction to typological classification.[23]

Rigorously methodological and based on formal analysis, Bloomfield's linguistics was highly conditioned by the positivism of America's behaviourist psychologists, reflecting the scientific interest of his era.[24] His *Language*, first published in the USA in 1933, became not only linguistic's best introductory description for two decades but also the leading university textbook on the subject, influencing the course of the discipline itself.[25] The 'Bloomfieldian era' saw most American linguists centring their studies on formal analysis through objectively describable operations and concepts. Here the phoneme and morpheme took centre stage, with sentence structure 'diagrammed' in terms of immediate constituent analysis; morphemes were connected in 'trees' that illustrated constructs of ascending size and complexity. The statemental model was one of distribution, with syntax and morphology less regarded.

American Kenneth L. Pike and colleagues built on immediate constituent analysis, using mostly Mesoamerican and South American languages, to create the tagmemic system of analysis, identifying the tagmeme as the fundamental grammatical unit or structural 'slot' – the position in a sentence into which a certain class of grammatical items can fit. Sentences could then be more precisely analysed not as successions of immediate constituents, as with Bloomfieldian linguistics, but as strings of collateral constituents.

After the Second World War, linguistic science began to fragment into various semi-autonomous subfields. This was necessitated by the complexity presented by each aspect of linguistic study, be it syntax, phonology, phonetics, semantics, semiotics (the study of signs and symbols and their relation to meaning), dialectology, historical linguistics, lexicography or other fields. Linguistic interest also expanded to include greater domains of ethnological, social and psychological aspects of language, leading to the emergence of the important fields of ethnolinguistics, sociolinguistics and psycholinguistics.

The second half of the twentieth century experienced an exponential increase in the number of linguists, linguistic courses and linguistic theories. Significantly, more was written about language in these 50 years than in the preceding 2,500. Out of this mountain of material a significant number of substantial advances in linguistic investigation was distilled. Also, a wholly new dynamic revealed what direction linguistic science is likely to take, at least for the new century.[26]

In Britain, in the 1940s and 1950s, J. R. Firth, concentrating on phonology, advanced his theory of 'prosodic analysis', what some have called the contextual theory of language. Component words and phrases of an utterance assume meaning only in relation to their various functions in the situational contexts of actual usage. All linguistic form comprises sets of abstractions at three different levels: lexical, grammatical and phonological. These refer to actual features and occurrences of phonic input, with elements and categories related to one another at each of the three levels in syntactic structures and paradigmatic systems. Here, phonology becomes the link between grammar and utterance (phonetics).[27]

Distinctive feature analysis in actual speech transmission was advanced by Roman Jakobson, originally of the 'Prague Linguistic Circle', who, after the Second World War, analysed phonemic features acoustically from the hearer's perspective to deconstruct the phonemes of the world's languages into combinations of as many as twelve binary contrasts (acuteness/gravity, diffuseness/compactness and so on), defined in terms of the distribution of energy at varying frequencies in their sound waves. A language's phonological system could then be analysed on a matrix of feature oppositions.[28]

The Russian revolution had signalled the area's break from Western linguistic tradition. Soviet language studies came to be rather eccentrically controlled by Nikolai Y. Marr (1864–1934), who had concocted his own theories of linguistic history. Marr rejected even Indo-European theory and adopted the old concept of gesture as language's source, which he combined with nineteenth-century typology as an indication of the 'stages' of language evolution. In 1950 Josef Stalin ordered the wholesale rejection of Marrist theory, as it was known, and since that time Russian linguists, in particular, have adopted the principles and methods of Western linguistics, excelling in lexicography (the principles and practices of dictionary making) which, in the 1950s and 1960s, achieved a componential status in linguistic science equal to phonology and grammar.

Several linguists in the 1940s and 1950s reinterpreted the Neogrammarian idea of sound laws and change to incorporate phonemic theory, seeing historical linguistic changes such as Germanic's 'First Sound Shift' as the change in a system – not in autonomous sounds – enabling an explanation of such change to represent the maintenance of phonological oppositions during successive alternations in speakers' articulation. Causes were now investigated, not just effects. One of the most significant was found to lie within languages' own phonological system. Every language strives towards symmetry at all levels, but the human vocal tract is anatomically asymmetric. It creates a permanent imbalance that causes readjustments, or change, automatically. Contrasts must be maintained to achieve meaningful communication and so languages constantly change on their own, independently of conscious human intervention, in order to maintain these necessary contrasts.

In another domain of investigation, American Sidney M. Lamb's 'stratificational grammar' posited four descending strata within language structure for sentence analysis: sememic (the smallest linguistic unit of meaning), lexemic, morphemic and phonemic, each level being hierarchically linked to the other. A conscious rejection of Bloomfield's distributional analysis, stratificational grammar made evident the various types of structural relation one may encounter, as well as the many ways a structure on one level of analysis might relate to another structure on a different level.[29]

A significant break in linguistic tradition came in 1957, the year American Noam Chomsky's *Syntactic Structures* appeared and presented the concept of a 'transformational generative grammar'.[30] A generative grammar is essentially one that 'projects' one or more given sets of sentences upon the greater, perhaps infinite, set of sentences that make up the language one is describing, a process characterizing human language's creativity. Modified in its theoretical principles and methods over succeeding years by many linguists, principally in the USA, a transformational generative grammar attempts to describe a native speaker's linguistic competence by framing linguistic descriptions as rules for 'generating' an infinite number of grammatical sentences.[31]

A generative grammar, as understood by Chomsky, must also be explicit; that is, it must precisely specify the rules of the grammar and their operating conditions. These rules fall into three sets: rules of phrase structure (described as 'trees', hierarchically ordered as noun phrase/verb phrase, then article/noun and verb/noun phrase and so on); specific transformations of these rules (re-ordering, embedding, additions, deletions and so forth) that affect the 'deep structure' to yield a 'surface structure'; and a morphophonemic component whose rules convert the output of the first two sets into actual sounds (utterance) or symbolizations of sounds (written language).[32]

Transformational generative grammar turned Bloomfieldian descriptive linguistics upside-down, devising rules that demonstrate and stress the creative nature of language itself, rather than describe the rules of one language. Its theoretical forerunners are found in the Latin grammarians, von Humboldt and the Port Royal grammarians who all pointed out certain transformational techniques, as Chomsky himself has acknowledged. But transformational generative grammar goes beyond these in providing a framework to generate an infinite linguistic competence. Also, Chomsky believes that linguistics, psychology and philosophy are no longer to be held as separate disciplines but comprise a unitary system of human thinking that should be understood as a larger whole. Though the passage of time has relativized Chomsky's place in linguistic history from 'the' direction to 'a' direction for future language studies, transformational generative grammar will remain the most important theoretical linguistic model that has emerged in the second half of the twentieth century.[33]

Traditional linguists still followed, and continue to follow, the model laid down by Bloomfield, Sapir, Boas and others. These are the Descriptivists, who generally adhere to Basic Linguistic Theory – working concepts fundamental to describing language and linguistic change and recognizing general linguistic properties. Descriptivists take exception with those Formalists (principally the Chomskyists), adherents of 'non-basic theories', as they claim, who seek to create a new model of language based not on a known natural language but on deeper linguistic universals theoretically applicable to all languages. Descriptivists adamantly claim there can be no agreement with the Formalists, since there can never be a complete theory of language: 'analysis' with the Formalists, they allege, means 'fitting a language into their axiomatic framework'.[34] Formalists ignore the debate altogether, since for them there is no debate, the entire issue being irrelevant. Many new Formalist theories have arisen, some augmenting, others competing with transformational generative grammar. That transformational generative grammar can be usefully applied in historical linguistics as well, succeeding in explaining certain phonological phenomena that traditional linguistics has hitherto failed to explain adequately, has been demonstrated since the 1960s by a number of leading historical linguists.[35]

Transformational generative grammar is the leading theoretical statement of language of the last half of the twentieth century, at the same time that Basic Linguistic Theory has been formalized as a contrasting field of applied linguistics with a strong theoretical foundation. Descriptivists may complain of the 'malaise of formalisms' and identify a lack of good descriptive grammars for most of the world's languages. But Formalists are making a large contribution to the field, too, especially in the associated area of computational linguistics (see below).

Wholly new directions have emerged. Discourse analysis, already pioneered in the 1950s by Chomsky's teacher Zellig Harris, who called the transformation between two or more actual sentences in texts a 'conversion relation', has shown itself to be an effective means of extending textual descriptive analysis beyond and across sentence boundaries. It makes use of the concept of language 'frames' to help interpret a text by placing it in a defining context; of 'turn-taking' or 'floors' in conversation to identify systems of noting speech conclusions or signalling listenership; of 'discourse markers' like 'and', 'oh', 'well' and 'but' that divide discourse into segments and show discourse relationships beyond mere dictionary definitions; and of 'speech act analysis' that investigates what an utterance achieves, such as complimenting to submit, ingratiate or indirectly claim possession, an important aspect of cross-cultural understanding.

Computational linguistics, also known as natural language processing, began in 1946 when computers were first used to generate machine translations from Russian into English.[36] (The field of machine translation has since become a highly sophisticated and commercially profitable discipline, with many varied systems in use.) In essence, computational linguists use computers to study natural languages, in contrast to programming languages like Java, C++, Fortran and so forth. Here linguists unite linguistic and computer science resources in order to enable computers to be used technologically as aids in analysing and processing natural language and psychologically to better understand, by analogy with computers, how human language is processed. Utilizing methods and tools from computer science and related disciplines, linguists can construct and test computational models of various theories and thereby gain insights from applied algorithms (rules of procedure for solving a recurrent computational problem), data structures and programming languages.

There are many subfields in computational linguistics, such as computational lexicography, computational phonology, controlled languages and constraint logic programming. Applied computational linguistics addresses machine translation, information extraction from text and speech synthesis and recognition. Speech understanding and generation – for the handicapped, for telephony-based information systems, for office dictation systems and so forth – are applied fields of computational linguistics with enormous commercial markets. Further aspects are the creation, administration and presentation of texts using a computer, removing the human agent to minimize cost and maximize efficiency. The presentation of textual information in hypertext, eliminating the need for standard (that is, linear) texts, is presently one of the greatest challenges in computational linguistics.

Computational linguistics is now a major field of research, with institutes, seminars, research centres and private corporations worldwide dedicated to its study and service provision. The discipline is growing exponentially, making it the most dynamic and lucrative branch of linguistic science at present.

Language studies have enjoyed a long and rich tradition. India's Sanskrit scholars achieved astonishingly profound insights into language's nature already in the first half of the first millennium BC. Ancient Greece and Rome solidly ordered and categorized their own languages, raising grammatical columns that supported many structures, even those of 'barbarians', for more than 2,000 years. Mediæval 'speculative grammars' combined Priscian's Latin declensions with Aristotelian philosophy. The Renaissance, discovering Hebrew and other languages, realized that Greek and Latin did not explain all observed linguistic phenomena after all. The eighteenth century compiled lexica and posed questions about language's origin and the nineteenth century provided the answers and, in the process, founded the science of linguistics. The twentieth century has abounded with exciting new linguistic theories and innovations, commencing with the phoneme and concluding with computer-generated languages, opening a window on a whole new universe of linguistic possibilities.

Linguistic science contributes greatly to the store of human knowledge. Other disciplines only now are able merely to confirm what historical linguists have earlier discovered. For example, linguistic comparisons made several decades ago clearly established that the Finnish language is Uralic from northern Asia; geneticists are presently announcing their 'discovery' that Finns are Asians because they can demonstrate that the Y polymorphisms (extremely rare male mutations) so abundant in Asia are also prevalent in Finnish populations. In a similar case, decades ago linguists identified the Māori of New Zealand, as Polynesians, to have originated in Asia, in particular Taiwan, around 5,000–6,000 years ago. In 1998, the world's media celebrated the 'discovery' by geneticists of the same fact – with no mention of linguistic science's earlier contribution. Perhaps more spectacularly, computational linguistics in particular is seemingly now offering to everyone's view an entire new world of discovery through programming languages, in ways one can yet scarcely comprehend.

Linguistics continually evolves, like the languages it investigates. This is not only because of new insights, but also because of the fluid social changes, interests and priorities that affect the course of language studies. The science of language, that 'step in the self-realization of man', now fully flowered and possessing its own unique dynamic, will doubtless continue to enhance humankind's evolving understanding and appreciation of language and its seemingly infinite potential for many centuries to come.

SEVEN

Society and Language

'I will set up my name in the place where the names of famous men are written', boasted the Sumerian king Gilgamesh nearly 4,000 years ago, signalling one of society's principal uses of language: to herald one's space. Societies' great and small issues have always been reflected in linguistic usage. Already ancient Egyptians appreciated that 'the word is father to the thought', acknowledging that language is both the foundation and building material of the social house. Society's final architecture and subsequent remodelling are also measured from and through language. Language gives all human action voice, achieving this in complex and subtle ways.[1] Multiple levels of social interaction, from international relations to intimate relationships, are borne, enabled and empowered through language.

Language not only signals where we come from, what we espouse and to whom we belong, but also operates tactically and strategically to invest our individual, gender or ethnic franchise; to authorize our pilgrimage through societies' orders; and to signal to others what we want and how we intend to achieve it.[2] Throughout history people have judged others – that is, consciously or unconsciously assessed their place in human society – based solely on their ethnic language, their regional dialect, indeed their personal choice of individual words. The linguistic verdict has been final and has fashioned all of human history.[3]

LANGUAGE CHANGE

All living languages experience constant change.[4] Linguistic change is most apparent in written language, as one immediately appreciates when reading Shakespeare, for example. Least apparent is occurring change or 'change in progress'. Only a word here or vowel there of one's grandparents' speech would seem a bit 'odd'. Conversely, every older generation finds the speech of the younger 'inappropriate'.

The expanded social domain of split infinitives became such a topic in Great Britain at the end of the nineteenth century – to mention one very protracted case of linguistic change – that the matter concerned the highest orders: 'This is the sort of English up with which I will not put!' quipped Sir Winston Churchill in a marginal comment on a state document, intuiting perhaps that, nearly a century later, the Oxford English Dictionary would at last 'condone' the split infinitive . . . which English has used with eminent success for centuries.

The hierarchical registers of linguistic usage – sacral, royal, professional, official, military, civil, familiar and intimate – contend with one another and with the speech usage of preceding and succeeding generations in all the world's tongues. Yet communication endures and language continues to thrive.

The causes of linguistic change are as varied and intricate as the personal lives of each speaker: foreign contact, bilingualism, substrates, written language, the phonological system itself that always seeks symmetry and other causes.[5] One major cause of the past 200 years has been unprecedented urbanization. In 1790, only one in twenty Americans lived in a town; in 1990, only one in 40 lived on a farm. The Third World is now experiencing a similar urban revolution, eradicating not only languages but entire language families. The inversion of traditional human settlement patterns brings about innumerable linguistic upheavals, a 'punctuation' causing innovation, dialect levelling and even language replacement. In contrast, during a protracted period of equilibrium that might last for thousands of years, areal diffusion might well be the major factor in linguistic change.

Recent technology has introduced an entirely new dimension to the dynamics of linguistic change: telephone, radio, cinema and television. For the first time in human history we are also listening 'blindly', as that so primeval element of speech – gesture – is missing in non-visual communication, though on the telephone Italians still wave, Japanese still bow and all of us still smile and frown as if our interlocutor were present, so immediate is gesture to speech. 'Everything that came out of this machine was believed', said the American actor, director and writer Orson Welles of the radio in the 1930s. At the same time, in Germany, the cheaply distributed *Volksempfänger*, or 'Peoples' Receivers', broadcast Berlin's High German propagandistic pronouncements throughout the Third Reich, effectively prescribing the pronunciation of a central government among a large population of dialect speakers, something that had never happened before. Throughout the world, radio's effect on spoken language was enormous, beginning a linguistic levelling that reverberates three generations later.

After the Second World War, television intruded far more dramatically: increased dialect levelling, contamination and superimposition have since been documented among large populations of viewers. At this moment, television is perhaps the single greatest cause of universal dialect levelling. With English, the Hollywood studios' predominance in international television programming in the last two decades of the twentieth century has ensured that the use of Standard American English is increasing at a rapid rate in those countries that broadcast this programming without 'dubbing' (voicing over actors' lines in a foreign language). In the 1970s, New Zealand, for example, knew nothing of American discourse fillers – 'like', 'sorta', 'kinda', 'ya know', 'and stuff' – but by the middle of the 1990s, once American television programming for economic reasons had all but replaced British and New Zealand programming, these generally adolescent expressions were polluting New Zealand speech as frequently as in the USA and Canada.

The phenomenon is occurring worldwide in other English-speaking countries, too, and is effectively reinterpreting International Standard English, which is presently becoming a hybrid British-American idiom. Immediate lexical introductions, particularly of slang words and expressions, have been witnessed worldwide as a result even of one favourite programme or striking news broadcast. The broadcasting of a metropolitan language programme to a small community of minority speakers can be socially devastating: Chilean television on tiny Easter Island, for example, has resulted in parents speaking to their children in traditional Polynesian Rapanui but the children responding only in Spanish, a phenomenon now occurring in similar fashion throughout the world.

The reflex of a rapidly changing society, vocabulary expansion and replacement is an almost daily process in all modern countries. With this one does not mean the Inuit's twenty words for 'snow', Irish Gælic's 40 words for 'green', or English's 226 words for 'money', which may be environmental or psycholinguistic phenomena. Of more concern to sociolinguists are words that appear, disappear or change meaning because of a society's technological growth, reassessment, maturation or suffering.

Migration into new territories with hitherto unknown objects and topographies and the invention of new technologies such as the computer, are commonly observed sociolinguistic motors causing languages to change. Around 4,500 years ago, the earliest Greeks encountered the pre-Greek inhabitants of the Ægean and learned from them of the *plínthos* 'brick, tile', *mégaron* 'type of hall', *símblos* 'domed beehive', *kypárissos/kypárittos* 'cypress' and even the *thálassa/thálatta* 'sea', things they had never known or seen before. These words soon became Greek. When the Brittonic Celts experienced the Romans' *strata* 'street', *ecclesia* 'church' and *fenestra* 'window' around 2,000 years ago, they borrowed these unknown concepts, which explains why the Welsh say *stryd*, *eglwys* and *ffenest* today. Massive lexical expansion has just occurred in many of the world's languages, for example, because of the introduction of personal computers: 'download', 'online', 'Internet', 'spreadsheet', 'database', 'modem' and scores of other words are now in daily use that, 30 years ago, did not exist. Borrowing new words and expanding the domain of old words are linguistic processes which have enriched human society since the emergence of articulate speech.

Societies also alter lexicons because of reassessment, sometimes reflecting a society's agonizingly slow progress towards maturation. Once a word of honour, 'war' now elicits general repugnance. 'Nigger' for 'Negro' is taboo, perhaps more emotionally charged than English's worst four-letter word; meaning the same as 'nigger', *keffir* is currently being purged from South

African vocabularies. Gone from English, either wholly or in certain meanings, are also 'fairy', 'queer', 'cohabitation', 'concubine' and other victims of the sexual revolution of the 1960s and 1970s that rendered these terms not only meaningless but offensive. 'Divorcée', 'spinster' and 'unwed mother' have all but disappeared since the 1970s, attesting to women's changed role in society. Many ancient generic terms – words relating to, or characteristic of, a whole group or class – are being semantically reassessed, too, in light of humankind's growing awareness and sensitivity at the beginning of the third millennium: 'animal', for example, is presently experiencing semantic re-interpretation, from 'beast' into 'fellow creature'. Such changes reveal much about the evolving human condition.

Sociolinguists also note negative changes. 'Music', 'literature', 'art' and 'theatre' are losing their traditional definitions by the mutating appearance of what they embrace; they are 'dissolving into meaninglessness'. Perhaps more alarmingly, 'family', 'marriage', 'honour', even 'God' are becoming indistinct concepts as society inverts and fails to maintain hitherto revered conventions and beliefs.[6] The single word 'partner' that until recently meant only 'pal', 'business associate' or 'colleague in a game' is presently expanding its semantic domain to replace such ancient relationships in English as 'husband', 'wife', 'spouse' and 'fiancée/fiancé'. (However, basic 'child', 'mother' and 'incest' remain untouched; 'father' is under reassessment.)

A society's reinvention is seen in such replacements. All the changes cited above have occurred within the author's lifetime, the latter half of the twentieth century, which has experienced a difficult reweaving of the social fabric that is still unfinished. The older one becomes, the more one must abandon inherited usages and redefine venerable concepts. For many it is a difficult, if not impossible, task.

Minor changes reflect humankind's penchant for change-for-change's-sake, that is, innovation for no other reason but the novelty of innovation itself. Perfectly good standard words are regularly replaced or supplemented merely for the additional spice, to flavour speech as thyme flavours soup. Most such words are fad words that disappear again almost immediately, especially among the young. A particularly vulnerable semantic 'slot' that invites regular supplementation is the word 'excellent' with its dozens of popular synonyms that come and go: 'awesome' (1990s), 'groovy' (1960s), 'hep' (1940s), 'absolute' (Shakespeare), 'ful faire' (Chaucer). Other words enter the vocabulary as a fad, then remain: in the eighteenth century English 'acute' became slang 'cute' signifying 'clever, sharp, cunning' and then, in the USA, 'attractive, pretty'; 'cuteness' meaning 'prettiness' is a recent derivation of this later redefinition.

Slang represents the usage of an informal non-standard vocabulary – both words and expressions – in order to creatively manipulate speech for a variety of reasons. Only since the eighteenth century has English slang been seen as something negative: Chaucer, Shakespeare, Dryden and Pope all used slang in their works as an integral part of their artistic statement.[7] From the eighteenth up to the end of the twentieth centuries, slang has been something to be avoided as English speakers strove towards prescriptive usage, the reflex of the general education movement with its idealized concept of a 'proper language'. Now, English speakers are becoming more like those of Shakespeare's era in their use of slang. Slang has even become acceptable in the higher social registers, particularly among American English speakers: a White House press secretary calling a satellite launch 'awesomely cool' exemplifies the USA's fast, innovative, commercial, multi-ethnic use of language.[8] In sober contrast, German and French, for example, would never tolerate slang in the higher social registers, slang being restricted in both languages to precisely defined 'lower' orders.[9] To have used slang in ancient Tahitian prayer, to cite the extreme, would have brought a swift blow to the head.

COMMON, CONTACT AND CONSTRUCTED LANGUAGES

One might imagine that there was an effort among early *Homo erectus* tribes to establish some sort of a common tongue to facilitate mutual understanding and promote trade. Throughout history, common languages have evolved in this way, usually along trade routes. If a dominant language was spoken in the area of such trade routes, then this dominant language became the 'interlanguage', as it is called. Such an interlanguage, or koiné, is a simplified dialect with which speakers of two or more quite different dialects communicate with one another. Commonly shared features of their language are retained and non-shared features ignored.

One of the earliest documented interlanguages was the *koinē diálektos* or 'common dialect' of the Hellenistic age (323–27 BC). Basically an Attic dialect from the Athens region, through influences from other dialects, particularly Ionian, *koinē* changed its phonology, morphology, syntax and lexicon and spread rapidly through trade and colonization. It also became the Greek standard language used in literature, especially in the writings of Hellenized foreigners, as in the New Testament. From the middle of the first century BC, scholars, striving to resurrect a 'pure' Attic literary language, showed antipathy towards this 'inferior' vulgar language. Nevertheless, *koinē* continued to dominate the ports and trading centres of the greater Mediterranean well into the first few centuries AD.

One of the major interlanguages of the Celtic peoples in the first few centuries BC, when *koinē* was dominating the Mediterranean, was perhaps the Gallo-Brittonic common language spoken among the Gaulish-speaking Celts of the mainland and the Brittonic-speaking Celts of Britain before Roman occupation. However, little is known of this presumed common idiom.

Lingua franca is what mediæval Arabs called the languages of the Romance peoples they came into contact with. In particular this was the vulgar Italian whose origin lay in Venetian and Genoese rule in the Levant and which served there as an interlanguage between the Semitic peoples and resident Europeans. The term *lingua franca*, like koiné, has since been borrowed by many languages to designate any interlanguage. *Lingua Geral* is the Portuguese language, in particular the interlanguages Tupi of the Amazon Basin and Guaraní in Paraquay and southern Brazil. Swahili, with Bantu grammar and a large portion of Arab vocabulary, became the *lingua franca* of East African trade routes and, in the nineteenth century, was used as far inland as the

Congo River. Swahili still represents one of the world's major interlanguages, possessing its own rich literature.

Unlike a naturally evolving language that derives from proto-languages, an artificial *pidgin language* can arise when speakers of several different languages converge for longer periods.[10] Its vocabulary is commonly from a dominant language but much smaller than this; its grammar is greatly simplified and, in most but not all cases, regularized. A pidgin language is generally used only as a second language, but there are exceptions. Examples of pidgin languages are the Zulu-based Fanagolo of South Africa, Swahili-based Settla of Zambia, French-based Tay Boi of Vietnam and many more. The pidginization process is commonly associated with colonial languages, such as Portuguese, Spanish, French and English.

As an example of an English-based pidgin, three forms of a new language emerged in the nineteenth century when Melanesian workers were transported by English-speaking plantation owners from the Solomon Islands, Vanuatu (formerly New Hebrides) and Papua New Guinea to cut sugarcane in Australia and Samoa. The pidgin they brought back became Tok Pisin in Papua, Pijin in the Solomons and Bislama in Vanuatu, consisting of 80 to 90 per cent English with a mixture of local vocabularies. These three now comprise a 'new and distinct language with its own phonology, grammar and lexicon'.[11]

If a pidgin language replaces the indigenous tongues, then the pidgin is called a *creole language*, such as the French-based Haitian of Haiti, Kongo-based Kituba of Zaïre, German-based Unserdeutsch of Papua New Guinea, Arabic-based Nubi of Uganda and many others. A creole language can emerge from a pidgin language, for example, if pidgin-speaking male workers are not allowed to return home and if women are brought in among them to allow the establishment of families of mixed linguistic origin. A pidgin then becomes a first language and only fragments of the mother tongues remain as relics in the new creole. Because of the African slave trade, a great number of such creole languages emerged in exactly this way in the many islands of the Caribbean.

A grey zone obtains between pidgin and creole languages, one occupied by those who speak the same language but either as a pidgin or a creole – that is, one and the same language can serve either group of speakers. Perhaps a redefinition of creole is necessary, seeing it instead as a shallow contact language whose underlying pidgin has not yet elaborated a solid linguistic structure. A generation of speakers growing up speaking only this 'unfinished' pidgin as a first language appear to gravitate towards stabilizing rules that suggest language universals. The recent Language Bioprogram Hypothesis alleges that specific grammatical features tend to show themselves in just such a creolization process.[12]

If one does not use an interlanguage, devise or adopt a pidgin, or grow up speaking a creole, then one can instead elaborate one's own invented language, a 'constructed human language'. This is an artificially created language, ideally easily learnable, fashioned to serve all nations in neutral manner. In earlier centuries in Europe such a construct was unnecessary, as all educated Europeans spoke and wrote Latin as a second language. However, already in the seventeenth century Descartes and Leibniz theoretically proposed the creation of a logically perfect symbolic system for communicating scientific knowledge. A constructed human language is often called 'naturalistic' because, though artificially constructed, it attempts to reduce one or more known natural languages to a common, simplified grammar and vocabulary. Historically, this has been through the incorporation of the most widely shared features of words in Western languages, in particular Indo-European ones. Of course this historical reliance on Indo-European – only one of many language families in the world – betrays the pretense of 'universality'.

The first practical constructed language was the south-west German Pastor Schleyer's Volapük from 1879; its complicated grammar and irregular vocabulary made learning difficult, however. The most successful has been Esperanto, devised by the Warsaw ophthalmologist Ludwig Zamenhof in 1887, that today can count some one million speakers. Influenced by Esperanto, several members of the Volapük Academy reorganized themselves and published in 1902 a new attempt: Idiom Neutral; this was hailed as a great advance in naturalistic language construction and had a major impact on subsequent attempts. At the same time, the Italian mathematician Giuseppe Peano offered a simplified (flexionless, or without variation in word endings) version of Latin called Interlingua. In 1907, a naturalistically reformed Esperanto called Ido, developed by Frenchman L. de Beaufront, was reworked and endorsed by a scientific committee in Paris, who then argued with the Esperantists and divided the artificial language movement.

Already by 1918 around 100 different constructed languages had been proposed. Esperanto's practical experience and Ido's theoretical innovations led to new suggestions, such as the German E. von Wahl's Occidental in 1922 and the Dane Otto Jespersen's Novial in 1928, whose vocabulary was based on Western European languages. New investigations followed, such as the wholly independent movements of C. K. Ogden's Basic English in 1930 and L. Hogben's Interglossa in 1943. In 1951, an Interlingua–English dictionary was published under the auspices of the International Auxiliary Language Association in New York.

There remains active interest today in constructed human languages, from both the theoretical-linguistic standpoint and the practical, with new languages now being created with the aid of personal computers. The field is historically fascinating, but the goal is no longer of practical use. Most constructed languages are Indo-European based and so lack 'linguistic universality' (whatever this is conceived to be). Further, it is simply unnatural to try to be natural. Living languages are of far greater influence in the world, particularly Mandarin Chinese, Spanish and English. The original idea behind constructed human languages was to avoid national identification in an era of emerging nations and competing colonization. This need is now gone, as most of the large metropolitan languages are no longer identified with any one single nation. That is, world languages are emerging naturally for the first time in history. Indeed, the English language – by historical circumstance, not by design – presently counts more second-language speakers than any other tongue on Earth and numbers are growing.[13]

Throughout history, people have identified with their own tongue and with those who speak it most closely. Indeed, through the identification with others speaking the same language the idea of a 'nation' of peoples emerged. More recent multi-ethnic, multilingual nations often stand on two-legged stools principally because of language – one need only think of Belgium, Canada, the Basques and other similarly troubled societies. A recognized national tongue further inherently comprehends the notion of a 'superior dialect' within this tongue, too, usually because those who speak this dialect are the richest and most powerful while those who do not speak it are poorer and less powerful. As with prescriptive grammars, which teach how a language 'should' be spoken, 'received pronunciations' from prestige dialects, as much a thing of fashion as a new hat, constantly reshape non-prestige dialects. Now, with radio, television and Internet, bombardment by the linguistically empowered can occur planet-wide.

In a contrasting process, the recent 'modernization' of the British Broadcasting Corporation (BBC) has essentially eliminated what had come to be called 'BBC English', an easily recognizable received pronunciation of the English language that had long been held in high regard. Now, older listeners, be they in Britain or New Zealand, register alarm at hearing in BBC broadcasts what they register as 'lower-class pronunciation'; they feel this not only 'lowers standards' but also demonstrates 'a beastly lack of good taste'. However, such protestations are meaningless in the larger saga of living languages. 'Superior' dialects are only a chimera, as special dialects themselves very soon mutate and/or lose what made them special.

All dialects of a nation – the geographical, ethnic, 'upstairs-downstairs' social, ethnic-social (black 'upstairs' with white 'downstairs', or vice versa), prestige, peer and other dialects – together with contact influences (such as French's influence on English for nearly 1,000 years) contribute to the linguistic amalgam that characterizes each of Earth's natural languages.[14] In urban sociolinguistics, one commonly follows the 'standard-vernacular model', whereby one invokes the dyads of 'power' versus 'solidarity', 'higher' versus 'lower' social class, 'open networks' versus 'closed networks' and so forth. However, in the smaller communities that have characterized most of human history these polarities are apparently irrelevant: linguistic variation is best conceptualized and ordered according to the speech norms of neighbourhood and ancestry, as studies of smaller African languages are now revealing.

It is true that some ethnic groups in multi-ethnic societies display greater regionalism than others, a consciousness of and loyalty to a distinct domain with a homogeneous population. Americans of European ancestry are far more regional (areally bound), for example, than Americans of African ancestry, who tend more towards an ethnic universal of behaviour and speech (areally independent, in contrast to communities in Africa). But the speech of all groups in a nation continuously moulds the language and changes it daily, as each spice added to the bouillabaisse changes and enriches its flavour. Black American speech, primarily through music, films and television, has tremendously affected Euro-American speech in recent years, especially among the young. A prestige dialect might superficially impress, certainly; but all dialects of a language together, as a dynamic whole, express. And it is its expressive constituents in dynamic orchestration that enable a living language to thrive.

It was mentioned earlier how, at the beginning of the fifth century BC, the historian Herodotus wrote of 'the whole Greek community, being of one blood and one tongue'. This is significant. For throughout most of human history, blood was tongue. Because of small human populations, those who spoke like you usually were related to you. Over tens of millennia, this consanguinity had engendered a conviction that similar speech embraces. Conversely, foreign speech threatens. As communities of like speakers banded together, first into city states, then principalities, then nations, encounters with non-like speakers at the same time led to ever larger conflicts. This defined more pronounced borders between neighbours, borders based on the lack of a common tongue.

One notes with sadness how the division between English and French speakers in Canada now threatens national unity;

how the violent disintegration of the former Soviet Union is chiefly following linguistic borders; and how the many wars in Africa are fought almost exclusively between tribes speaking different tongues. In the USA, the recent incursion of millions of Spanish speakers from southern nations has so aroused sensitivities that many Americans are calling for an 'English-only' amendment to the US constitution – a legislative proposal to make English the 'official' language of the USA. A similar folly was instituted by the Russian-speaking Soviet Union and added to internal dissent.

The idea of 'linguistic isolation' fails to appreciate human languages' driving force, the power to absorb and link in order to foster cooperation and ensure human survival. Middle English was not polluted or destroyed by Norman French after 1066; it was extraordinarily enriched. A similar enrichment – Spanish into English – might now be enjoyed by North Americans over 900 years later.

Such topics argue for the status of national and vernacular languages as effective indicators of social harmony in developing nations. Since the articulation of speech, humankind's varied appreciation of language's role in society has either united or divided communities, formed them or invited warfare. Caught in-between, multilingual cultures experience constant friction. The creation of nation-states in recent times has increased this friction, adding artificial pressure from the top down.[15] In most multilingual countries, national liberation movements after the Second World War forced anew the question of an official language(s) after independence from colonial powers. Since this time, the social impact of languages has been studied in depth: the need to identify with a linguistic community defining one's concept of 'home' is now recognized to be one of society's most basic requirements. Further, the issue of minority rights has at the same time effected an acknowledgement of the equality of minority languages and dialects in most Western countries, such as Chicano Spanish and Afro-American and Afro-British English. It is an ancient concern, one that troubled the Putaans and Libyans on Minoan Crete in 1600 BC, the Greeks in Egypt in 200 BC and the Romans and Germans in Britain in AD 200 – indeed, minority peoples in every age.

The Afro-American story is remarkable. Brought to America by force, Africans were commonly forbidden to speak West African languages and educated English. The Black English Vernacular they developed in order to communicate lay uncomfortably atop an inherited African substrate. It lies there still, a readily identifiable ethnic emblem. In particular, Afro-American phonology abounds with features not found in Euro-American phonology. It is generally assumed that these derive from original West African languages, though this need not be the case: such features might well have originated among the slave communities on American soil as early as the seventeenth century.[16]

However, many West African lexical items not only have survived, often hidden as English homonyms, but have entered the international mainstream: 'dig', 'jive', 'jazz', 'hep', 'cat', 'boogie-woogie' and many more.[17] Supplementing the inherited Germanic homonym, slang 'cool' might perhaps derive from a West African *kul* meaning 'admirable, excellent'; a 'cool cat' would have been an 'admirable person', for example. However, for the past twenty years young people throughout the world have been using Afro-American 'cool' as an all-inclusive term for 'excellent' – making 'cool' the most widely borrowed adjective in the world today. From an initial position of persecution, because of the civil rights movement beginning in the 1950s Black English Vernacular has attained a position of influence in International Standard English.

In dramatic contrast, Bulgaria's minority Turks, resident for centuries, have recently been forbidden not only their Turkish language but also their Turkish names; as a result, thousands have fled to neighbouring Turkey. And in 1998, to suppress the former colonial language, French, Algeria's government passed a law making it an offence to use any other language but Arabic; Algeria's minority Berbers, speaking the country's earliest known tongue, took to the streets to protest. The two examples describe minority languages' all-too-common fate.

Since the late 1960s, the women's liberation movement has prompted linguists to study gender differences in language, in particular whether language usage helps to reinforce and perpetuate sexual inequality.[18] The movement has even caused a partial 'neutering' of the English language – the removal of traditional 'gender markers' – in order to help women, gays and lesbians achieve social equality through the medium of language. For those whose social indoctrination and schooling predated this movement, it has necessitated a constant revision of spoken and written English as well as of inherited attitudes and concepts.

In many languages such neutering is simply impossible, since gender distinction (particularly differentiated noun classes) is the bearer of grammar. For example, the Welsh sentence *Rydw i yn chwarae ei biano* 'I am playing his piano' contrasts with *Rydw i yn chwarae ei phiano* 'I am playing her piano' only through a consonantal mutation operating on *piano* that is governed by gender. In French, adjectives must agree both in gender and number with their nouns: in *les soeurs sont belles* 'the sisters are beautiful' and *les frères sont beaux* 'the brothers are handsome', feminine plural *belles* contrasts with masculine plural *beaux*. In German, gender inflection is an indispensable marker of grammatical function: *das Kind gehört der Frau* 'the child belongs to the woman', whereby *die Frau* 'the woman' here becomes dative (indirect object) singular *der Frau* 'to the woman'. In many languages, gender differences (that is, noun classes) carry essential semantic distinctions, too. In German, for example, masculine *der Band* means 'the volume (of a book)', feminine *die Band* 'the (musical) band' and neuter *das Band* 'the string, cord, band'. In Welsh, which like French uses only two genders, masculine *gwaith* is 'work' but feminine *gwaith* is 'time'. Lacking such explicit gender rules and distinctions, English perhaps finds itself in an eminent position to achieve, at least linguistically, partial gender equality.

What has actually transpired in the past 25 years in the English language has been an unprecedented 'gender purge', facilitated by a concomitant explosion of mass communication. This has prompted a conscious reassessment by every educated speaker and writer of the English language of his or her vocabulary in order to avoid any word that might negatively affect the rights of not only women but also gays and lesbians.[19] Sometimes the debate has been absurb. Women's advocates, thinking English 'human' to be a 'man' word, tried for example to replace this with 'huperson'. Fortunately, the attempt failed, perhaps not so much because 'human' is actually from Latin *hūmānus* that has nothing to do with Germanic *mann/mannon* 'man, human being', but because the word is core vocabulary. (Humorists queried at the time whether 'women's libbers' wished also to rename Manhattan 'Personhattan'.)

However, other words have indeed been dropped from the active English vocabulary, particularly those that patently express masculineness when this is unnecessary. For example, in this book the author has consciously suppressed each 'mankind' with a gender-correct 'humankind'. Despite the Prime Minister of Australia's attempt in 1998 to reintroduce it, 'chairman' has effectively been replaced everywhere with 'chairperson'. Most occupational categories in English have been neutered: 'stewards' and 'stewardesses' are now collectively 'flight attendants', for example. Such venerable words as 'forefathers', 'fatherhood' and 'manservant' – that is, 'ancestors', 'parenthood' and 'domestic' – will perhaps disappear from the active vocabulary, too, to join that vast store of archaisms that inflate the historical lexica. This is not only language's fate, it is language's duty . . . when warranted.

The past has known similar ventures, usually of religious, ethnic or nationalistic nature (see below). In the nineteenth century, British politician Thomas Massey railed against Catholicisms in the English language and proposed to the House of Commons that Christmas should be renamed 'Christ-tide' to avoid reference to the Catholic mass. When Prime Minister Benjamin Disraeli stood up, however, to ask Thomas Massey whether he was then also prepared to change his own name to 'Tom-tide Tidey', the matter was closed.

Rather than altering inherited language in order to effect social change, linguistic purists wish to return to an intuited 'purer' form of their tongue. Perhaps the prime motive of early Sanskrit, Greek, Latin and Arabic grammarians was not so much to 'understand' language (in the modern scientific sense) as to prescribe it – that is, to define and petrify its 'purest' form in written language. The myth of an ancient, unadulterated tongue of wiser antecedents always seemed to underlie this activity. When Renaissance scholars introduced a profusion of borrowings from Greek and Latin into all European tongues in order to create a new philosophical and scientific vocabulary, the flood of foreign words this generated subsequently pro-voked, in the seventeenth century, 'linguistic purges' that sought to rid one's tongue of all perceived foreign elements and to prescribe 'proper', that is, earlier, language usage. Only in the eighteenth century was a rational balance between the two extremes finally achieved.

In Florence, Italy, several scholars and poets convened in 1582 to found the *Accademia della Crusca* with the intention of purging the national tongue of all foreign words and elevating the sensed national characteristics of Italian, basing their ideal particularly on the revered texts of Dante and Boccaccio. The Accademia flourished for two centuries and inspired similar societies throughout Europe. Germany had several, the oldest and most highly respected being Weimar's *Fruchtbringende Gesellschaft* (1617–80) to which all important German poets of the seventeenth century belonged. In similar fashion, France established the *Académie Française* in 1635, which today remains France's most highly respected, prescriptive institution for lan-guage supervision.

England's Royal Society was founded in 1662, principally to emulate France. By then England had long complained of lan-guage impurity. In the late fifteenth century London printer William Caxton had remonstrated against 'over curyous termes which coude not be vnderstande of comyn people'. Hundreds of French borrowings were then competing with native English words: rock/stone, realm/kingdom, stomach/belly, velocity/speed, aid/help, cease/stop, depart/leave, parley/speak. English's solution: to keep both, but to impart to each a different nuance or social value (with much accompanying displacement and replacement, too). This enriched the English language as few languages on Earth have experienced and made English essentially the product of two separate language families, Germanic and Italic. By 1577, historian Ralph Holinshed could claim, 'There is no one speeche vnder the sonne spoken in our time, that hath or can haue more varietie of words and copie [copiousness] of phrases than English'.

Others were critical of unrestrained borrowing, however, chastising those who 'patched vp the holes with peces and rags of other languages, borrowing here of the french, there of Italian, euery where of the Latine, not weighing how il those tongues accorde with themselues, but much worse with ours: So now they haue made our English tongue a gallimaufray or hodgepodge of al other speches'. Samuel Johnson, who attempted in the eighteenth century to write the first 'complete' dictionary of English, declared his goal was to 'redefine our language to grammatical purity and to clear it from colloquial barbarisms'. Johnson was of course doomed from the start, since there is no such thing as a 'pure language'. For English in particular, of the 10,000 most frequent words, only 31.8 per cent are inherited Germanic, with the remaining consisting of 45 per cent French, 16.7 per cent Latin and several minor contributing languages. (English also displays a French superstratum in its grammar and phonology, but this is not so pronounced as in its vocabulary.) However, of the 1,000 most frequent words of English, 83 per cent derive from Old English, 12 per cent from French and 2 per cent from Latin.

The error of linguistic purists has always been their failure to realize that borrowing is one of a language's greatest strengths. Human languages are not stones, they are sponges. This quality bestows on them their wonderful creativity as well as their adaptability and viability. Yet throughout history linguistic purges have occurred time and time again. Often war is the cause. In the First World War, for example, German or German-related words and names in English were Anglicized:

'German shepherd' became 'Alsatian', 'Battenberg' became 'Mountbatten' and so forth. Similarly, because of their Aryan aberration in the 1930s and 1940s the Nazis tried to purge the German language of all foreign influences, particularly Jewish ones. At the same time, Russia was purging the Russian language throughout the vast Soviet Union of all capitalist words in order to create a 'pure, socialist vocabulary', similarly a mirage.

When Indonesia became independent of Holland after the Second World War, the new government replaced Dutch with Bahasa Indonesia – up until then only one of scores of separate languages there – as the language of government, the courts, media and education. A Language and Literature Council was established to create a new terminology and to translate the necessary Dutch materials into Bahasa Indonesia using this terminology. This meant a wholly 'pure' Bahasa Indonesia planned, sanctioned and implemented by central government. All instruction in Indonesia has since been held in this new artificial language, bringing about the rapid depletion of Indonesia's rich linguistic diversity.

The Māori of New Zealand make up approximately eleven per cent of the population but only around one in twenty Māori actively speaks the Māori language, a Polynesian tongue (all Māori speak fluent English). Nevertheless, because of New Zealand's indigenous rights campaign inspired by the USA's black civil rights movement, a language council similar to Indonesia's has been established to create a new Māori vocabulary of Western cultural and technological items that are unknown in Māori. Since this is a prejudiced action to 'protect' Māori from English, it is neither needed nor often applied. The plan cannot compare with undertakings elsewhere in the world to preserve a national majority tongue.

As an example of the latter, Iceland is another country that practises linguistic purification. Icelandic is the Germanic majority language of the descendants of largely Norse (but also Irish) colonists who settled Iceland in and after AD 874. Because of Iceland's very small population of around 270,000, making Icelandic particularly vulnerable to foreign influences, and because of a strong ethnic pride, a special language council meets regularly to Icelandicize any new, mostly technical terms entering the language, such as *sjónvarp* 'television' (literally 'sight-throw'). The council's work has helped Icelandic to survive.

PROPAGANDA AND LANGUAGE

A society also obfuscates, lies and deceives through language, with dire consequences for the personal freedoms of its members who are thereby deprived of their right of achieving a democratic consent. Such misuse of language is a symptom of an ill society. In the past, governments which have practised this misuse for a protracted period have invariably perished.

'Political correctness' is first and foremost linguistic. One suffers harm if one does not speak the speech of those in power.[20] Ancient Athenians had to use those *lógoi* that disparaged the Spartans and upheld Attic values. After the Roman invasion, London Celts were cautious to avoid any Latinisms that might insult their *domini novi*. While mediæval monks exercized chastity of speech, the Vikings who slew them chose the *tal* that exalted their prowess among fellow warriors. With the printing press came more stringent censorship, whereupon scribes became writers and editors who were careful to elect that *usus scribendi* that would not imperil the precious imprimatur of the local prince or bishop.

The media in particular, with the advent of the first newspapers at the end of the sixteenth century, had to be especially cautious of their vocabulary in reporting and criticizing. For this reason, the printed word linguistically has usually represented deferential compromise rather than actual spoken usage. The printed word has also all too often misled. In the USA in the first half of the nineteenth century, 'Manifest Destiny' was the journalistic provocation to slaughter Native Americans and confiscate their homeland. A century later, the anti-colonial movements after the Second World War often came to be called, if fighting against the Western Alliance, 'guerrilla groups' or 'communist insurgents', or, if opposing the East Block, 'capitalist rebels', 'fascists', 'bandits' and so on. East

Germany's *antifaschistische Schutzmauer* or 'anti-fascistic bulwark' was in reality a prison wall keeping millions incarcerated. Even after the Cold War the propagandistic rhetoric persists.

Propaganda works in subtle ways. In a Johannesburg radio interview in 1998, a white interviewer used the expression 'you Afro-Americans' while his North American interviewee responded with 'you whites', an ironic reversal of earlier linguistic offences there. (South Africa is now in an age that white newspapers label as 'post-apartheid' but black newspapers 'post-liberation'.) Similar linguistic convolutions are often employed at the highest level to mask multinational corporate excesses: radioactive pollution, bio-invasion, excessive carbon-dioxide emissions, unchecked rainforest clearance, increased ozone depletion and more. When this masking occurs solely for corporate profit, then some believe that 'manufacturing consent' – that is, the media's misuse of language to communicate disinformation and a composed reality on behalf of a privileged minority – can lead in our age of instant global communication to serious harm for democratic systems, for humanity in general and for all of nature.[21]

One recoils with horror before linguistic sanitization. Adolf Hitler's *Endlösung* or 'Final Solution' chillingly cloaked an order for the mass murder of Europe's Jews. In the USA's Vietnam war, the expressions 'to take someone out' and 'sanitize' replaced 'kill' and 'murder'. Even at the end of the twentieth century, after the Cold War, the Pentagon was still calling bombs 'vertically deployed anti-personnel devices'. Human deaths are 'body counts'. Many believe linguistic sanitization is necessary, as it enables humans to perform inhuman acts. In a similar phenomenon, soldiers reduce an enemy to collective non-entities in order to convince themselves that their potential victims are different from normal human beings and thus killable. For ancient Greeks, enemy Persians were only *bárbaroi* or 'stammerers'. In the American Revolutionary War, one fought either 'Redcoats' or 'Yankees'; in the American Civil War, the 'Johnny Rebs' or, again, 'Yankees'; in the Sudan, the 'Fuzzy-wuzzies'; in the First World War, the 'Huns'; in the Second World War, the 'Heinies', 'Jerries', 'Krauts', 'Fritz' or 'Japs'; and in Vietnam, simply 'Charley'.

Officers are actually taught to encourage such usage. Sometimes this is too much for principled statesmen. In General Eisenhower's headquarters in London during the Second World War, British Prime Minister Winston Churchill heard an American colonel asking after a battle, 'How many ICPs have been counted?' Churchill demanded, 'What are ICPs?' 'Impaired Combatant Personnel', replied the colonel. 'Never let me hear that detestable phrase again', railed Churchill. 'If you are talking about British troops, you will refer to them as "wounded soldiers"'.

Debauching reason and feeling, the stilted language of officialdom is also endemic in every nation with writing. 'Officialese' in its broadest sense pollutes nearly all ancient Egyptian and Mayan monumental inscriptions, as these to a large degree communicate stylistically convoluted messages about and from self-aggrandizing central powers. Today, the abuse abounds. In English, countless occupational titles have recently received nearly incomprehensible reincarnations: 'undertaker' or 'mortician' became 'funeral director' then 'bereavement care expert'; 'caretaker' (British) or 'janitor' (Scotland, Canada and the USA) is now 'sanitary engineer'. More ominously, perfectly understandable concepts increasingly disappear because of more ambiguous expressions that hide unpleasant or politically incorrect realities. Texts are often written so confusingly as to defy common sense; sometimes this is the goal of an author.

To counter such linguistic abuses, the Plain English Campaign was launched in Britain in 1979 to persuade organizations to communicate with the public in plain language. Opposed to bad style, ambiguity and obfuscation, the directors of the movement mediate in grievances about officialese, legalese and 'small print', that is, implicit linguistic deception. The work of the Campaign has 'transformed the language and design of public information in the UK', with international repercussions. The editor of the *Oxford Companion to the English Language* has recently written, 'In all the history of the [English] language, there has never been such a powerful grass-roots movement to influence it as the Plain English Campaign'. An example of rewriting in Plain English: 'High-quality learning environments are a necessary precondition for facilitation and enhancement of the ongoing learning process' becomes: 'Children need good schools if they are to learn properly'.

SIGN LANGUAGE

That all of the world's known living languages combine gestures with speech indicates that a 'signing' of some sort has always been part and parcel of human communication. Some believe that primitive signing prompted the development of vocal language in early humans. But a 'sign language' *per se* can also stand alone as an organized system of naturally, mechanically or electronically created symbols for transmitting messages over greater distances; and of hand gestures and/or pantomime in place of spoken language among peoples without a common tongue or among individuals physically incapable of speech and/or hearing. *Semiotics* is the general philosophical theory of signs and symbols that deals particularly with their function in both artificially constructed and natural languages.

Humans have always transmitted messages over distances using some form of sign language: with smoke, drums, conch shells, arrows, trumpets, bugles and a vast array of other means.[22] Ancient Greeks could signal to offshore ships by reflecting the sun on polished bronze shields. Romans used trumpets and standards to signal in battle. Chinese employed colour-coded rockets and fired powders. North Americans often sent one another special signals over wide valleys by use of series of smoke puffs, like a primitive Morse Code. Flag codes have been used by merchantmen and navies for millennia. With the advent of railways in the nineteenth century, a system of general lantern signals meant 'release brakes', 'stop', 'back' and so on. With telegraphy came elaborate language codes that could also be used for various means of physical signalling, too: the Morse Code, for example, has been used with hand flags, sun flashes, or by night with torches, lanterns or other lights; if close at hand, Morse can also be transmitted by means of a whistle, bugle, drum and other things.

Spoken language is also transmitted by prearranged gestures.

Monastic sign language has been used within Europe's monasteries since the Middle Ages as a second language enabling communication without breaking one's vow of silence. There are no 'mother-tongue' speakers of monastic sign language. The Plains Indian sign language, shared by speakers of mutually unintelligible language groups, is an elaborate manual language that can express natural objects, concepts, emotions and sensations in a sophisticated syntax bearing grammar. It was devised in North America after the Spaniards had introduced horses from the south of the Great Plains and after the French had circulated guns from the east. Permitting detailed conversation, Plains Sign allowed the exchange of trade, hunting and social information not only with other Native American nations but also with Europeans. Within individual nations, Plains Sign is still used today for legends, prayers, rituals and storytelling; it is no longer used between nations, as all Native Americans speak fluent English. Plains Indian sign language is not a deaf sign language and remains a second language only.

For the deaf who sign, sign language is a first language. With well over 100 individual natural languages being transmitted – from Catalan to Chinese and from Mongolian to Mayan – deaf sign language is the major group of sign languages being used in the world today. Indeed, sign language primarily concerns deaf culture, with a significant amount of research and other activity in this field currently engaging tens of millions of practitioners.

The Abbé de l'Épée, who in 1770 founded in Paris the world's first deaf-and-dumb school, personally devised a one-hand alphabet for his charges. Later, a two-hand alphabet was elaborated, which method is generally used for most deaf signing today. Deaf sign language is not a separate language but, in general, the coding of the alphabet of a natural language through manual signs. Copying the Plains Indian sign language and the French example, North American experts for the deaf elaborated two types of manual gesture languages, from which most of the world's current deaf sign languages derive: first, *natural signs* which, like the Plains peoples' system, signal objects, concepts and so on based on the spoken language; and second, *systematic signs* which signal individual words or letters of the alphabet based on the written language. The greatest number of 'signers' in the world today use Ameslan, the American Sign Language. This is also used to communicate with animals (see Chapter 1).

ENDANGERED LANGUAGES AND LANGUAGE EXTINCTION

Languages more often die than the peoples who speak them. Indeed, the human history of Europe over the past 50,000 years comprises an overwhelmingly linguistic, not genetic, replacement. Though textbooks usually cite approximately 5,000 languages as being extant, probably only around 4,000 are still spoken today and the number is rapidly declining. It is estimated that perhaps less than 1,000 of these will still be spoken at the beginning of the twenty-second century. Social integration and ethnic dissolution have never been more pronounced in human history.[23] Languages have always disappeared, for economic, cultural, political, religious and other reasons. One need not be a minority to lose one's language: most of Europe's majority languages were replaced by minority Indo-European tongues in various waves of incursion from the east. Language endangerment is presently one of humanity's greatest cultural challenges, posing enormous scientific and humanistic problems.[24]

Contrary to general opinion, language extinction as a result of catastrophe – drought, warfare, earthquake, vulcanism, landslips, tsunamis, flooding – is extremely rare. Though in earlier epochs murder, disease and proscription may have been a statistically more frequent cause of language loss, in more recent human history language loss, which is nearly always language replacement, has much more often been 'voluntary'; that is, it is 'reluctantly desired'. In this way, pre-Indo-European Aquitanian yielded to the Celts' Gaulish, then Gaulish itself to the Romans' Latin. Most Brittonic Celts of Britain similarly accepted the Latin language of their minority occupiers, but then finally adopted the German of the later minority occupiers who followed. Polabian, the Slavic language of the West Slavs between the Elba and Oder rivers, was finally assimilated into

German language and culture around AD 1750 after 800 years of close contact; yet the Wends or Sorbs, West Slavs of the upper and middle Spree south-east of Berlin, have managed to maintain their Slavic language and culture up to the present day as a result of a series of fortuitous circumstances. After 500 years of colonization, almost all of Latin America is now Spanish-speaking. Tiny Easter Island, no longer the world's last refuge, is finally yielding to Spanish, too, trading its Polynesian patrimony for income. Once contact has occurred with a 'superior' foreign power, parents the world over have always urged their children to accommodate themselves, wishing their safety and betterment. It is usually they who replace their language with another by encouraging or tolerating bilingualism. The children themselves then eventually become monolingual in the new tongue.

Despite the immediate gains language replacement brings, those who voluntarily give up their language invariably sense a loss of ethnic identity, a defeat by a colonial or metropolitan power (with concomitant sensations of inferiority) and a distressing defection from one's sacred ancestors. This also entails the loss of oral histories, chants, myths, religion and technical vocabulary, as well as of traditions, customs and prescribed behaviour. All old society collapses and often the new language cannot fill the vacuum that results, leading to lost generations searching for a new identity, for 'something of value'.

An alternative to language replacement is permanent bilingualism. That is, a people will continue to speak their indigenous tongue among themselves while also actively using a metropolitan language such as International Standard English or Spanish to communicate with all outsiders. Among large populations of speakers, such a solution works eminently. Among smaller populations, it almost invariably leads to replacement by the metropolitan tongue. True minority languages, that is, those tongues spoken by around 20,000 or less, depending on circumstances, can be preserved only by complete isolation. Anything else means certain annihilation.

Not only languages are being lost at an unprecedented rate. Dialects are disappearing, too. All regional dialects of languages that are heard in broadcasting are yielding to the prestige dialect that governments or corporate centres have chosen to be represented in the media (this is usually the governing class's own dialect). It is a levelling of language's variety that is comparable to rainforest clearance. In addition, since the early nineteenth century education has also traditionally been held in the prestige language of a nation and in the prestige dialect of that language. This has likewise resulted in great uniformity of speech, as, most commonly, 'prescriptive' modes have been imposed.

Most attempts to save endangered languages have failed. One sometimes argues that similar to maintaining faunal and floral diversification it is essential for humankind to maintain linguistic diversification, too, in order to avoid a culturally depleted world.[25] However, each culture changes to adapt and survive; this is not loss, but social evolution. There is far more enthusiasm among foreign linguists to save endangered languages than among those indigenous communities speaking them. For scientific purposes endangered languages must of course be documented in formal descriptions, at once and with all available resources. But they cannot be saved.

Once dead, languages cannot be 'resurrected' either. Among languages, there is no Lazarus. One often hears the claim that Hebrew is a modern 'revival'. However, Hebrew never died. Always the prestige language of its speakers, for religious and ethnic reasons, Hebrew was the written and sung language of Jewish religious services, so it was constantly heard and spoken. Eventually, because of political necessity with the founding of a Jewish state in 1948, Hebrew was raised from a ritual second language to an active first language. Modern linguistic revival attempts, such as with Manx and Cornish, invariably remain the diversion of small interest groups, without large-scale linguistic repercussions: the metropolitan languages that replaced these remain the first language. Most linguists accept that the mass extinction of human languages is already a foregone conclusion, the price humanity is paying for the new global society.

VERBAL HUMOUR

Of the many types of humour – pantomimic, gestural, situational, musical, illustrative, graphic, symbolic and so forth –
verbal humour is by far the most common and constitutes an
equally essential element of human society. All societies use
verbal humour. This involves playing with language in multiple
levels, from the ridiculous to the sublime, to appeal to a sense of
the ludicrous or absurdly incongruous. Often with interplay
between different levels at the same time, the linguistic manipulation brings together opposites in sudden or unexpected
fashion to effect, initially at least, surprise and delight.[26]
One can assume that more sophisticated forms of verbal
humour such as satire, irony and parody have always existed.
However, an unusually large part of ancient humour that has
survived appears to be of a sexual nature, a form of verbal
humour that is evidently universal. This does not mean that earlier societies were more promiscuous. On the contrary, it
indicates the opposite. Verbal humour reveals what is commonly suppressed in a society and as most ancient societies
maintained strict decorum within small, tight communities
with often suffocating rules of speech and conduct, risqué or
even ribald stories were the more welcome for their gift of a
'social enema'.[27] The humour lay in revealing the concealed and
mentioning the unmentionable – the shock of the sudden juxta-
position then elicited immediate laughter. Enjoyed, too, was the
biting social critique one could only risk when it was couched in
humour.
    In ancient Egypt, the 'country that possesses so many won-
ders', in the words of Herodotus, humour doubtless spiced the
daily diet. 'A boy's ears are on his back', explained an early
scribe, 'for he hears best when he is beaten!' A lover on the Nile
penned about his dearest (in free translation): 'If I kiss her and
her lips are open, I am drunk even without beer!'
    Europe's earliest known verbal humour is Homer's story of
Odysseus telling the Cyclops Polyphemus his name is 'No-
man'. When other Cyclopes, hearing Polyphemus's cries of
pain and rushing to his aid, asked who was harming him,

Polyphemus shouted back: 'No-man!' So they left.

The Roman poet Martial wrote of Pompeii's burial from the eruption of Mount Vesuvius in AD 79: 'Even for gods this was going too far'. Among the graffiti one has since uncovered from Pompeii: 'Do you think I'd mind if you dropped dead tomorrow?' A Roman husband wrote to a wife who bought expensive creams: 'You lie stored away in a hundred little jars . . . your face does not sleep with you!' And in the eighteenth century the Romans' descendants said of Grand Tour collecting: 'If the Colosseum were portable, the English would carry it away!'

The Middle Ages was a particularly rich period of humour, a fact often overlooked in scholarship. A fragment on the last page of the 'Cambridge Songs' copied around AD 1050 preserves the Latin lyric, sung by a girl to her lover (a favourite literary genre at the time):

> Come to me, my dearest love – with ah! and oh!
> Visit me, what joys you'll have – with ah! and oh! and ah!
>   and oh!
> I am dying with desire – with ah! and oh!
> How I long for Venus's fire – with ah! and oh! and ah!
>   and oh! . . .
> If you come and bring your key – with ah! and oh!
> How easy will your entry be – with ah! and oh! and ah!
>   and oh!

In an early twelfth-century Spanish song from al-Andalus (Andalusia), a young girl sings to her paramour: 'I'll give you such love – but only if you'll bend my anklets right over to my earrings!'

Guillaume IX d'Aquitaine (1071–1127), the first poet of secular lyric in France whom we know by name, one of the most colourful personalities of the Middle Ages, Duke of Poitou and Aquitaine and grandfather of Eleanor of Aquitaine, later Queen of England, sang to his band of *companhos* (knights and soldiers) about his 'two splendid horses and [I] can mount either'. But they cannot stand each other; if only he could tame them, he'd have 'better riding than any other man'. So he turns to his audience to ask them to 'resolve my predicament: Never has a choice caused such embarrassment. I don't know which to keep now – Agnes, or Ermensent!' (naming two noble ladies from his court).

The earliest reconstructed Polynesian chant from Easter Island, composed around AD 1800, ends with the chanting adolescent boys affectionately taunting the adolescent girls:

Why the song-devotion? – to stay within the hole.
Within the hole where? – [on the] *tī* leaves for top-tossing
When [So that] there runs non-rain, squirming rain,
    filling rain.
Put up a fight, young women, lest the flower be tamed, ha!

Verbal humour was exalted as seldom before or since under William Shakespeare's genius when, in his play *The Tragedy of King Lear* of 1606, he allowed the Fool to reveal humour's profoundest purpose: to cushion life's ugliest truths.

When Lear protests, 'Dost thou call me fool, boy?' the Fool replies, 'All thy other titles thou hast given away. That, thou wast born with'.

Later, 'Who is it that can tell me who I am?' cries Lear. 'Lear's shadow', replies the Fool.

Whereupon, 'If a man's brains were in 's heels', says the Fool, 'were 't not in danger of kibes [sore on the heel]?' 'Ay, boy', says Lear. 'Then, I prithee, be mercy; thy wit shall ne'er go slipshod'. To which Lear naively laughs: 'Ha, ha, ha!'

Near Lear's tragic end, the Fool counsels Kent: 'Let go thy hold when a great wheel runs down a hill, lest it break thy neck with following it; but the great one that goes up the hill, let him draw thee after. When a wise man gives thee better counsel, give me mine again: I would have none but knaves follow it, since a fool gives it'.

For the first time in human history, language's supreme role in transmitting, shaping and reflecting all social phenomena is appreciated and one has begun to apply this appreciation to broadly based social, educational and political problems. This is the charge of the sociolinguist who, through studying language's use in society, unites theory, description and application.

The primary concern of the sociolinguist is language change that marks the friction points in human activity; signals dying beliefs and emerging concepts; defines the limits of the tolerable; reveals the machinations of those in power; and, perhaps most importantly, registers the evolution of humanity's awareness and sensitivity as revealed through language. The use of common tongues and artificially constructed languages demonstrates human societies' fundamental need to communicate on equal footing. Throughout history, societies have identified more with those speaking similarly; because of this, nations of a single speech have emerged. Ethnic minorities within such nations strive to express their unique contribution, too, through language. Colonial independence for multi-ethnic regions has revealed language's importance in establishing a sense of nationhood.

Over the past generation the reinvention of women's role in society has seen a 'gender purge' in the English language. Linguistic purges or purifications have taken place throughout human history when society changes in some salient fashion, when 'too many' foreign borrowings intrude, or when a regime declares a nationalistic agendum. Propaganda and political correctness are social phenomena that have always polluted languages; indeed, both have enabled humanity's most heinous acts. Most welcome, therefore, are those movements to 'clean up' and 'simplify' the linguistic obfuscations and deceits of officialdom.

Sign language in its several forms is the demonstration of a society's need to communicate when vocal language physically fails, a biological phenomenon that many societies address through a systematized language of gesture. The more than 100 deaf sign languages in the world today testify to this language form's wonderful plasticity and utility. A social phenomenon linked with human language is language death. Tens of thousands of languages have disappeared since human speech first emerged. Contrary to common belief, most simply evolved into something new or were voluntarily replaced with an intrusive language because one expected to benefit by this. All linguistic contact is enrichment.

These manifestations occurred alongside life's triumphs and

tragedies always with verbal humour, that linguistic art which allows humankind to mock adversity and laugh in the face of affliction while probing life's profundities.

In these and many more fascinating ways, language is the ultimate measure of human society. More than any other of life's faculties, it is language that tells us who we are, what we mean and where we are going.

EIGHT

Future Indicative

What will Earth's languages be like in future? One cannot reliably predict a linguistic future, since so many non-linguistic factors are constantly reshaping a society's language: economic turns, civil insurrections, mass migrations, the sudden rise of prestige nations, new technologies, social fads and many other phenomena. However, reference to past linguistic changes and recognition of present linguistic trends can provide possible linguistic scenarios, at least for the near future. One might also wish to consider the activities of – mainly English-speaking – governmental and corporate strategists who are earnestly expanding their bailiwicks at present, increasing the likelihood of their (English) language prevailing over those languages of non-strategists in the coming decades.

Merely drawing analogies to past linguistic changes and dynamics no longer holds unqualified validity. All traditional relations of political, cultural and economic power between Western nations and the rest of the world are in the process of unprecedented transformation. This now appears to be a permanent global feature which will perhaps create a new world order whose nature and quality are still largely unknown. But it will most probably entail larger nations, larger corporations and larger, that is, fewer, languages.

Not simply change and loss (replacement), as in the past, is currently describing linguistic history, but also expansion of the domain of language to a degree hitherto unprecedented in human society. This is currently reinventing what one means with the word 'language' itself. New technologies such as programming (computer) languages are elaborating innovative extensions of human speech, allowing a new medium of language to artificially communicate with itself.

Though Earth's surviving languages will continue to change in familiar ways, a traditional linguistic dimension has been altered forever. Language throughout history has meant geographical territory – land. Now, the linguistic atlas has become all but meaningless. Language primarily means technology and wealth, a new borderless world with the only directions up and down, separating the haves from the have-nots. Proficiency in the planet's single 'corporate language' – perhaps ultimately English – will soon define each person's place on Earth . . . and beyond.

PROGRAMMING LANGUAGES

Computers expedite the manipulation of descriptions of values, properties and methods in order more readily to provide solutions to particular problems. The result of a programming process is a program for text processing, operating systems, databases and other computer activities. The specific tool that allows programming processes is a programming (or computer) language, a convention for writing descriptions which can be evaluated.[1] A programming language can also be used for linguistic research, compiler research, teaching and other things.

Many contrasting definitions attempt to succinctly capture the essence of a programming language. It is a language, yes, because it is a 'medium of information exchange'. But it is wholly different from all previous forms of language known to humankind, except perhaps written language with its many types and forms of scripts reproducing natural language.[2] To some, a programming language is simply a tool to aid the programmer. To others, it is a notational system for describing computation in machine-readable and human-readable arrangement. Some understand a programming language to be a notation for formally expressing algorithms (a rule of procedure for solving any computational problem) so that these may be understood by both humans and computers. And others see it simply as a sequence of instructions for a machine.

The purpose of all language is communication and so the

main objective of a programming language is to communicate with literal-minded machines.[3] In its essence a programming language, with certain exceptions, is a mechanism for describing computation and solutions to problems. It must, above all, be machine-readable; that is, a computer must be able to translate data, problems and instructions into its own language. And a programming language must be human-readable, too; that is, a person will have to be able to read and understand the solution's description.[4]

Each programming language reveals different perspectives and features on the description and design of algorithms, on data structures and on program governance. Like a natural human language, each programming language has specific and unique characteristics. This determines its suitability for a given computational task.[5] The theory of computer language programming commonly recognizes three primary aspects of a programming language:

syntax: the programming language determines the symbols and their allowable ('legal') combinations;

semantics: these are the meanings programmers assign to the constructs of the programming language;

language model: this is the program's inherent domain, philosophy or paradigm (that is, the ways of approaching computation in order to solve a specific problem).

There exists at present a wide variety of language models or approaches to problem-solving. Among the most important (and the following is only a small selection of all those currently available):[6]

An *imperative language* applies an algorithm to an initial set of data. Here, programs are sequences of basic commands, usually assignments; these use associated control structures such as sequencing, conditionals and loops that govern the commands. Examples are Fortran, Pascal, C and Assembly Code.

An *object-oriented language* has programs that are collections of communicating objects. Examples are C++, Java, Eiffel, Simula and Smalltalk-80.

A *logic language* sequences deductive steps guaranteeing the solution stands in a specific relationship to the initial set of data. It consists of programs that are collections of statements from a specific logic, usually predicate logic, as with the Prolog language. *Equational-logic languages* are OBJ, Mercury and Equational.

A *functional language* applies (mathematical) functions to an initial set of data. Examples are ML, Haskell, FP and Gofer.

A *parallel* or *concurrent language* consists of programs that are collections of communicating or mutually cooperating processes. Examples are Ada, Modula-2 and C*.

A *declarative language* contains programs that are simply collections of facts. Several logic and functional languages are included in this category.

Scripting languages adopt any of the foregoing models, but are usually used as a larger package support.

In adopting one or more of the above and other approaches, programming languages begin to resemble the traditional model of 'language families' commonly, if not wholly appropriately, associated with natural human languages – they are 'branching off' from one another, in other words, to create new 'families' of programming languages. But the main differences with programming languages lie in the fact that they are non-biological, non-vocal (until now) and claim no geographical territory. They are a system-internal keyboard process that exists only in cyberspace.

However, this too appears to be evolving. Researchers at Raytheon Systems and the University of Texas at Dallas have recently developed an electronic neural switch for an artificial nervous system to be elaborated in the near future. The latter will mimic the processes of the human brain and its communications network, enabling the creation of an autonomous robot that can receive information from various sensors and arrive at independent decisions. Ultimately, even 'speech' should be possible between robots and humans and between robots and other robots and computer systems.

Throughout the world, computers are already 'communicating' among themselves using a wide range of programming languages, very much like human-animal communication but this time human-induced without necessarily being human-guided. 'Language' in its very broadest sense is quickly transcending human governance to become also the provenance of artificial electronic systems. No one at present can say where this development will ultimately lead.

INTERNET, E-MAIL AND NEWSGROUPS

One of the Internet's most widely used resources is language teaching and learning.[7] Benefiting schools, governments, businesses and private individuals, this usage promotes and preserves in hitherto unprecedented fashion not only living languages but extinct tongues as well, the most popular being Classical Latin. Language instructors around the world have found that effective language education is achieved by weaving the Internet's linguistic resources into personal lesson plans. The Internet is thus not an end, but an effective tool, a means to an end: the best quality language instruction. The Internet cannot replace face-to-face linguistic interaction.[8]

A study conducted in 1989–90 with secondary students in Finland, Britain, the USA, Austria, Canada, the then West Germany and East Germany, Sweden, Japan and Iceland revealed that on-line, e-mail communication resembles oral communication that makes use of a casual linguistic style which includes colloquialisms and elliptical speech – that is, great economy of expression.[9] All non-verbal communication (gesturing) is substituted on-line by textual visualizations. Off-line writing, in contrast, displays more textual and linguistic coherence; it is more highly structured and hierarchically organized. The study therefore indicated that e-mail (and, through inference, newsgroup) linguistic usage appears to occupy a special position between spoken and written language.[10]

All natural (that is, non-artificial) linguistic situations involve 'viewer-listeners'. With e-mail and newsgroup communications, however, one loses viewing and hearing, unless these are electronically enabled, such as through v-mail, video-messages sent by e-mail. With the loss of viewing and hearing, one also loses facial expressions, hand gestures, posture, suprasegmentals (pitch, length, stress, juncture and tone), loudness/softness distinctions, speed of speech and much more that are all an integral part of human communication. Subliminal signals, such as scent, that address a more primeval, but no less important, level of communication, also fail to be transmitted with the new electronic media. With our obvious gain, we are apparently also losing a good deal of what it presently means to be human.

At present, International Standard English is the universal language of the Internet. English holds no 'official' status as such, since the Internet is still largely unregulated; only a few countries, such as China, exercise rigorous censorship of the Internet. Some allege that English commands the Internet because of the economic and political 'imperialism' of English-speaking countries. However, English prevails on the Internet because the Internet is the creation of English-speaking countries and because, at the beginning of the twenty-first century, English is the world's most popular second language. The fact that the Internet has evolved into a mainly English-language medium is not by design but historical circumstance.[11]

It is to be hoped that there never will be an 'official' language for the Internet, only the language or languages that Internet users both want and need. At the moment English happens to prevail (some would say 'dominate'). But some other language might replace English on the Internet in future. A constructed language might be chosen by a regulatory body as an alternative (though this seems unlikely). Automatic computer translation might make the entire question of a prevailing natural language superfluous, leaving one's choice merely that of which programming language to use. The Internet would then, with this scenario, transcend the need for the prevalence of any kind of natural language, including English.

However, one should recognize that bilingualism is a world trend, beyond the cyberspacial jurisdiction of the Internet.

Worldwide, more and more people are choosing English as a second (or additional) language. When possible, people are retaining their indigenous tongue as a first language for a smaller, more immediate sphere of interaction. It appears that the Internet itself will, at least in the near future, remain the experimentee of such real human developments.

The Internet, e-mail and newsgroups are themselves actively affecting the world's vocabularies, too. International Standard English has added a large number of lexical items to its vocabulary (or expanded the meaning of older words) that were unknown only one generation ago: *bit* (binary digit), *browser* (a client software program used to peruse Internet resources), *click on* (to use the 'mouse' to access a site), *cyber-space* (the range of information resources available through computer networks), *e-mail* (messages people send one another via a computer), *v-mail* (video messages), *gopher* (a method of making menus of material available over the Internet), *hypertext* (any text that holds 'links' to other documents), *modem* (from *Mo*dulator, *Dem*odulator, the device that connects the computer to a phone line and allows intercomputer communication) and scores of others. Most modern nations are borrowing these English terms directly, without translation into the local tongue.

Soon, voice-recognition systems will allow a person to speak directly to a computer and for it to provide a vocal answer. Simultaneous translations will also be possible in this manner. At present, an ever-increasing number of people are spending more hours per day using written, that is, keyboard, language rather than actual spoken language. This is especially true of students, office workers, journalists, editors, writers, researchers, computer programmers, pensioners and many other active computer users. In the Middle Ages, only scribes were to be found in the scriptoria, who then comprised a very small percentage of mediæval society's population. Within a few years, computers will be enriching nearly every household of the developed world. Human life in these countries is centring on, and contracting to, electronic texts and international networking and moving away from immediate visual and vocal speech. A different sort of language is emerging from this artificial interfacing: an 'oral written language'. No doubt this, too, will change as the new technology further evolves.

THE FUTURE OF LANGUAGE

Before Thomas Edison's invention of the phonograph in 1877 only venerable elders and older written texts, whose precise spoken qualities were unknown, could reveal previous stages of language. Now, from listening to those scratchy voices from over a century ago one can appreciate how quickly language actually changes. By analysing written texts, hearing recent changes and following broad trends linguists can approach a consensus – despite the general 'unpredictability' of language change – about where the world's spoken languages are heading in the near future.

All linguists agree that the natural linguistic changes to come will, to a large degree, but not exclusively, remain within already known phonological, morphological, syntactic, lexical and semantic parameters. The largest changes, the fates of entire languages and language families, cause linguists perhaps the greatest concern. This is because the next two centuries will doubtless see unprecedented language replacement; the homogenization and levelling of what few dialects and languages survive; and then, ultimately, everyone apparently speaking English as a first or second language as the global society becomes at least a linguistic reality.

Among those few languages that will survive the next two centuries, cyclic typological evolution will continue. That is to say, Mandarin Chinese, for example, will become even less isolating and more agglutinative in its structure, tending more strongly towards polysyllabicism (using words of several syllables) and forming derivative or compound words by joining together single-meaning constituents. The Indo-European languages, on the other hand, in various stages of their own linguistic evolution, will no doubt continue their drift away from earlier fusional status towards an increased isolating structure. At the same time, because of modern media, the lexica of Earth's languages will continue to fill with common borrowings. If in earlier centuries borrowings took years to find acceptance in one language and spread throughout many further languages (*chocolate*, *coffee*, *tobacco*, *taboo*, *verandah*), because of radio, television and now the Internet such borrowings can become native vocabulary within weeks or even days: *fatwa* 'religious edict', *Scud* 'type of guided missile', *ayatollah* 'religious leader', *glasnost* 'political transparency', to name but a few recent examples.

Social transformations occurring simultaneously in many countries are also leaving their mark, causing fascinating linguistic changes whose effects will doubtless continue to ripple in future. In those Indo-European languages still preserving the distinction between informal and formal pronouns of address – German *du* and *Sie*, French *tu* and *vous*, Spanish *tú* and *usted* and so forth – the informal pronoun is encroaching more and more upon the domain of the formal. That is, children in these countries, for example, are no longer addressing their parents with the formal forms they had used since time immemorial: they are using the informal pronouns instead, reflecting a fundamental change in attitude towards parents and elders in general.

However, a Welsh teenager will still tell his mother 'Peidiwch â phoeni!' ('Don't worry!') using formal grammar – not the informal to be heard in the same context in German ('Mach' Dir keine Sorgen!') or French ('Ne t'inquiète pas!'). That is, though most metropolitan languages of Indo-European origin have expanded the domain of the informal form of address since the Second World War, smaller Indo-European languages have generally resisted this trend. Perhaps it is a conscious effort by the speakers of these smaller languages to stave off 'invading' metropolitan influences, especially among bilingual speakers (such as the Welsh, Wends, Catalans, Galicians, Occitans and others).

There are innumerable examples of identifiable trends now occuring in the world's languages. In German, for example, the reported discourse tense (that is, 'eyewitness/non-eyewitness evidentiality contrast'), in the form of 'Er sagte, er sei . . . ' ('He said he was . . .') is becoming superfluous in modern speech, being replaced by neutral declarative discourse: 'Er sagte, er ist . . .' The syntax of the conjunction *weil*, 'because', that always used to place the verb at the end of the dependent clause ('weil er alt ist'), now allows the verb to immediately follow the subject, as in English ('weil er ist alt'), though this is still regarded as non-standard usage by more formal and elderly speakers. This new usage might be generalized in future to include similar conjunctions, radically altering German syntax in the process. The German lexicon also abounds with modern English borrowings: *der Computer*, *der Supermarket*, *der Soft Drink*, *die Jeans*. German will doubtless absorb hundreds of similar introductions in the years to come.

In the Rapanui language of Easter Island, which will probably be replaced by Chilean Spanish within the next twenty years, the *ku . . . ʻā* tense/aspect marker, embracing a past action or state that still continues, has recently been replaced by *ko . . . ʻā*. For over 100 years the Tahitian glottal stop has been replacing *k*'s in the language, producing historically identifiable doublets: *kino/ʻino* 'bad, wicked, perverse'. Much of the older Rapanui lexicon has been replaced by Tahitian, a process now becoming rampant: Rapanui *kī* 'to speak' is now Tahitian *parau*; *raʻā* 'sun, day' has been replaced by *mahana*; *taʻu* 'year' is now *matahiti* and many more, including the Rapanui counting system, which is now almost wholly Tahitian. The Tahitian connective *ʻē* 'and' has been introduced (there had been no connective in the Rapanui language), as well as Spanish *pero* 'but'. However, these Tahitian borrowings, too, will soon fall victim to Chilean Spanish on the island.

Welsh is similarly displaying significant 'changes in progress'. In its phonology, one of the most evident is Welsh's gradual loss of terminal *f*: *tref* [pronounced TRAVE] 'town' is now most often simply *tre* [TRAY]. All terminal *f*'s will probably soon disappear in Welsh. After *yn* in its meaning of 'in', many Welsh speakers now favour the soft mutation (with its wider domain of usage) over the grammatically 'more proper' but less general nasal mutation, so that *yn Gaerdydd* 'in Cardiff' is now heard more often than traditional *yngh Nghaerdydd*. Welsh's new decimal counting system has only in the last generation replaced the ancient Celtic counting system. Thus, 11 *un deg un*, 12 *un deg dau*, 15 *un deg pump*, 16 *un deg chwech*, 20 *dau ddeg*, 30 *tri deg* and so on, to name but a few, have replaced – particularly among younger speakers – the traditional numbers 11 *un ar ddeg*, 12 *deuddeg*, 15 *pymtheg*, 16 *un ar bymtheg*, 20 *ugain*, 30 *deg ar hugain* and so forth.

Since English is at present the world's most popular language (and also the language of this book), with which most readers will perhaps be more familiar than with the above languages, the following examples will demonstrate future trends in English. English is at the forefront of international linguistic change, riding the new techno-language wave. Though one may not be aware of it, English is also experiencing rapid change on many different levels: phonological, morphological, syntactic, lexical and semantic. And though most of Earth's languages face imminent extinction, English continues to gain thousands of new speakers each day. Indeed, English is becoming something totally new: a natural world language.

In its phonology, English is displaying characteristic trends which doubtless will greatly change the sound of English to come, both regionally and internationally. In British English, for example, *t* between vowels and at the end of words is now being replaced by a glottal stop (') in dialects far beyond the Cockney (London) area where this change was first innovated, particularly in the Midlands: *Ge' the le'uce tha's a li'o bi'a* ('Get the lettuce that's a little bitter'). The old innovation's recent and sudden diffusion – in the variety of modified regional speech called Estuary English, as identified by linguist David Rosewarne in 1984 – might derive from London-centred television and films and be spread by mainly younger speakers imitating this formerly snubbed but now preferred dialect.

American English's greatest 'change in progress' reveals a similar innovation. Here, *t* between vowels has, for many decades now, been increasingly replaced by *d* (that is, *t*'s vocalic environment has caused it to be voiced): *Get the ledduce that's a liddle bidder*. In American English there no longer obtains, then, a spoken distinction between *writer* and *rider*, *matter* and *madder*, *boating* and *boding*, *whitest* and *widest* and so forth, the distinction being drawn by the listener only from context. The enormous influence of American English at present suggests that this phonological innovation might soon spread beyond America. (In contrast, it appears unlikely that the Cockney innovation mentioned above will experience international diffusion.)

As a demonstration of its linguistic strength, the American innovation seems to have become productive. That is, it is bringing about a further change. In 1998 a young white female speaker of American English from the Midwest was heard to say *My dar was sin* – in perhaps more comprehensible International Standard English, 'My daughter was sitting'. This reflects a relatively new and increasingly widespread form of American speech. Here, a derivative *My daughder was siddin'* has experienced a weakening of the *d*'s between vowels until they have disappeared altogether, leaving only *dar* for 'daughter' and *sin* for 'sitting'. It might be that this trend marks a long-term development of intervocalic *d*'s and of terminal *-ing*'s in American English. Then again, it might prove to be a short-lived alternative pronunciation. Only time will tell.

Adjectives are assuming an ever larger nominalized role in English syntax. For many centuries now, English adjectives have served as nouns. Some of these uses even date from Old French, such as 'at present', 'in the past' and 'in future' whereby the noun 'time' is understood. A 'professional' means a 'professional person', for example; a 'profligate' is a 'profligate person'; 'the blind' signifies 'blind people'; and 'a white' means 'a white person'. This elliptical or absolute sense has known a venerable history in both the Italic and Germanic families from which Modern English derives. However, the usage has experienced a recent sudden expansion, especially among American speakers (who in turn have affected British speakers), so that a previously limited adjectival qualification can now serve as a generic name, too: a 'historical' is a 'historical novel', a 'botanical' is a 'herbal drug or medicine' and so forth. As such usage appears to be increasing, one may imagine in future more adjectives will assume nominal tasks hitherto unimaginable: 'a reasonable' meaning 'an acceptable proposal', for example, or 'a timely' being 'a recent news item'.

Adjectives are losing ground to nouns, too. Whereas most British speakers would talk of 'a Californian wine' and 'a Texan rancher', thus maintaining the systemic adjectival endings, American speakers would now say 'a California wine' and 'a

Texas rancher'. That is, the proper nouns themselves are doing service for their adjectives in American English. Already now, most writers of English draw no distinction between 'linguistic change' and 'language change', for example. If this trend becomes universal, then one might expect to hear in one or two decades 'the Britain royal family' or 'an Australia kangaroo'.

Even prepositional phrases are not spared such reinterpretative assaults, reversing inherited syntax: what used to be 'children at risk' and 'patients at risk' are now 'at-risk children' and 'at-risk patients', both spelled with a hyphen, turning a post-positive phrase into a pre-positive adjective. This syntactic trend is particularly rampant at present, so that in future one might well expect to hear of 'on-time trains' and 'with-a-grudge colleagues'. A similar innovation was used in a leading British professional journal that recently wrote of 'a biophysicist-turned-expert on technology and society at Oxford', a compression of English syntax that would hardly have passed a senior editor's scrutiny only a decade ago.

In a similar vein, 'folk semantics' is also changing the English language, very often in ways that go unnoticed by the general public. The word 'chemical' seems now to mean 'synthetically manufactured chemical compound' as in the way it is used in the advertising phrase, 'This product is 100 per cent chemical free'. (As it happens, nothing in existence is 'chemical free'.) And 'natural' has recently been bestowed a positive connotation, since one can no longer imagine the perfectly fine English phrase 'natural bubonic plague', though 'natural hair shampoo' and 'natural washing powder' both pass the public scrutiny without censure.

While English dialect forms such as *sommat* 'something', *anyroad* 'anyway', *aught/ought* 'anything' and *naught/nought* 'nothing' will probably be replaced by their universally understood synonyms within one or two generations, again through media levelling, international slang – principally American in origin – will continue to diffuse rapidly. However, this international slang, originating as it does chiefly from the Hollywood (principally using both Californian and New York dialects) film, television and popular music industries that dominate the world entertainment market, is coming under increasing pressure from Spanish, too. One can imagine that future slang, as well as the English lexicon in general, will demonstrate in coming decades an ever more frequent use of words and expressions from Spanish than from any other foreign language.

In similar fashion, local varieties of English will continue to supplement their vocabularies from indigenous resources: Australian English will borrow more Native Australian words and expressions, New Zealand English more Māori, South African English more Zulu, Xhosa, Sotho, Tswana and so forth. All these developments are to be greeted as enrichments of the English language, contributing to the evolving distillation of a new International Standard English.

None the less, international English is continuing to lose most of its dialect features, amalgamating rather quickly into the amorphous International Standard English – in reality a statistical norm that exists nowhere and claims no official body determining its nature and regulating its usage. International Standard English has emerged through global communication, allowing immediate comprehension of radio, television and Internet interviews whether in New Delhi, Tokyo or St Petersburg. It is still the product of historical circumstance, not design (though this might soon change), and will continue to mutate and evolve.

Before radio and films, most Britons had never heard American speech, which many found 'vulgar' on first encounter, especially American nasalization. Most Americans had never heard 'proper' English either. Now, only three generations later, the two dialects, rather than turning into two daughter languages, as normal linguistic processes should have produced, are growing even closer. Indeed, they are evolving towards each other, if somewhat unevenly at present, because of new technology. British English, Standard American English and all other forms of English spoken throughout the world are contributing to the linguistic amalgam that is International Standard English, an emergent tongue.

Mention has often been made in this book of English as a 'world language'. This has good reason. For the first time in human history, global communication is a daily reality. The emergence of this technological achievement has coincided with, and has partially been the result of, the emergence of English as the world's most popular second, or additional, language. This latter development comes from a combination of factors: the internationalization of English beyond Great Britain with the establishment of English-speaking colonies throughout the world, the outcome of two world wars in the twentieth century, the enormous economic growth of English-speaking countries and recent political developments.

The rise of English in the twentieth century has occurred at the same time that the influence of former powers, in particular France and Germany, has rapidly declined.[12] Among the world's languages, only Spanish currently displays a similar dynamic to that of English, but to a much smaller degree. As for Mandarin Chinese, the language spoken by most people as a first language, the Chinese are presently learning English. Few English speakers are learning Chinese.

English is currently spoken by first-language (or native) speakers; second-language (or additional) speakers in English-speaking nations, not only Britain, the USA and New Zealand, for example, but also South Africa, India, Fiji, the Cook Islands and many more; and exclusively foreign-language speakers. The future of English as a world language rests with the two latter groups.[13] Eighty per cent of Internet data is currently in the English language. Judging by the growth rate of Internet usage, this alone might ensure English's position as the world's most popular language well into the twenty-second century, if not longer.[14] The world's economic and political future is now being secured on a technological base that is English-speaking and English-defined. The world's population in this way is being 'forced' to adopt English and prosper, or ignore English and decline. At the beginning of the twenty-first century, English learning has become a question of simple economics: the world's best-paid jobs require English. It is a trend that will perhaps determine Earth's linguistic profile for the next two centuries, at least.

Scandinavia, Holland, Singapore and a few other regions of the world might already represent the linguistic situation that will soon prevail everywhere: bilingual adult populations who speak the local (metropolitan) language as well as English. After this, perhaps in the late twenty-fourth century, only English could well be left as the world's sole surviving language, together with its sign language counterpart. However, history has taught that such global predictions are usually invalid. German or Japanese might well be Earth's dominant tongue in 200 years, despite the current trend that makes this seem unlikely. At present, because of sheer numbers only the three languages (and their sign languages) will perhaps survive the next 300 years: Mandarin Chinese, Spanish and English. None the less, smaller, rich societies (such as Japan, the German-speaking nations, France, Italy and others) might be able to retain their tongues as local vestiges for several hundred years more, for cultural reasons. And like Latin, Arabic and Hebrew will certainly continue to be spoken and signed, for many centuries, principally for religious reasons.

And thereafter? Once humankind settles the Solar System then a new form of – perhaps – English might be spoken in the not-too-distant future. One can imagine the descendants of the multi-ethnic, presumably International Standard English-speaking colonists on Mars, for example, displaying by the end of the twenty-second century characteristic linguistic innovations not known in Earthen English. In this case a separate dialect will emerge, a Martian English that is immediately identifiable to those who do not speak it. But because of regular interplanetary communication this new form of English will probably remain a dialect and not become a separate language and mutual comprehension between speakers of Martian English and Earthen English will be easily maintained. Diachronically replacing International Standard English, an Interplanetary English might eventually emerge.

'Language is the most precious human resource', Australian linguist Robert Dixon has recently asserted.[15] Indeed, human society is inconceivable without language. Language defines our lives, it heralds our existence, it formulates our thoughts, it enables all we are and have. But as the above material has perhaps demonstrated more cogently than anything else, language is not something that is permanent, stable and fixed. As the river of history itself, language is in constant flux, ever changing, ever mutating, replacing, dying, rejuvenating, growing. Though one can identify common characteristics of linguistic change over millennia, new innovations such as the personal computer can change the very dynamics of change itself, so that hitherto unprecedented processes of linguistic change and usage emerge. In this way language remains, and doubtless will always remain, one of the most volatile features of human society: as long as humankind survives there will always be language, but it will not remain language as we know it now.

Soon all of Earth's languages but a small vestigial number will disappear, leaving one language for all humankind (with its sign language counterpart). With this loss the new global society will simultaneously attain to a degree of communication hitherto unimaginable, with concomitant benefits for all aspects of human activity. We will lose most of Earth's cultural diversity, but at the same time we will gain, with one world language, a new sense of belonging, a new world order, a new common understanding of our place in the greater universe. However, many fear with one world language the possibility of unprecedented political manipulation, propaganda and control. In addition, loss of local languages will initially lead, through loss of ethnic identity, to an increased feeling of alienation, not of universal brotherhood. One world language may bring benefits, but perhaps at too great a cost. Whatever Earth's linguistic future may be, language will continue to evolve as humankind evolves, as language has done for the past million or so years since primitive hominids first began communicating orally.

For language – in all its myriad forms: chemocommunication, 'dance', infrasound, ultrasound, gesture, oral speech, writing, computer language – is the very nexus of Nature . . . and of Nature's communicating creations.

References

ONE · ANIMAL COMMUNICATION AND 'LANGUAGE'

1 Donald H. Owings and Eugene S. Morton, *Animal Vocal Communication* (Cambridge, 1998).
2 William C. Agosta, *Chemical Communication: The Language of Pheromones* (New York, 1992).
3 D. A. Nelson and P. Marler, 'Measurement of Song Learning Behavior in Birds', in *Methods in Neurosciences*, XIV: *Paradigms for the Study of Behavior*, ed. P. Conn (Orlando, FL, 1993), pp. 447–65.
4 Irene M. Pepperberg and R. J. Bright, 'Talking Birds', *Birds, USA*, II (1990), pp. 92–6.
5 Irene M. Pepperberg, 'Functional Vocalizations by an African Grey Parrot (*Psittacus erithacus*)', *Zeitschrift für Tierpsychologie*, LV (1981), pp. 139–60.
6 Irene M. Pepperberg, 'Cognition in an African Grey Parrot (*Psittacus erithacus*), Further Evidence for Comprehension of Categories and Labels', *Journal of Comparative Psychology*, CIV (1990), pp. 42–51.
7 L. E. L. Rasmussen, 'The Sensory and Communication Systems', in *Medical Management of the Elephant*, ed. S. Mikota, E. Sargent, and G. Ranglack (West Bloomfield, MI, 1994), pp. 207–17.
8 George Harrar and Linda Harrar, *Signs of the Apes, Songs of the Whales: Adventures in Human–Animal Communication* (New York, 1989).
9 John C. Lilly, *Communication Between Man and Dolphin* (New York, 1987).
10 Francine Patterson, *The Education of Koko* (New York, 1981).
11 Francine Patterson, 'In Search of Man: Experiments in Primate Communication', *Michigan Quarterly Review*, XIX (1980), pp. 95–114.
12 Francine Patterson and C. H. Patterson, 'Review of Ape Language: From Conditioned Response to Symbol', *American Journal of Psychology*, CI (1988), pp. 582–90.
13 Eugene Linden, *Silent Partners: The Legacy of the Ape Language Experiments* (New York, 1986).
14 R. Allen Gardner and Beatrix T. Gardner, *Teaching Sign Language to Chimpanzees* (Albany, NY, 1989).
15 Duane M. Rumbaugh, *Language Learning by a Chimpanzee: The Lana Project* (New York, 1977).
16 Sue Savage-Rumbaugh, *Kanzi: The Ape at the Brink of the Human Mind* (New York, 1996).
17 Duane M. Rumbaugh, 'Primate Language and Cognition', *Social Research*, LXII (1995), pp. 711–30.

18 Sue Savage-Rumbaugh, Stuart Shanker, and Talbot Taylor, *Apes, Language, and the Human Mind* (Oxford, 1998).
19 Sue Taylor Parker and Kathleen Rita Gibson, eds, *'Language' and Intelligence in Monkeys and Apes: Comparative Developmental Perspectives* (Cambridge, 1991).
20 Stephen Hart and Franz De Waal, *The Language of Animals* (New York, 1996).
21 Judith De Luce and Hugh T. Wilder, *Language in Primates: Perspectives and Implications* (New York, 1983).

TWO · TALKING APES

 1 Richard Leakey, *The Origin of Humankind* (New York, 1996).
 2 Donald Johanson and Blake Edgar, *From Lucy to Language* (New York, 1996).
 3 Jean Aitchison, *The Seeds of Speech: Language Origin and Evolution* (Cambridge, 1996).
 4 Christopher Stringer and Robin McKie, *African Exodus: The Origins of Modern Humanity* (New York, 1997).
 5 Alan Walker and Pat Shipman, *The Wisdom of the Bones: In Search of Human Origins* (New York, 1997).
 6 Clive Gamble, *The Palaeolithic Settlement of Europe* (Cambridge, 1996).
 7 Ian Tattersall, 'Out of Africa Again . . . and Again?', *Scientific American*, CCLVI/4 (1997), pp. 60–7.
 8 Derek Bickerton, *Language and Species* (Chicago, 1992).
 9 Bernard Comrie, *Language Universals and Linguistic Typology: Syntax and Morphology*, 2nd edn (Chicago, 1989).
10 Herbert Clark and Eve Clark, 'Language Processing', in *Universals of Human Language*, ed. Joseph Greenberg (Stanford, 1978), I, pp. 225–77.
11 Simon Kirby, 'Function, Selection and Innateness: The Emergence of Language Universals', PhD thesis, University of Edinburgh, 1998.
12 Ian Tattersall, *The Last Neandertal: The Rise, Success, and Mysterious Extinction of Our Closest Human Relatives* (New York, 1996).
13 Philip Lieberman, *Eve Spoke* (New York, 1998). See also Philip Lieberman *et al*, 'Folk Psychology and Talking Hyoids', *Nature*, CCCXLII/6249 (1990), pp. 486–7.
14 Derek Bickerton, *Language and Human Behavior* (Seattle, 1995).
15 James Shreeve, *The Neandertal Enigma: Solving the Mystery of Modern Human Origins* (New York, 1995).
16 Roger Lewin, *Bones of Contention: Controversies in the Search for Human Origins* (Chicago, 1997).
17 Milford Wolpoff and Rachel Caspari, *Race and Human Evolution* (New York, 1997).
18 Ian Tattersall, *The Fossil Trail: How We Know What We Think We Know About Human Evolution* (Oxford, 1997).
19 Robert M. W. Dixon, *The Rise and Fall of Languages* (Cambridge, 1997).

1 Morris Swadesh, 'Linguistic Overview', in *Prehistoric Man in the New World*, ed. Jesse D. Jennings and Edward Norbeck (Chicago, 1964), pp. 527–56.
2 Sydney M. Lamb and E. Douglas Mitchell, eds, *Sprung from Some Common Source: Investigations into the Prehistory of Languages* (Stanford, 1991).
3 Ernst Pulgram, 'The Nature and Use of Proto-Languages', *Lingua*, x (1961), pp. 18–37.
4 Johanna Nichols, *Linguistic Diversity in Space and Time* (Chicago, 1992).
5 Terry Crowley, *An Introduction to Historical Linguistics*, 3rd edn (Auckland, 1997).
6 Joseph Greenberg, *Studies in African Linguistic Classification* (New Haven, 1955).
7 Ian Maddieson and Thomas J. Hinnebusch, eds, *Language History and Linguistic Description in Africa*, Trends in African Linguistics 2 (Lawrenceville, NJ, 1998).
8 Saul Levin, *Semitic and Indo-European: The Principal Etymologies, with Observations on Afro-Asiatic*, Amsterdam Studies in the Theory and History of Linguistics (Amsterdam, 1995).
9 Jerry Norman, *Chinese* (Cambridge, 1988).
10 Malcolm D. Ross, 'Some Current Issues in Austronesian Linguistics', in *Comparative Austronesian Dictionary: An Introduction to Austronesian Studies, Part 1: Fascicle 1*, ed. Darrell T. Tryon (Berlin and New York, 1995), pp. 45–120.
11 Daniel Mario Abondolo, ed., *The Uralic Languages*, Routledge Language Family Descriptions (London, 1998).
12 Peter Hajdu, *Finno-Ugrian Languages and Peoples*, translated G. F. Cushing (London, 1975).
13 Ives Goddard, 'The Classification of the Native Languages of North America', in *Handbook of North American Indians*, XVII: *Languages* (Washington, 1996), pp. 290–323.
14 Lyle Campbell, *American Indian Languages: The Historical Linguistics of Native America*, Oxford Studies in Anthropological Linguistics 4 (Oxford, 1997). Please consult this outstanding study for the latest research on the classification, history of investigation, and most recent theories concerning the North American, Central American and South American languages.
15 William Bright, *American Indian Linguistics and Literature* (Berlin, New York, Amsterdam, 1984).
16 Harriet E. Klein and Louisa R. Stark, eds, *South American Indian Languages: Retrospect and Prospect* (Austin, TX, 1985).
17 Nichols (see note 4).
18 Stephen A. Wurm, 'Classifications of Australian Languages, Including Tasmanian', in *Current Trends in Linguistics*, VIII: *Linguistics in Oceania*, ed. Thomas A. Sebeok (The Hague and Paris, 1971), pp. 721–803.
19 A. Capell, 'History of Research in Australian and Tasmanian

Languages', in *Current Trends in Linguistics*, VIII: *Linguistics in Oceania*,
ed. Thomas A. Sebeok (The Hague and Paris, 1971), pp. 661–720.

20 Robert M. W. Dixon, *The Languages of Australia* (Cambridge, 1980).

21 Capell (see note 19).

22 C. F. Voegelin *et al.*, 'Obtaining an Index of Phonological
Differentiation from the Construction of Non-Existent Minimax
Systems', *International Journal of American Linguistics*, XXIX/1 (1963), pp.
4–29.

23 Capell (see note 19).

24 Pamela Swadling, *Papua New Guinea's Prehistory: An Introduction* (Port
Moresby, 1981).

25 Stephen A. Wurm, 'The Papuan Linguistic Situation', in *Current Trends
in Linguistics*, VIII: *Linguistics in Oceania*, ed. Thomas A. Sebeok (The
Hague and Paris, 1971), pp. 541–657.

26 Stephen A. Wurm, *The Papuan Languages of Oceania* (Tübingen, 1982).

27 Darrell T. Tryon, 'The Austronesian Languages', in *Comparative
Austronesian Dictionary: An Introduction to Austronesian Studies, Part 1,
Fascicle 1*, ed. Darrell T. Tryon (Berlin and New York, 1995), pp. 5–44.

28 Isidore Dyen, 'The Austronesian Languages and Proto-Austronesian',
in *Current Trends in Linguistics*, VIII: *Linguistics in Oceania*, ed. Thomas A.
Sebeok (The Hague and Paris, 1971), pp. 5–54.

29 Malcolm D. Ross, 'Some Current Issues in Austronesian Linguistics', in
*Comparative Austronesian Dictionary: An Introduction to Austronesian
Studies, Part 1, Fascicle 1*, ed. Darrell T. Tryon (Berlin and New York,
1995), pp. 45–120.

30 Sanford B. Steever, ed., *The Dravidian Languages*, Routledge Language
Family Descriptions (London, 1998).

31 Colin Renfrew, *Archaeology and Language: The Puzzle of Indo-European
Origins* (London, 1987).

32 Robert S. P. Beekes, *Comparative Indo-European Linguistics: An
Introduction* (Amsterdam, 1995).

33 Björn Collinder, *An Introduction to the Uralic Languages* (Berkeley and
Los Angeles, 1965). See also Bela Brogyanyi and Reiner Lipp, eds,
*Comparative Historical Linguistics: Indo-European and Finno-Ugric. Papers
in Honor of Oswald Szemerenyi*, III (Amsterdam, 1993).

34 Philip Balsi, *An Introduction to the Indo-European Languages* (Carbondale,
IL, 1983).

35 Anna Giacalone Ramat and Paolo Ramat, eds, *The Indo-European
Languages*, Routledge Language Family Descriptions (London, 1998).

36 Crowley (see note 5).

37 Robert M. W. Dixon, *The Rise and Fall of Languages* (Cambridge, 1997).

FOUR · WRITTEN LANGUAGE

1 M. W. Green, 'The Construction and Implementation of the Cuneiform
Writing System', *Visible Language*, XV/4 (1981), pp. 345–72.

2 Archibald A. Hill, 'The Typology of Writing Systems', in *Papers in
Linguistics in Honor of Léon Dostert*, ed. W. M. Austin (The Hague, 1967),

pp. 92–9.

3 Wayne M. Senner, ed., *The Origins of Writing* (Lincoln, NB, 1991).

4 Hans Jensen, *Sign, Symbol and Script. An Account of Man's Efforts to Write*, 3rd edn (London, 1970).

5 Edward B. Tylor, *Anthropology* (New York, 1881).

6 David Diringer, *Writing* (London, 1962).

7 George L. Trager, 'Writing and Writing Systems', in *Current Trends in Linguistics*, XII: *Linguistics and Adjacent Arts and Sciences*, ed. Thomas A. Sebeok (The Hague, 1974), pp. 373–96.

8 Geoffrey Sampson, *Writing Systems* (London, 1985).

9 For the most comprehensive and up-to-date, see Peter T. Daniels and William Bright, eds, *The World's Writing Systems* (New York, 1996). Also recommended are George L. Campbell, *Handbook of Scripts and Alphabets* (London, 1997); Florian Coulmas, *The Blackwell Encyclopedia of Writing Systems* (Oxford, 1996); Sampson (see note 8); Diringer (note 6); and Jensen (note 4).

10 Denise Schmandt-Besserat, *How Writing Came About* (Austin, TX, 1997).

11 John D. Ray, 'The Emergence of Writing in Egypt', *World Archaeology*, XVII/3 (1986), pp. 307–16.

12 Hilary Wilson, *Understanding Hieroglyphs: A Complete Introductory Guide* (Lincolnwood, IL, 1995).

13 Jaromir Malek, *The ABC of Hieroglyphs: Ancient Egyptian Writing* (Gilsum, NH, 1995).

14 W. V. Davies, *Egyptian Hieroglyphs*, Reading the Past, vol. VI (Berkeley and Los Angeles, 1990).

15 David P. Silverman, *Language and Writing in Ancient Egypt*, Carnegie Series on Egypt (Oakland, CA, 1990).

16 E. A. Wallis Budge, *An Egyptian Hieroglyphic Dictionary*, 2 vols (Mineola, New York, 1978).

17 Denise Schmandt-Besserat, *Before Writing: From Counting to Cuneiform* (Austin, TX, 1992).

18 Stuart Schneider and George Fischler, *The Illustrated Guide to Antique Writing Instruments* (New York, 1997).

19 Marvin A. Powell, 'Three Problems in the History of Cuneiform Writing: Origins, Direction of Script, Literacy', *Visible Language*, XV/4 (1981), pp. 419–40.

20 C. B. F. Walker, *Cuneiform*, Reading the Past, vol. III (Berkeley and Los Angeles, 1989).

21 Green (see note 1).

22 Gregory L. Possehl, *The Indus Age: The Writing System* (Philadelphia, 1996).

23 Walter A. Fairservis, Jr, 'The Script of the Indus Valley Civilization', *Scientific American* (March 1983), pp. 41–9.

24 Asko Parpola, 'The Indus Script: A Challenging Puzzle', *World Archaeology*, XVII/3 (1986), pp. 399–419, and *Deciphering the Indus Script* (Cambridge, 1994).

25 Maurice W. M. Pope, 'The Origin of Near Eastern Writing', *Antiquity*,

XL (1965), pp. 17–23.

26 G. R. Driver, *Semitic Writing* (London, 1948).

27 Roger D. Woodard, *Greek Writing from Knossos to Homer: A Linguistic Interpretation of the Origin of the Greek Alphabet and the Continuity of Ancient Greek Literacy* (Oxford, 1997). The new theory that Minoan Greeks elaborated the hieroglyphic and Linear A scripts can be read in Steven Roger Fischer, *Evidence for Hellenic Dialect in the Phaistos Disk* (Berne, Frankfurt am Main, New York, Paris, 1988); a popular version of his theory can be read in Steven Roger Fischer, *Glyphbreaker* (New York, 1997).

28 Brian Colless, 'The Byblos Syllabary and the Proto-Alphabet', *Abr-Nahrain*, XXX (1992), pp. 55–102.

29 Brian E. Colless, 'Recent Discoveries Illuminating the Origin of the Alphabet', *Abr-Nahrain*, XXVI (1988), pp. 30–67.

30 John F. Healey, *Early Alphabet*, Reading the Past, vol. IX (Berkeley and Los Angeles, 1991).

31 Steven Roger Fischer, *Rongorongo: The Easter Island Script. History, Traditions, Texts*, Oxford Studies in Anthropological Linguistics, 14 (Oxford, 1997).

32 S. Robert Ramsey, *The Languages of China* (Princeton, NJ, 1990).

33 Sampson (see note 8).

34 John S. Justeson, 'The Origin of Writing Systems: Preclassic Mesoamerica', *World Archaeology*, XVII (1986), pp. 439–56.

35 John S. Justeson and Terrence Kaufman, 'A Decipherment of Epi-Olmec Hieroglyphic Writing', *Science*, CCLIX (1993), pp. 1703–11.

36 Michael D. Coe, *Breaking the Maya Code* (London, 1992).

37 Michael D. Coe and Justin Kerr, *The Art of the Maya Scribe* (London, 1998).

38 Joyce Marcus, *Mesoamerican Writing Systems: Propaganda, Myth, and History in Four Ancient Civilizations* (Princeton, NJ, 1992).

39 D. Gary Miller, *Ancient Scripts and Phonological Knowledge*, Amsterdam Studies in the Theory and History of Linguistic Science (Amsterdam, 1994).

40 Henri Jean Martin, *The History and Power of Writing*, translated by Lydia G. Cochrane (Chicago, 1995).

41 John L. White, ed., *Studies in Ancient Letter Writing* (Atlanta, GA, 1983).

FIVE · LINEAGES

1 Ross Clark, 'Language', in *The Prehistory of Polynesia*, ed. Jesse D. Jennings (Cambridge, MA, and London, 1979), pp. 249–70.

2 Donald Macaulay, *The Celtic Languages* (Cambridge, 1993).

3 James Fife and Martin J. Ball, eds, *The Celtic Languages* (London, 1993).

4 Kenneth Hurlstone Jackson, *Language and History in Early Britain* (Portland, OR, 1994).

5 Janet Davies, *The Welsh Language* (Cardiff, 1993).

6 R. S. Conway, *The Italic Dialects* (Cambridge, 1897).

7 Carl Darling Buck, *A Grammar of Oscan and Umbrian: With a Collection of Inscriptions and a Glossary* (Boston, MA, 1904).

8 M. S. Beeler, *The Venetic Language*, University of California Publications in Linguistics, IV/1 (Berkeley and Los Angeles, 1949).

9 Helena Kurzova, *From Indo-European to Latin: The Evolution of a Morphosyntactic Type*, Amsterdam Studies in the Theory and History of Linguistic Science, Series 4 (Amsterdam, 1993).

10 Roger Wright, ed., *Latin and the Romance Languages in the Early Middle Ages* (University Park, PA, 1995).

11 Tracy K. Harris, *Death of a Language: The History of Judeo-Spanish* (Newark, DE, 1994).

12 Peter A. Machonis, *Histoire de la langue: du latin à l'ancien français* (Lanham, MD, 1990).

13 Peter Rickard, *A History of the French Language*, 2nd edn (London, 1989).

14 Paul M. Lloyd, *From Latin to Spanish: Historical Phonology and Morphology of the Spanish Language*, Memoirs of the American Philosophical Society, 173 (Philadelphia, PA, 1987).

15 Ralph Penny, *A History of the Spanish Language* (Cambridge, 1991).

16 Martin Maiden, *A Linguistic History of Italian*, Longman Linguistics Library (London, 1994).

17 D. H. Green, *Language and History in the Early Germanic World* (Cambridge, 1998).

18 Johan van der Auwera and Ekkehard K. Fonig, *The Germanic Languages* (London, 1994).

19 Joseph B. Voyles, *Early Germanic Grammar: Pre-, Proto-, and Post-Germanic Languages* (San Diego, CA, 1992).

20 Orrin W. Robinson, *Old English and Its Closest Relatives: A Survey of the Earliest Germanic Languages* (Stanford, CA, 1994).

21 Charles V. J. Russ, *German Language Today: A Linguistic Introduction* (London, 1994).

22 Rolf Berndt, *History of the English Language* (Leipzig, 1982).

23 Malcolm Guthrie, *Comparative Bantu: An Introduction to the Comparative Linguistics and Prehistory of the Bantu Languages*, 4 vols (Farnborough, 1967–70).

24 Derek Nurse and Thomas J. Hinnebusch, *Swahili and Sabaki: A Linguistic History*, University of California Publications in Linguistics, CXXI (Berkeley and Los Angeles, 1993).

25 Harry H. Johnston, *A Comparative Study of the Bantu and Semi-Bantu Languages* (New York, 1997).

26 Jan Vansina, *Paths in the Rainforests* (Madison, Wisconsin, 1990).

27 *Ibid.*

28 Jerry Norman, *Chinese* (Cambridge, 1988).

29 Victor Krupa, *The Polynesian Languages: A Guide*, Languages of Asia and Africa, IV (London, 1982).

30 Clark (see note 1).

31 Andrew Pawley, 'The Relationships of Polynesian Outlier Languages', *Journal of the Polynesian Society*, LXXVI (1967), pp. 259–96.

32 Carleton T. Hodge, 'The Linguistic Cycle', *Language Sciences*, XIII, pp. 1–7.

1 Leonard Bloomfield, *An Introduction to Linguistic Science* (New York, 1914).
2 Bimal Krishna Matilal, *The Word and the World: India's Contribution to the Study of Language* (Oxford, 1990).
3 Giulio Lepschy, ed., *History of Linguistics: The Eastern Traditions of Linguistics* (London, 1996).
4 Esa Itkonen, *Universal History of Linguistics: India, China, Arabia, Europe*, Amsterdam Studies in the Theory and History of Linguistic Science 65 (Amsterdam, 1991).
5 Robert H. Robins, *A Short History of Linguistics*, 3rd edn, Longman Linguistics Library (London, 1996).
6 Pieter A. M. Seuren, *Western Linguistics: An Historical Introduction* (Oxford, 1998).
7 Giulio Lepschy, ed., *History of Linguistics: Classical and Medieval Linguistics* (London, 1996).
8 Roy Harris and Talbot J. Taylor, *Landmarks in Linguistic Thought: The Western Tradition from Socrates to Saussure*, Routledge History of Linguistic Thought Series (London, 1997).
9 Robert H. Robins, *The Byzantine Grammarians: Their Place in History*, Trends in Linguistics, Studies and Monographs 70 (Berlin, New York, Amsterdam, 1993).
10 Seuren (see note 6).
11 Lepschy (see note 7).
12 Kees Versteegh, *Landmarks in Linguistic Thought III: The Arabic Linguistic Tradition*, Routledge History of Linguistic Thought Series (London, 1997).
13 Itkonen (see note 4).
14 Lepschy (see note 3).
15 Vivien Law, ed., *History of Linguistic Thought in the Early Middle Ages*, Amsterdam Studies in the Theory and History of Linguistic Science (Amsterdam, 1993).
16 Lepschy (see note 7).
17 Law (see note 15).
18 Robins (see note 5).
19 Seuren (see note 6).
20 Ferdinand de Saussure, *Course in General Linguistics*, translated by Wade Baskin (New York, 1966).
21 Jindrich Toman, *The Magic of a Common Language: Jakobson, Mathesius, Trubetzkoy, and the Prague Linguistic Circle*, Current Studies in Linguistics, 26 (Cambridge, MA, 1995).
22 Randy Allen Harris, *The Linguistics Wars* (Oxford, 1995).
23 Edward Sapir, *Language: An Introduction to the Study of Speech* (New York, 1921).
24 P. H. Matthews, *Grammatical Theory in the United States from Bloomfield to Chomsky*, Cambridge Studies in Linguistics, 67 (Cambridge, 1993).
25 Leonard Bloomfield, *Language* (London, 1935).
26 William O'Grady, *Contemporary Linguistics: An Introduction*, 3rd edn

(London, 1997).

27 J. R. Firth, *Papers in Linguistics 1934–1951* (Oxford, 1957).

28 Roman Jakobson, *Selected Writings I: Phonological Studies* (The Hague, 1962).

29 Sidney M. Lamb, 'The Sememic Approach to Structural Semantics', *American Anthropologist*, LXVI (1964), pp. 57–78; and *Outline of Stratificational Grammar* (Washington, DC, 1966).

30 Noam Chomsky, *Syntactic Structures* (The Hague, 1957).

31 Emmon Bach, *Introduction to Transformational Grammars* (New York, 1964).

32 Noam Chomsky, *Aspects of the Theory of Syntax* (Cambridge, MA, 1965).

33 On 12 November 1998, as I was writing this chapter, Noam Chomsky visited me at my home on Waiheke Island, New Zealand, where we spent the afternoon together discussing, among other things, transformational generative grammar and its place in the history of linguistics. When I asked Chomsky whether he agreed with my assessment, he replied yes, that 'generative grammar' would perhaps be the most important theoretical linguistic model of the second half of the twentieth century. The 'transformational' aspect might be debatable, he added, though he believed a transformational element must be present in the process of language generation.

34 Robert M. W. Dixon, *The Rise and Fall of Languages* (Cambridge, 1997).

35 Robert D. King, *Historical Linguistics and Generative Grammar* (Englewood Cliffs, New Jersey, 1969); Hans Henrich Hock, *Principles of Historical Linguistics* (Berlin, New York, Amsterdam, 1986).

36 James Allen, *Natural Language Understanding*, 2nd edn (London, 1995). Noam Chomsky informed me during our meeting on Waiheke Island (see above) that he initially drew his model of transformational generative grammar from the computational linguistics being innovated in the USA after the war, specifically in the area of machine translating.

SEVEN · SOCIETY AND LANGUAGE

1 Ronald Wardhaugh, *An Introduction to Sociolinguistics* (Oxford, 1997).

2 Suzanne Romaine, *Language in Society: An Introduction to Sociolinguistics* (Oxford, 1994).

3 Peter Trudgill, *Sociolinguistics: An Introduction to Language and Society*, rev. edn (New York, 1996).

4 Jean Aitchison, *Language Change: Progress or Decay?*, 2nd edn (Cambridge, 1991).

5 Roger Lass, *Historical Linguistics and Language Change* (Cambridge, 1997).

6 R. L. Trask, *Language Change* (London, 1994).

7 Jonathan Green, *Slangs Through the Ages* (Lincolnwood, IL, 1996).

8 Robert L. Chapman, *American Slang* (New York, 1998).

9 Karl Sornig, *Lexical Innovation: A Study of Slang, Colloquialisms, and Casual Speech* (New York, 1981).

10 Suzanne Romaine, *Pidgin and Creole Languages* (New York, 1988).

11 Terry Crowley, *An Introduction to Historical Linguistics*, 3rd edn (Auckland, 1997).

12 Derek Bickerton, *Roots of Language* (Ann Arbor, 1981).

13 David Crystal, *English as a Global Language* (Cambridge, 1998).

14 J. K. Chambers and Peter Trudgill, *Dialectology* (Cambridge, 1990).

15 Joshua A. Fishman, *In Praise of the Beloved Language: A Comparative View of Positive Ethnolinguistic Consciousness* (Berlin, New York, Amsterdam, 1997).

16 Joey Lee Dillard, *Black English: Its History and Usage in the United States* (New York, 1973).

17 Clarence Major, *Juba to Jive: A Dictionary of African-American Slang* (New York, 1994).

18 Dale Spender, *Man-Made Language* (New York, 1990).

19 Anna Livia, *Queerly Phrased: Language, Gender, and Sexuality* (Oxford, 1997).

20 John W. Young, *Totalitarian Language* (Charlottesville, VA, 1991).

21 Edward S. Herman and Noam Chomsky, *Manufacturing Consent: The Political Economy of the Mass Media* (New York, 1988).

22 William C. Stokoe, *Semiotics and Human Sign Languages* (The Hague, 1972).

23 Matthias Brenzinger, ed., *Language Death* (Berlin, New York, Amsterdam, 1992).

24 Lenore A. Grenoble and Lindsay J. Whaley, eds, *Endangered Languages: Current Issues and Future Prospects* (Cambridge, 1997).

25 Trudgill (see note 3).

26 Alison Ross, *Language of Humour* (London, 1998).

27 Jan Gavan Bremmer and Herman Roodenburg, eds, *A Cultural History of Humour: From Antiquity to the Present Day* (Oxford, 1997).

EIGHT · FUTURE INDICATIVE

1 Robert W. Sebesta, *Concepts of Programming Languages* (Don Mills, Ont., 1998).

2 Alice E. Fischer and Frances S. Grodzynsky, *The Anatomy of Programming Languages* (New York, 1993).

3 Ryan Stansifer, *The Study of Programming Languages* (New York, 1994).

4 Doris Appleby and Julius J. Vandekopple, *Programming Languages: Paradigm and Practice*, 2nd edn, McGraw-Hill Computer Science Series (New York, 1997).

5 Kenneth C. Louden, *Programming Languages: Principles and Practice*, PWS-Kent Series in Computer Science (Boston, MA, 1993).

6 C. A. R. Hoare and C. B. Jones, *Essays in Computing Science*, Prentice Hall International Series in Computer Science (New York, 1989).

7 Mark Warschauer, ed., *Virtual Connection: Online Activities and Projects for Networking Language Learners*, National Foreign Language Center Technical Reports No. 8 (Honolulu, 1995).

8 Seppo Tella, 'The Adoption of International Communications Networks and Electronic Mail into Foreign Language Education',

Scandinavian Journal of Educational Research, XXXVI (1992), pp. 303–12.

9 Seppo Tella, Introducing International Communications Networks and Electronic Mail in Foreign Language Classrooms: A Case Study in Finnish Senior Secondary Schools. Doctoral dissertation, University of Helsinki, 1991.

10 Seppo Tella, *Talking Shop Via E-Mail: A Thematic and Linguistic Analysis of Electronic Mail Communication* (Helsinki, 1992).

11 Dave Sperling, *The Internet Guide for English Language Teachers* (New York, 1997).

12 Robert Phillipson, *Linguistic Imperialism* (Oxford, 1992).

13 Jenny Cheshire, ed., *English Around the World* (Cambridge, 1991).

14 The British Council, *The Future of English?* (London, 1997).

15 Robert M. W. Dixon, *The Rise and Fall of Languages* (Cambridge, 1997).

Select Bibliography

Agosta, William C., *Chemical Communication: The Language of Pheromones* (New York, 1992)

Aitchison, Jean, *Language Change: Progress or Decay?*, 2nd edn (Cambridge, 1991)

—, *The Seeds of Speech: Language Origin and Evolution* (Cambridge, 1996)

Allen, James, *Natural Language Understanding*, 2nd edn (London, 1995)

Anttila, Raimo, *An Introduction to Historical and Comparative Linguistics* (New York, 1972)

Appleby, Doris, and Julius J. Vandekopple, *Programming Languages: Paradigm and Practice*, 2nd edn, McGraw-Hill Computer Science Series (New York, 1997)

Arlotto, Anthony, *Introduction to Historical Linguistics* (Boston, 1972)

van der Auwera, Johan, and Ekkehard K. Fonig, *The Germanic Languages* (London, 1994)

Baldi, Philip, ed., *Linguistic Change and Reconstruction Methodology* (Berlin, 1990)

Benveniste, Émile, *Problèmes de linguistique générale* (Paris, 1966)

Berndt, Rolf, *History of the English Language* (Leipzig, 1982)

Bickerton, Derek, *Roots of Language* (Ann Arbor, MI, 1981)

—, *Language and Species* (Chicago, 1992)

Bloomfield, Leonard, *An Introduction to Linguistic Science* (New York, 1914)

—, *Language* (London, 1935)

Bolinger, Dwight, *Aspects of Language* (New York, 1968)

Bremmer, Jan Gavan, and Herman Roodenburg, eds, *A Cultural History of Humour: From Antiquity to the Present Day* (Oxford, 1997)

Brenzinger, Matthias, ed., *Language Death* (Berlin, New York, Amsterdam, 1992)

Budge, E. A. Wallis, *An Egyptian Hieroglyphic Dictionary*, 2 vols (Mineola, NY, 1978)

Bynon, Theodora, *Historical Linguistics* (Cambridge, 1979)

Campbell, George L., *Handbook of Scripts and Alphabets* (London, 1997)

Cheshire, Jenny, ed., *English Around the World* (Cambridge, 1991)

Chomsky, Noam, *Syntactic Structures* (The Hague, 1957)

—, *Aspects of the Theory of Syntax* (Cambridge, MA, 1965)

Coe, Michael D., *Breaking the Maya Code* (London, 1992)

Conroy, Glenn C., *Reconstructing Human Origins: A Modern Synthesis* (New York, 1997)

Coulmas, Florian, *The Blackwell Encyclopedia of Writing Systems* (Oxford, 1996)

Crowley, Terry, *An Introduction to Historical Linguistics* (Auckland, 1997)

Daniels, Peter T., and William Bright, eds, *The World's Writing Systems* (New York, 1996)

Deacon, Terrence, *The Symbolic Species: The Co-Evolution of Language and the Brain* (New York, 1997)

De Luce, Judith, and Hugh T. Wilder, *Language in Primates: Perspectives and Implications* (New York, 1983)

Diringer, David, *Writing* (London, 1962)

Dixon, Robert M. W., *The Languages of Australia* (Cambridge, 1980)

—, *The Rise and Fall of Languages* (Cambridge, 1997)

Driver, G. R., *Semitic Writing* (London, 1948)

Fife, James, and Martin J. Ball, eds, *The Celtic Languages* (London, 1993)

Fischer, Alice E., and Frances S. Grodzynsky, *The Anatomy of Programming Languages* (New York, 1993)

Fischer, Steven Roger, *Glyphbreaker* (New York, 1997)

—, *Rongorongo: The Easter Island Script. History, Traditions, Texts*, Oxford Studies in Anthropological Linguistics 14 (Oxford, 1997)

Gardner, R. Allen, and Beatrix T. Gardner, *Teaching Sign Language to Chimpanzees* (Albany, NY, 1989)

Green, D. H., *Language and History in the Early Germanic World* (Cambridge, 1998)

Grenoble, Lenore A., and Lindsay J. Whaley, eds, *Endangered Languages: Current Issues and Future Prospects* (Cambridge, 1997)

Guthrie, Malcolm, *Comparative Bantu: An Introduction to the Comparative Linguistics and Prehistory of the Bantu Languages*, 4 vols (Farnborough, 1967–70)

Haas, Mary R., *The Prehistory of Languages* (The Hague, 1969)

Harrar, George, and Linda Harrar, *Signs of the Apes, Songs of the Whales: Adventures in Human–Animal Communication* (New York, 1989)

Harris, Randy Allen, *The Linguistics Wars* (Oxford, 1995)

Harris, Roy, and Talbot J. Taylor, *Landmarks in Linguistic Thought: The Western Tradition from Socrates to Saussure*, Routledge History of Linguistic Thought Series (London, 1997)

Hart, Stephen, and Franz De Waal, *The Language of Animals* (New York, 1996)

Hock, Hans Henrich, *Principles of Historical Linguistics* (Berlin, 1991)

Itkonen, Esa, *Universal History of Linguistics: India, China, Arabia, Europe*, Amsterdam Studies in the Theory and History of Linguistic Science, 65 (Amsterdam, 1991)

Jablonski, Nina G., and Leslie C. Aiello, eds, *The Origin and Diversification of Language* (San Francisco, CA, 1998)

Jeffers, Robert J., and Ilse Lehiste, *Principles and Methods for Historical Linguistics* (Cambridge, MA, and London, 1980)

Jensen, Hans, *Sign, Symbol and Script. An Account of Man's Efforts to Write*, 3rd edn (London, 1970)

Jespersen, Otto, *Language: Its Nature, Development and Origin* (London, 1922)

Johnston, Harry H., *A Comparative Study of the Bantu and Semi-Bantu Languages* (New York, 1997)

Krupa, Victor, *The Polynesian Languages: A Guide*, Languages of Asia and
Africa, IV (London, 1982)

Lass, Roger, *Historical Linguistics and Language Change* (Cambridge, 1997)

Lehmann, Winfred P., *Historical Linguistics: An Introduction* (New York, 1962)

Lepschy, Giulio, ed., *History of Linguistics: Classical and Medieval Linguistics*
(London, 1996)

—, ed., *History of Linguistics: The Eastern Traditions of Linguistics* (London, 1996)

Lieberman, Philip, *The Biology and Evolution of Language* (Cambridge, MA,
1987)

—, *Eve Spoke: Human Language and Human Evolution* (New York, 1998)

Lilly, John C., *Communication Between Man and Dolphin* (New York, 1987)

Linden, Eugene, *Silent Partners: The Legacy of the Ape Language Experiments*
(New York, 1986)

Lloyd, Paul M., *From Latin to Spanish: Historical Phonology and Morphology of
the Spanish Language*, Memoirs of the American Philosophical Society
173 (Philadelphia, PA, 1987)

Macaulay, Donald, *The Celtic Languages* (Cambridge, 1993)

Maiden, Martin, *A Linguistic History of Italian*, Longman Linguistics Library
(London, 1994)

Mallory, J. P., *In Search of the Indo-Europeans: Language, Archaeology and Myth*
(London, 1989)

Martin, Henri Jean, *The History and Power of Writing*, translated by Lydia G.
Cochrane (Chicago, 1995)

Matthews, P. H., *Grammatical Theory in the United States from Bloomfield to
Chomsky*, Cambridge Studies in Linguistics, 67 (Cambridge, 1993)

Miller, D. Gary, *Ancient Scripts and Phonological Knowledge*, Amsterdam
Studies in the Theory and History of Linguistic Science (Amsterdam,
1994)

Nichols, Johanna, *Linguistic Diversity in Time and Space* (Chicago, 1992)

Noble, William, and Iain Davidson, *Human Evolution, Language and Mind: A
Psychological and Archaeological Inquiry* (Cambridge, 1996)

Norman, Jerry, *Chinese* (Cambridge, 1988)

O'Grady, William, *Contemporary Linguistics: An Introduction*, 3rd edn
(London, 1997)

Owings, Donald H., and Eugene S. Morton, *Animal Vocal Communication*
(Cambridge, 1998)

Patterson, Francine, and Ronald H. Cohn, *Koko's Story* (New York, 1988)

Pei, Mario, *The Story of Language* (London, 1966)

Penny, Ralph, *A History of the Spanish Language* (Cambridge, 1991)

Phillipson, Robert, *Linguistic Imperialism* (Oxford, 1992)

Ramsey, S. Robert, *The Languages of China* (Princeton, NJ, 1990)

Renfrew, Colin, *Archaeology and Language: The Puzzle of Indo-European
Origins* (London, 1987)

Rickard, Peter, *A History of the French Language*, 2nd edn (London, 1989)

Robins, Robert H., *A Short History of Linguistics*, 3rd edn, Longman
Linguistics Library (London, 1996)

—, and Eugenius M. Uhlenbeck, eds, *Endangered Languages* (Oxford, 1991)

Robinson, Andrew, *The Story of Writing* (London, 1995)

Robinson, Orrin W., *Old English and Its Closest Relatives: A Survey of the Earliest Germanic Languages* (Stanford, 1994)

Romaine, Suzanne, *Pidgin and Creole Languages* (New York, 1988)

—, *Language in Society: An Introduction to Sociolinguistics* (Oxford, 1994)

Russ, Charles V. J., *German Language Today: A Linguistic Introduction* (London, 1994)

Sampson, Geoffrey, *Writing Systems* (London, 1985)

Sapir, Edward, *Language: An Introduction to the Study of Speech* (New York, 1921)

de Saussure, Ferdinand, *Course in General Linguistics*, translated by Wade Baskin (New York, 1966)

Savage-Rumbaugh, Sue, *Ape Language: From Conditioned Response to Symbol* (New York, 1986)

—, *Kanzi: The Ape at the Brink of the Human Mind* (New York, 1996)

—, Stuart Shanker, and Talbot Taylor, *Apes, Language, and the Human Mind* (Oxford, 1998)

Schmandt-Besserat, Denise, *Before Writing: From Counting to Cuneiform* (Austin, TX, 1992)

—, *How Writing Came About* (Austin, TX, 1997)

Sebeok, Thomas A., *Speaking of Apes: A Critical Anthology of Two-Way Communication with Man* (New York, 1980)

Sebesta, Robert W., *Concepts of Programming Languages* (Don Mills, Ont., 1998)

Senner, Wayne M., ed., *The Origins of Writing* (Lincoln, NB, 1991)

Seuren, Pieter A. M., *Western Linguistics: An Historical Introduction* (Oxford, 1998)

Shibatani, Masayoshi, *The Languages of Japan* (Cambridge, 1990)

Stansifer, Ryan, *The Study of Programming Languages* (New York, 1994)

Stokoe, William C., *Semiotics and Human Sign Languages* (The Hague, 1972)

Tella, Seppo, *Talking Shop Via E-Mail: A Thematic and Linguistic Analysis of Electronic Mail Communication* (Helsinki, 1992)

Trask, R. L., *Language Change* (London, 1994)

Trudgill, Peter, *Sociolinguistics: An Introduction to Language and Society*, rev. edn (New York, 1996)

Vansina, Jan, *Paths in the Rainforests* (Madison, WI, 1990)

Von Frisch, Karl, and Thomas D. Seeley, *The Dance Language and Orientation of Bees* (Cambridge, MA, 1993)

Voyles, Joseph B., *Early Germanic Grammar: Pre-, Proto-, and Post-Germanic Languages* (San Diego, CA, 1992)

Wardhaugh, Ronald, *An Introduction to Sociolinguistics* (Oxford, 1997)

Warschauer, Mark, ed., *Virtual Connection: Online Activities and Projects for Networking Language Learners*, National Foreign Language Center Technical Reports, 8 (Honolulu, 1995)

Wenner, Adrian M., and Patrick Wells, *Anatomy of a Controversy: The Question of a Language Among Bees* (New York, 1990)

Wright, Roger, ed., *Latin and the Romance Languages in the Early Middle Ages* (University Park, PA, 1995)

Index

Ægean 67, 86, 96
African languages 65, 112
Afrikaans 125
Afro-American speech 183, 185
Afro-Asiatic languages 66–7, 90
Ainu 70, 104
Akkadian 67, 94
Alighieri *see* Dante
alphabet 87, 88, 91, 93, 96–9, 105,
    108–9, 111, 124, 144, 195
Altaic languages 69
American languages 63, 68, 70–2, 164
Ameslan 26–8, 32, 196
animal communication 11–34
ants 13–14, 45
apes, great 16, 25–33, 35
Arabic 121-2, 126, 142, 149–50, 153,
    185, 188, 219
areal diffusion 60, 74, 84, 127–8, 173
Aristotle 144–6, 149, 154, 156, 170
articulation 29, 35, 37, 39, 44, 46, 48,
    50–51, 56–8, 141, 150
Asian languages 67–70
Australia 39, 53, 56, 63, 125, 187, 217,
    219
Australian languages 63, 72–6
Austro-Asiatic languages 68, 78
Austronesian languages 62, 63, 68,
    77, 133
Aztec 60, 106

Babel, Tower of 158
Bacon, Roger 152–3

Bahasa Indonesia 113, 190
Bantu languages 112, 126–8, 136
Basque 62, 78–9, 81, 154, 182
bats 12, 17
bees *see* honey-bees
Berber 66–7, 185
bilingualism 197, 209–10, 218
Bilzingsleben 43
bioacoustics 11–13, 17, 25
birds 15–16
Bloomfield, Leonard 139, 161,
    164–5, 168
Boas, Franz 164, 168
bonobos 25, 30–31, 36
Bopp, Franz 159
borrowing 127, 129, 188–9, 202, 212
Boxgrove 42
Breton 115–17, 118

case theory 146
Catalan 118, 121, 154, 195, 212
Caucasian languages 69–70, 79
Celtic languages 62, 79, 85, 100, 112,
    115–18, 121–3, 136, 147, 157,
    159, 178
Chadic 66
change, linguistic 172–7, 211
chemocommunication 11, 13, 20, 220
chimpanzees 25, 28–31, 36
Chinese 61, 63, 68, 81, 84, 102–5,
    107–8, 111–13, 125, 129–33, 136,
    150–51, 154, 160, 181, 195, 211,
    218, 219; *see also* Mandarin

Chinese

Chomsky, Noam 46–7, 51, 167–8, 169, 229

Churchill, Sir Winston 173, 193

classification 60, 61
    genetic 61
    typological 61

Coe, Michael 107

common language 177–8, 202

computational linguistics 142, 169–70, 171, 229

constructed languages 112, 180–81, 209

convergence 74, 127, 128

Corded Ware culture 80–81

Cornish 115, 116, 118, 198

creole language 179–80

Crete 67, 96, 184

'Cro-Magnon' 52

Cumbric 118

cuneiform 93–4, 108

Cushitic 66

Danish 124, 135

Dante 158

death, language see extinction

deer 18

descriptive grammar 140, 163–4

dialects 17, 21, 23–5, 58, 75–6, 111, 122, 124, 130, 133–5, 143, 144, 151, 161–2, 172, 174, 182–3, 197–8, 211

dictionaries 142–3, 150, 154, 158, 166

discourse analysis 169

Dixon, Robert 219

dolphins 12, 16–17, 24–5

Dravidian 78, 95

Dutch 125, 126

e-mail language 208–9

Easter Island 77, 87, 101–2, 134–6, 175, 197, 201, 213

echo-location 17, 20, 21, 24

Egyptian 62, 66–7, 86–93, 108, 137

elephants 12, 19–20

endangered languages 196–7

English 109–11, 125–6, 174, 182, 186–9, 193, 209, 214–19

equilibrium, linguistic 57–8, 74–5, 84, 128, 173

Esperanto 112, 180–81

Estuary English 214

ethnic language 183–5, 202

Etruscans 79, 99–100, 115, 119–20

etymology 142, 145, 147

Euskara see Basque

evolution 11, 35–59
    cyclic 76, 137
    linguistic 81, 88, 156, 171, 220
    neural 8, 16, 29, 35–6, 38, 44–6, 51, 56–7

extinction, language 63, 84, 112, 136, 138, 197–8, 202

'family tree' 58, 60, 63, 74–5, 82–4, 127–8, 160–61, 207

Faroese 124

Finnish 69

Finno-Ugric 69, 80, 171

'First Grammarian' 152, 158

'first language' 62

Firth, J. R. 165–6

fish 12

Flemish 125

Flores Island 39

Fossey, Dian 26

French 61, 81, 114, 117, 120–21, 125, 131, 135, 137, 154, 177, 179, 182, 184–6, 212, 215

frequencies, hearing 11–12, 19, 21

Frisch, Karl von 14

Galápagos 24

Galician 118, 212

Gaulish 79, 109, 115, 117, 121, 178, 196

gender 186–7, 202
generative grammar 142, 167–9, 229
German 110, 115, 117, 121–2, 124,
    126, 158, 174, 177, 186, 189, 197,
    212–13, 218
Germanic languages 61, 62, 80–81,
    85, 99, 100, 112, 121–7, 136, 147,
    159
gesture 11, 29, 30, 33, 49, 156, 194–6,
    208–9, 220
Gilgamesh 172
glottochronology 128
gorillas 25, 26–8, 36
Gothic 79, 99, 123, 157
grammar 46
Greek 95–9, 108–9, 144–6, 175, 178
Grimm, Jacob 158–9

Harris, Zellig 169
Hawai'i 135–6
Hebrew 67, 87, 97, 142, 153–4, 156,
    158, 170, 198, 219
Herodotus 144, 183, 199
hieroglyphs 90–3
Hittites 94
Homer 145, 199
hominids 8, 18, 20, 25, 34–59, 220
Homo erectus 37–49, 50–51, 53, 55–7,
    67, 177
Homo ergaster 37
Homo habilis 36–7, 55
Homo heidelbergensis 43
Homo sapiens 7, 8, 33, 37–8, 43–7,
    49–58, 63, 65, 67, 70, 73–4, 79
honey-bees 14, 45, 46
horses 18
Humboldt, Wilhelm von 159–60,
    161, 164, 168
humour 199–201, 203
Hungarian *see* Magyar

Icelandic 124, 126, 152, 158, 190–91
ideolects 17

India 60, 78, 139, 140–41, 143, 145,
    150–51
Indian languages 78, 95
Indo-European 61–3, 67, 78–85,
    94–5, 115, 118–20, 122–3, 126,
    157, 159–60, 180, 196, 211
Indus Valley 78, 86–7, 89, 94–5, 140
infrasound 11–12, 19–21, 220
insects 12–13
interlanguage 178
International Standard English 126,
    174, 209–10, 217, 219
Internet 208–11, 218
Irish 99, 115–17, 152, 175, 190
Italian 61, 120–22, 154, 178, 188
Italic languages 79, 81, 112, 115,
    119–22, 126, 136

Jakobson, Roman 166
Japanese 70, 104–5, 108, 111, 130,
    132, 218
'Java man' 38
Jones, Sir William 157

Kanzi 30–31
Khoisan languages 65
koiné 178
Koko 26–30
Korean 70, 105, 130, 132

Lamb, Sidney M. 167
language
    agglutinative 61, 132, 137, 160, 164
    artificial 46–7
    body 18, 194
    'dance' 11, 14, 45–6, 220
    definition of 11–12, 33
    fusional 61, 137
    future of 204–20
    inflectional 61, 104, 130, 147,
        159–60, 164
    isolating 61, 129, 137, 160, 164

Lappish 69
Latin 146–9, 151–3
lexicon 45–7, 58, 84, 120, 127, 133–4, 136, 151, 171, 175
lexicostatistics 127–8
Libya 67
Ligurians 79
Lilly, John C. 24–5
lingua franca 126, 132, 136, 178–9
linguistic equilibrium *see under* equilibrium
linguistics 81, 109, 139–71

Magyar (Hungarian) 67, 69
Mandarin Chinese 61, 68, 81, 84, 113, 125, 129, 131–2, 151, 181, 211, 218–19
'manufacturing consent' 192
Manx 115, 116–18, 198
Māori 135–6, 171, 190
marking 48
Mayan 72, 106–8, 195
Mesoamerican languages 71–2, 89, 105–8
Mesopotamia 67, 87, 89, 95
Mexicans 60, 106–8
Mongol languages 69
morpheme 61, 86, 129–30, 145, 149, 165
morphology 46, 114, 127, 137, 142, 145, 148, 164, 165
Morse Code 194

Nahuatl 60
national languages 182–4, 202
Neandertal 43, 45, 47, 49–56, 57
Neogrammarians 142, 161–2, 166
New Guinea *see* Papuan languages
New Zealand 79–80, 125, 135, 171, 174, 182, 190, 217–18, 229
'Niger-Congo' 62–3, 65, 126
Nilo-Saharan languages 65
Norse 123–4

Norwegian 124

Occitan 118
officialese 193
Omotic 66
orangutans 25, 26

Palæo-Asiatic 70
Paṇini 140–1
Papuan languages 63, 72–3, 76–7
Patterson, Francine 26–8, 29, 33
Pepperberg, Irene 15–16
pheromones 13–14, 20, 45
Phoenician 67, 96, 98
phoneme 46, 111, 131, 141, 152, 163, 165–6, 171
phonetics 46, 87, 130, 139–71
phonology 46, 58, 75, 84, 113–14, 120, 127–8, 136–7, 139–71, 185, 214
Picts 79, 117
pidgin language 179–80
Pike, Kenneth L. 165
Plain English Campaign 193–4
Plato 144, 146
Polynesian languages 62, 77, 112, 133–6, 137, 160, 171, 175, 190, 197, 201
Port Royal schools 155–6, 168
Portuguese 121, 154, 178, 179
Prague Linguistic Circle 163, 166
primates 25–31
Priscian 148, 151–3, 155, 170
programming languages 11, 111, 170–71, 204–8, 220
propaganda 107, 174, 191–3, 202, 220
prosody 143, 150
Provençal 120–21, 154
'punctuation', linguistic 57–8, 74, 128, 173
purification, linguistic 188–91, 202

Ramée, Pierre 154–5

Rask, Rasmus 158–9
received pronunciation 182
reconstruction 60, 63, 71, 84, 109,
    112, 126, 128, 130, 160
Renaissance 139, 146, 153–5, 170–71,
    188
replacement, language 84–5, 112,
    128, 135, 196–7, 202, 204, 211
Rhaetian 109, 119
Romance languages 61–2, 120–2,
    130, 136, 154
Romanian 121–2
Romany 118

Sahul 63, 72–7
Sanskrit 60, 81, 95, 139, 140–3, 150,
    157–60, 162, 170, 188
Sapir, Edward 164, 168
Saussure, Ferdinand de 162–3
Savage-Rumbaugh, Sue 30–31, 33
Schlegel, Friedrich 158
Schleicher, August 160–61
Scots Gaelic 115–18
semantics 87, 104, 114, 137, 140–41,
    143, 153, 156, 164, 216
semiotics 165, 194
Semitic languages 63, 66–7, 94, 97,
    108, 160
Siberian languages 68–9, 70
sign language 29, 194–6, 202
Sinitic languages see Chinese
Sino-Tibetan 63, 68, 77, 129
slang 174–7, 216–17
Slavic 99–100
South American languages 72
Spanish 113, 121–2, 133, 135, 149,
    154, 175, 179, 181, 184, 197, 200,
    213, 217–18, 219
'speculative grammars' 152, 170
Stoics 144–5
stress, word 137
structural linguistics 162–3
Sumerian 67, 86, 89, 91, 93–4, 108
Sunda 38–9, 44, 74

Swahili 126, 178–9
Swedish 124, 135
symbolic thought 39, 45, 54, 56–57
syntax 28, 31, 33, 39, 45–8, 51–2, 57–8,
    114, 131, 137, 139–71, 195, 216

Tahitian 135, 136, 213
Taiwan 68, 77, 132, 171
Tasmanian 63, 72–3
Tibeto-Burman 68
Tolkien, J. R. R. 117
transformational generative
    grammar see generative grammar
Turkish 61, 69, 160, 185
typology 60, 137, 157, 164

ultrasound 12, 17, 220
'universal grammar' 152–3, 156
universals, language 45–9, 57
'Ural-Altaic' 67–9
Uralic languages 69, 80, 171

Varro 147–8
vocabulary see lexicon

Wallace's Line 39, 42, 44
Washoe 26, 28–9, 30
Welsh 99, 115–18, 152, 163, 175, 186,
    212–14
whales 12, 16, 17, 20–25
Wittgenstein, Ludwig 3
words, emergence of 45–6
world language 81, 181, 217–18, 220
writing 11, 63, 81, 86–111, 129, 132,
    136, 144–6, 149, 168, 172, 188,
    208, 220

Yiddish 121, 124

Zulu 126